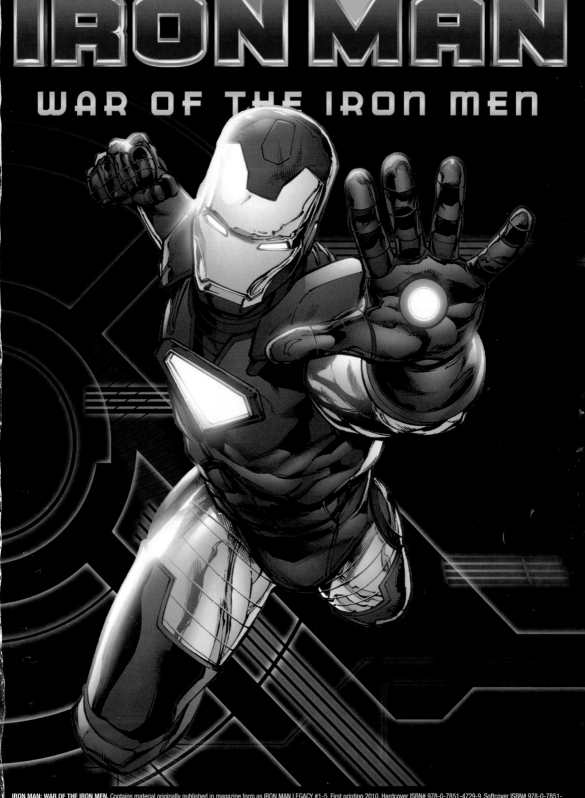

IRON MAN
WAR OF THE IRON MEN

IRON MAN: WAR OF THE IRON MEN. Contains material originally published in magazine form as IRON MAN LEGACY #1-5. First printing 2010. Hardcover ISBN# 978-0-7851-4729-9. Softcover ISBN# 978-0-7851-4730-5. Published by MARVEL WORLDWIDE, INC., a subsidiary of MARVEL ENTERTAINMENT, LLC. OFFICE OF PUBLICATION: 417 5th Avenue, New York, NY 10016. Copyright © 2010 and 2011 Marvel Characters, Inc. All rights reserved. Hardcover: $19.99 per copy in the U.S. and $22.50 in Canada (GST #R127032852). Softcover: $16.99 per copy in the U.S. and $18.99 in Canada (GST #R127032852). Canadian Agreement #40668537. All characters featured in this issue and the distinctive names and likenesses thereof, and all related indicia are trademarks of Marvel Characters, Inc. No similarity between any of the names, characters, persons, and/or institutions in this magazine with those of any living or dead person or institution is intended, and any such similarity which may exist is purely coincidental. **Printed in the U.S.A.** ALAN FINE, EVP - Office of the President, Marvel Worldwide, Inc. and EVP & CMO Marvel Characters B.V.; DAN BUCKLEY, Chief Executive Officer and Publisher - Print, Animation & Digital Media; JIM SOKOLOWSKI, Chief Operating Officer; DAVID GABRIEL, SVP of Publishing Sales & Circulation; DAVID BOGART, SVP of Business Affairs & Talent Management; MICHAEL PASCIULLO, VP Merchandising & Communications; JIM O'KEEFE, VP of Operations & Logistics; DAN CARR, Executive Director of Publishing Technology; JUSTIN F. GABRIE, Director of Publishing & Editorial Operations; SUSAN CRESPI, Editorial Operations Manager; ALEX MORALES, Publishing Operations Manager; STAN LEE, Chairman Emeritus. For information regarding advertising in Marvel Comics or on Marvel.com, please contact Ron Stern, VP of Business Development, at

IRON MAN
WAR OF THE IRON MEN

WRITER: **FRED VAN LENTE**
PENCILER: **STEVE KURTH**
INKER: **ALLEN MARTINEZ** WITH **VICTOR OLAZABA**
COLORIST: **JOHN RAUCH** WITH **CHRIS CHUCKRY**
LETTERER: **ARTMONKEYS' DAVE LANPHEAR**
COVER ARTISTS: **FRANCIS TSAI, BRANDON PETERSON, JUAN DOE & TRAVEL FOREMAN**
ASSISTANT EDITORS: **ALEJANDRO ARBONA & CHARLIE BECKERMAN**
EDITOR: **RALPH MACCHIO**

"HEAVY RAIN"

WRITER: **MATTEO CASALI**
PENCILER: **STEVE KURTH**
INKER: **ALLEN MARTINEZ**
COLORIST: **SUNNY GHO**
LETTERER: **DAVE SHARPE**
COVER ARTIST: **DAVID YARDIN**
EDITOR: **MICHAEL HORWITZ**
SENIOR EDITOR: **RALPH MACCHIO**

COLLECTION EDITOR: **CORY LEVINE**
EDITORIAL ASSISTANTS: **JAMES EMMETT & JOE HOCHSTEIN**
ASSISTANT EDITORS: **ALEX STARBUCK & NELSON RIBEIRO**
EDITORS, SPECIAL PROJECTS: **JENNIFER GRÜNWALD & MARK D. BEAZLEY**
SENIOR EDITOR, SPECIAL PROJECTS: **JEFF YOUNGQUIST**
SENIOR VICE PRESIDENT OF SALES: **DAVID GABRIEL**
BOOK DESIGNER: **RODOLFO MURAGUCHI**

EDITOR IN CHIEF: **JOE QUESADA**
PUBLISHER: **DAN BUCKLEY**
EXECUTIVE PRODUCER: **ALAN FINE**

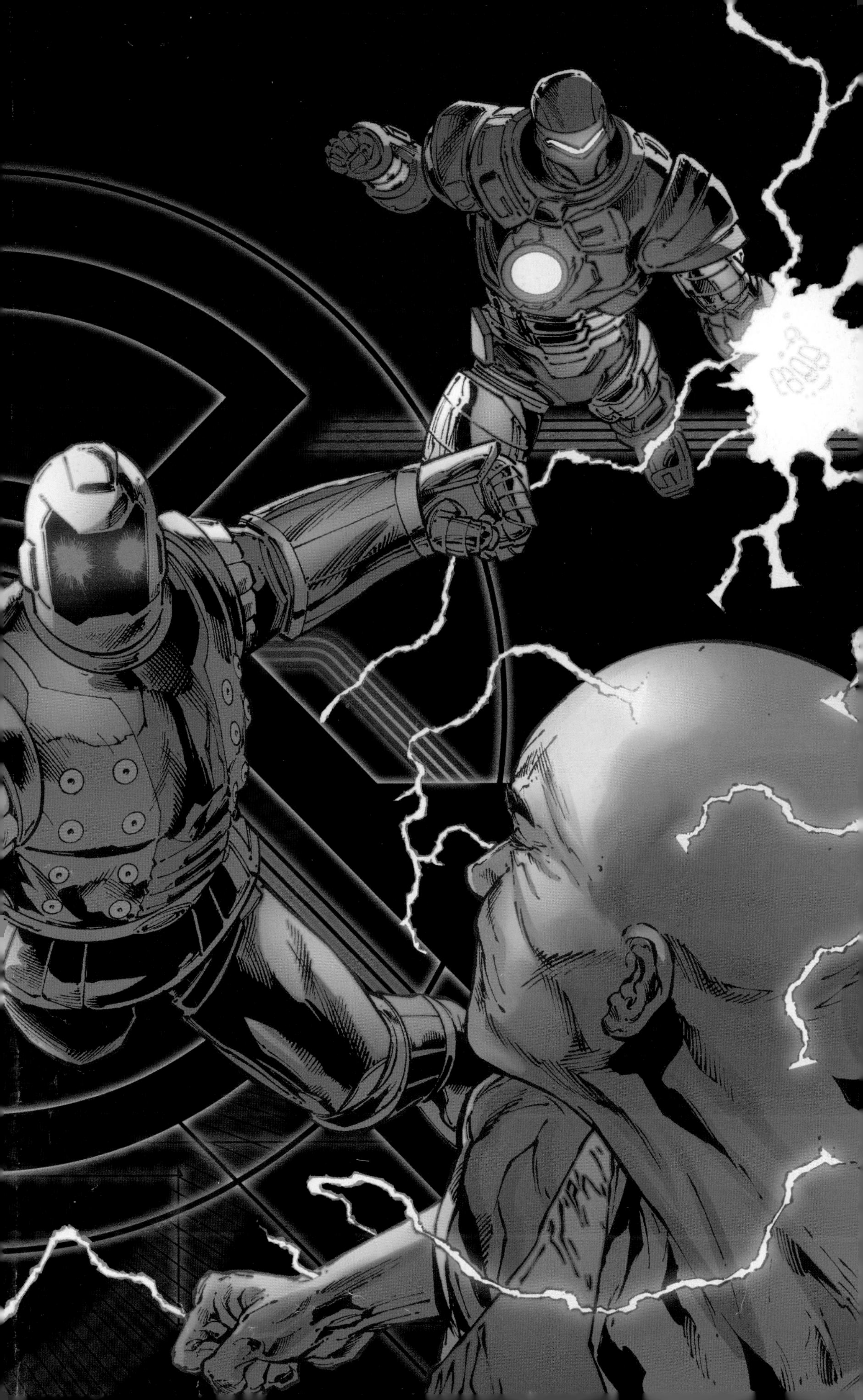

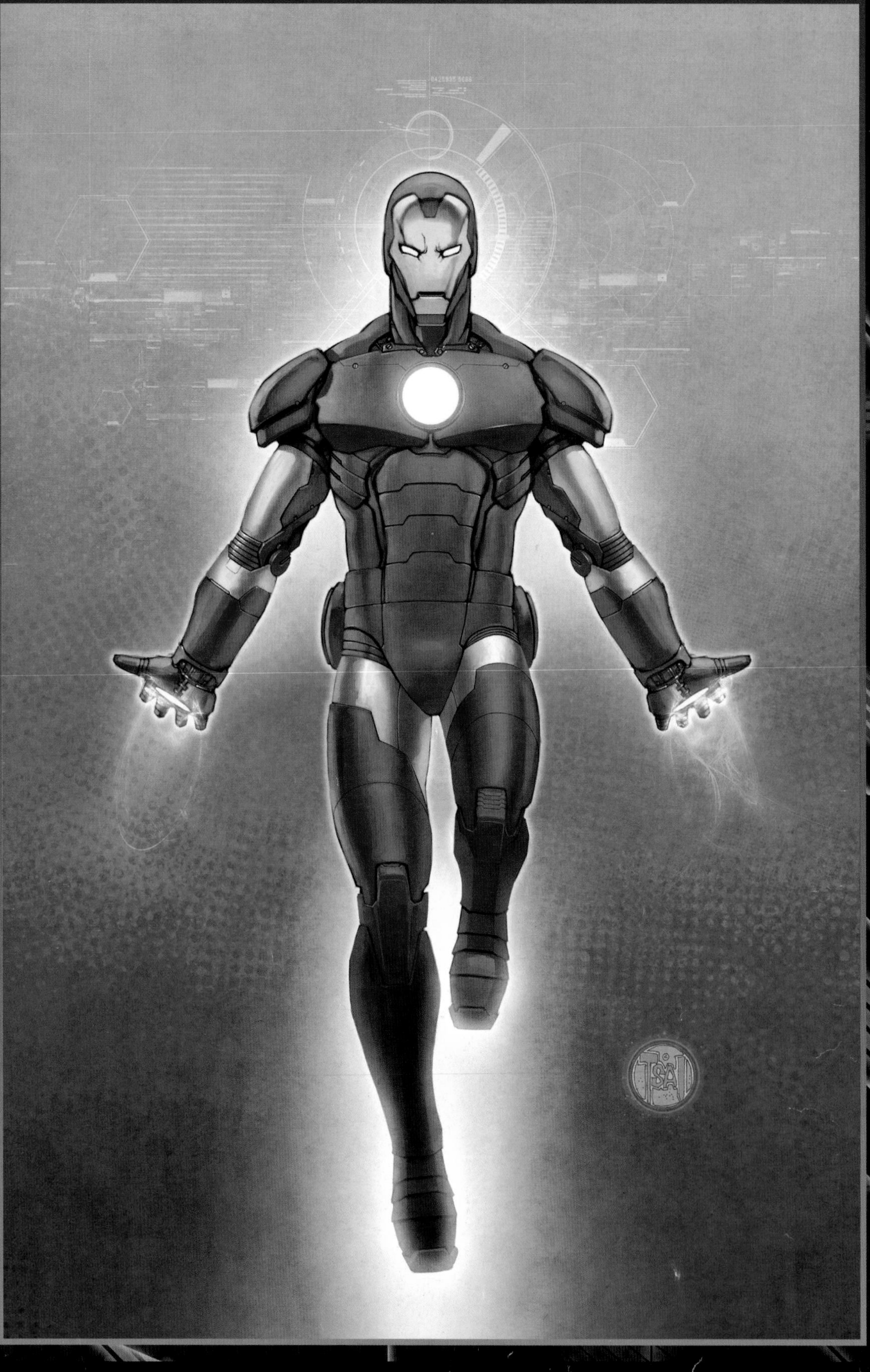

IRON MAN LEGACY 1

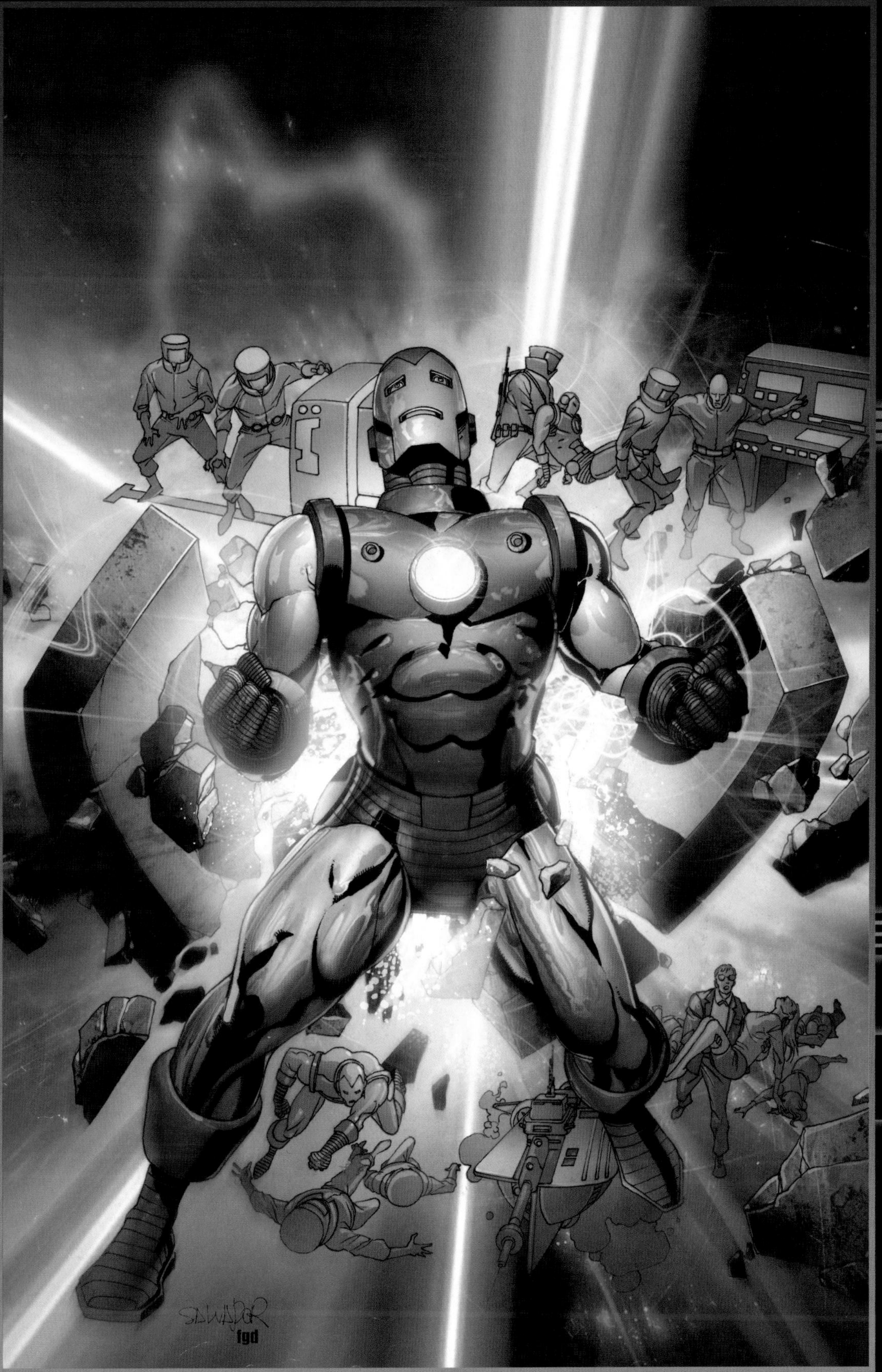
SALVADOR
fgd

#1 VARIANT
BY SALVADOR LARROCA

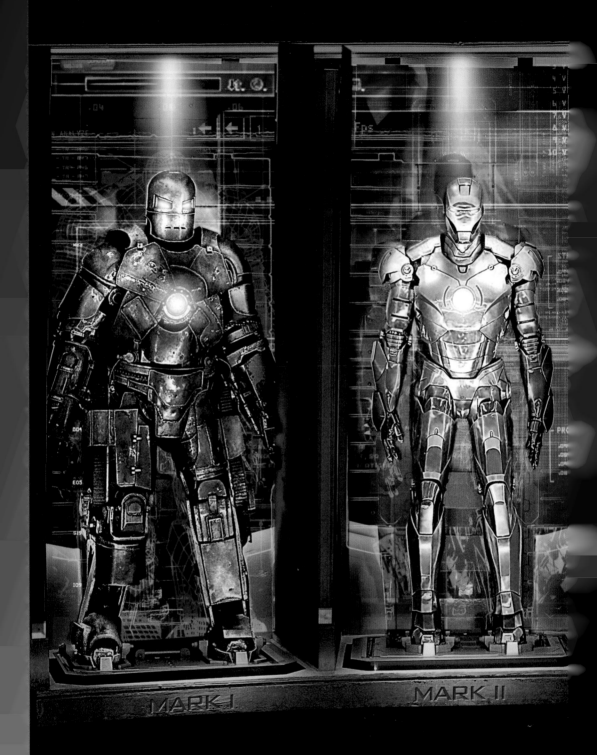

MARK I

MARK II

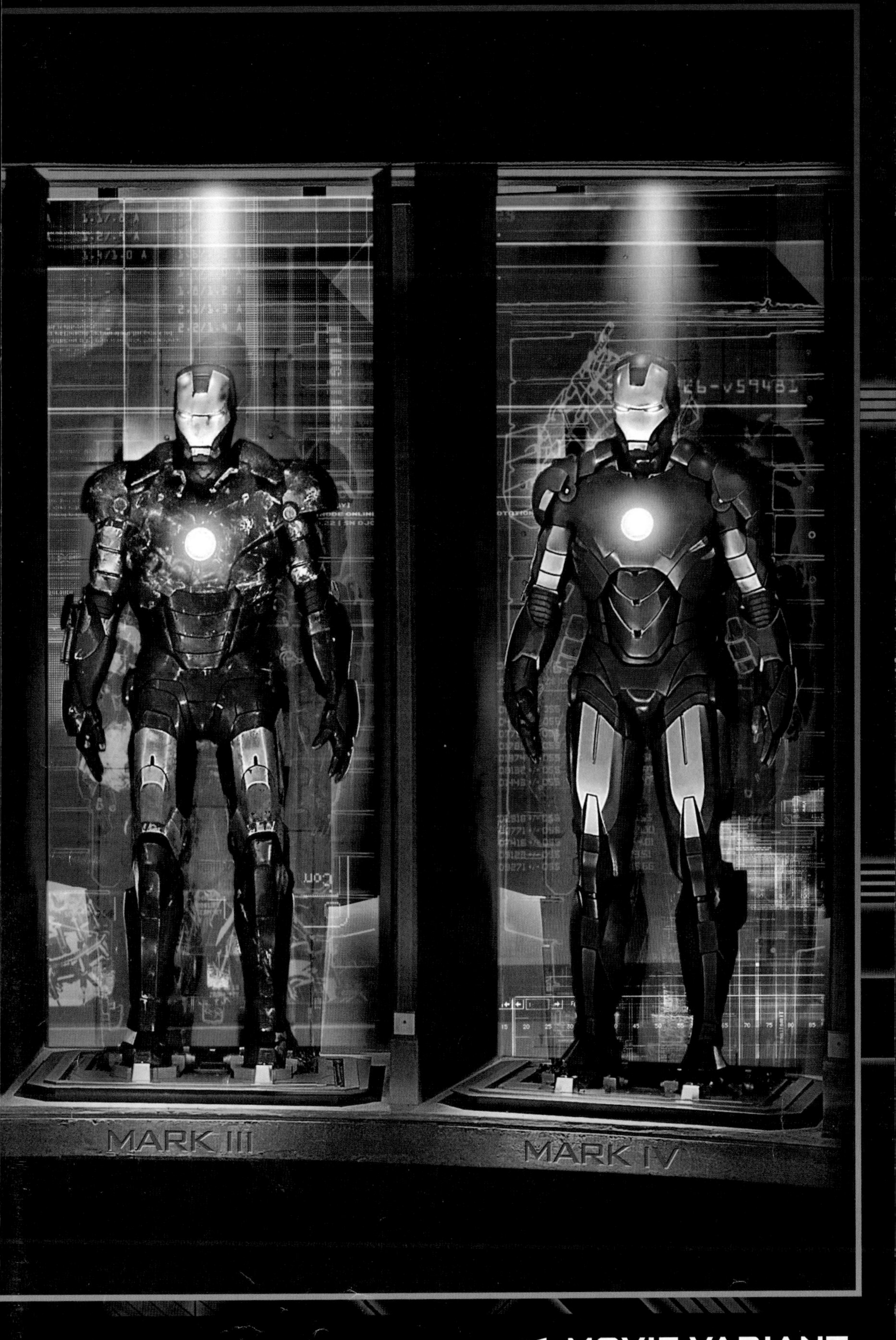

MARK III
MARK IV

#1 MOVIE VARIANT

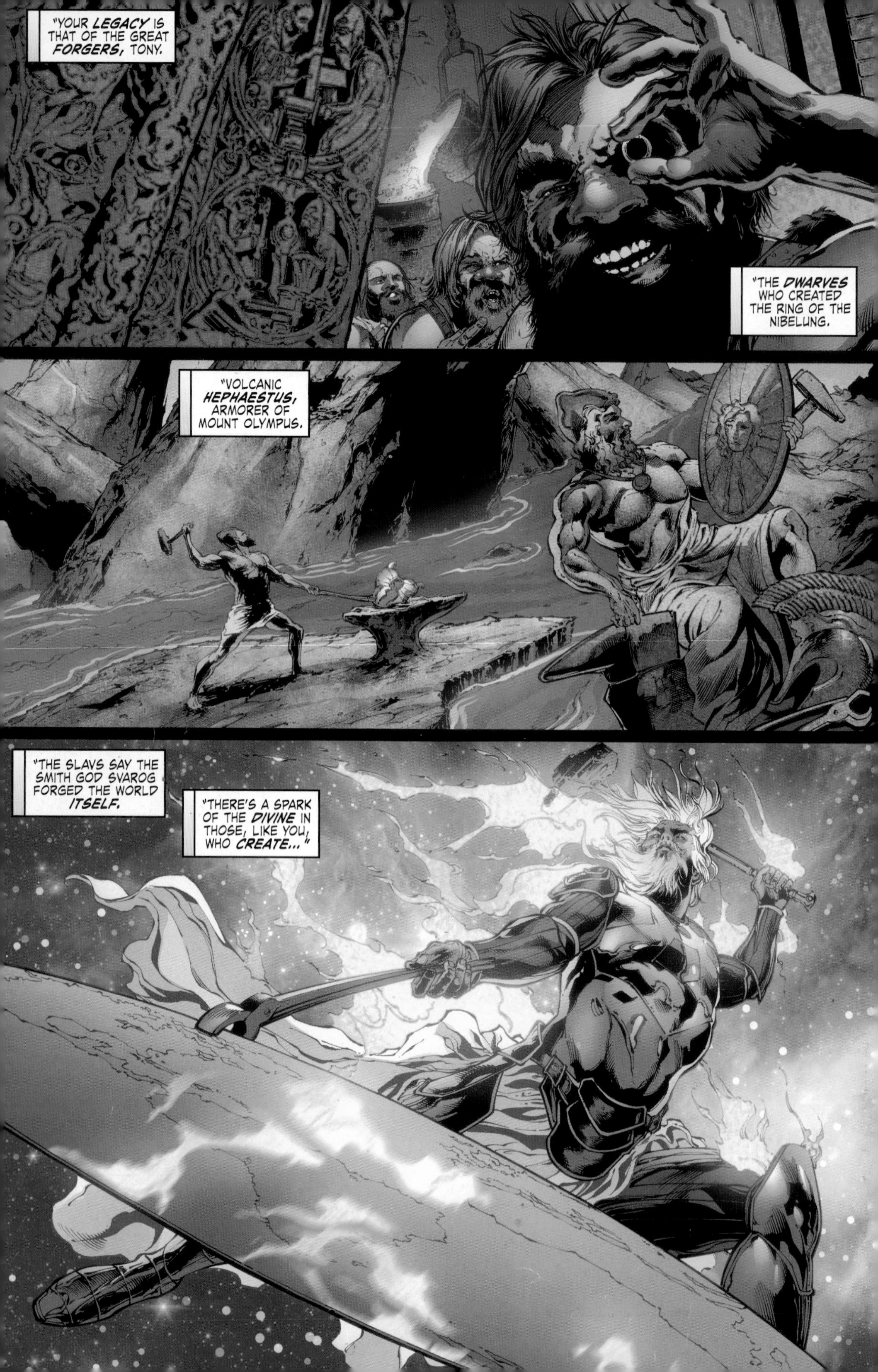
"YOUR LEGACY IS THAT OF THE GREAT FORGERS, TONY.
"THE DWARVES WHO CREATED THE RING OF THE NIBELUNG.
"VOLCANIC HEPHAESTUS, ARMORER OF MOUNT OLYMPUS.
"THE SLAVS SAY THE SMITH GOD SVAROG FORGED THE WORLD ITSELF.
"THERE'S A SPARK OF THE DIVINE IN THOSE, LIKE YOU, WHO CREATE..."

...WHO MAKE *SOMETHING* OUT OF *NOTHING.*

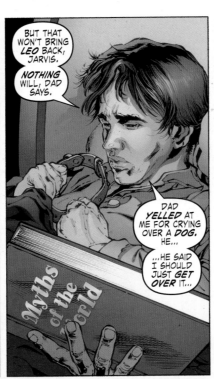

BUT THAT WON'T BRING *LEO* BACK, JARVIS.

NOTHING WILL, DAD SAYS.

DAD *YELLED* AT ME FOR CRYING OVER A *DOG.* HE...

...HE SAID I SHOULD JUST *GET OVER* IT...

THAT'S MY POINT *EXACTLY,* MASTER TONY.

THAT'S *HOW* YOU'LL GET THROUGH IT.

YOU'LL *CREATE* YOUR WAY OUT.

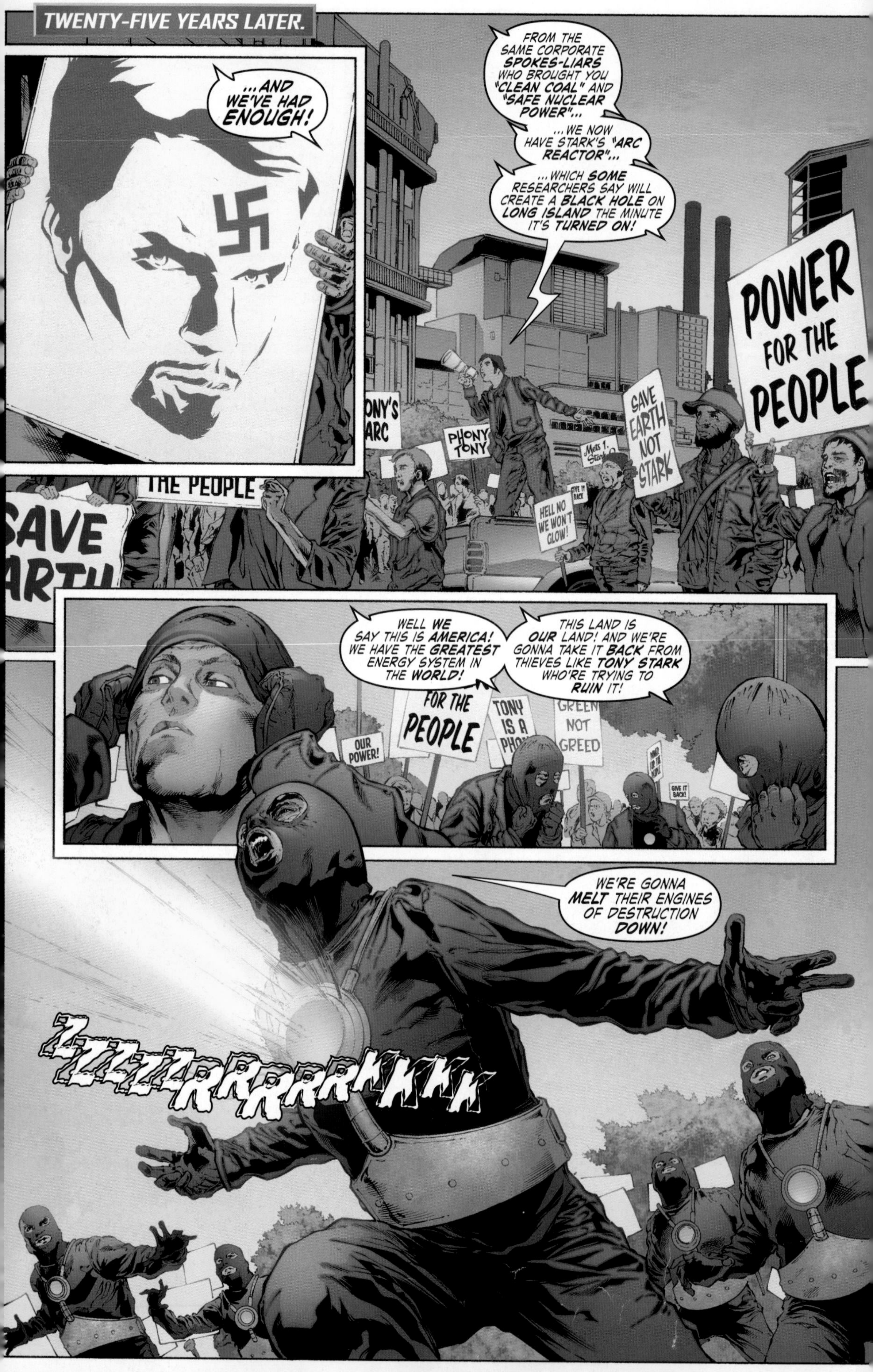

TWENTY-FIVE YEARS LATER.
...AND WE'VE HAD ENOUGH!
FROM THE SAME CORPORATE SPOKES-LIARS WHO BROUGHT YOU "CLEAN COAL" AND "SAFE NUCLEAR POWER"...
...WE NOW HAVE STARK'S "ARC REACTOR"...
...WHICH SOME RESEARCHERS SAY WILL CREATE A BLACK HOLE ON LONG ISLAND THE MINUTE IT'S TURNED ON!
POWER FOR THE PEOPLE
SAVE EARTH NOT STARK
PHONY TONY
HELL NO WE WON'T GLOW!
GIVE IT BACK
THE PEOPLE
WELL WE SAY THIS IS AMERICA! WE HAVE THE GREATEST ENERGY SYSTEM IN THE WORLD!
THIS LAND IS OUR LAND! AND WE'RE GONNA TAKE IT BACK FROM THIEVES LIKE TONY STARK WHO'RE TRYING TO RUIN IT!
FOR THE PEOPLE
OUR POWER!
GREEN NOT GREED
GIVE IT BACK!
WE'RE GONNA MELT THEIR ENGINES OF DESTRUCTION DOWN!
ZZZZZZRRRRRRRRKKKK

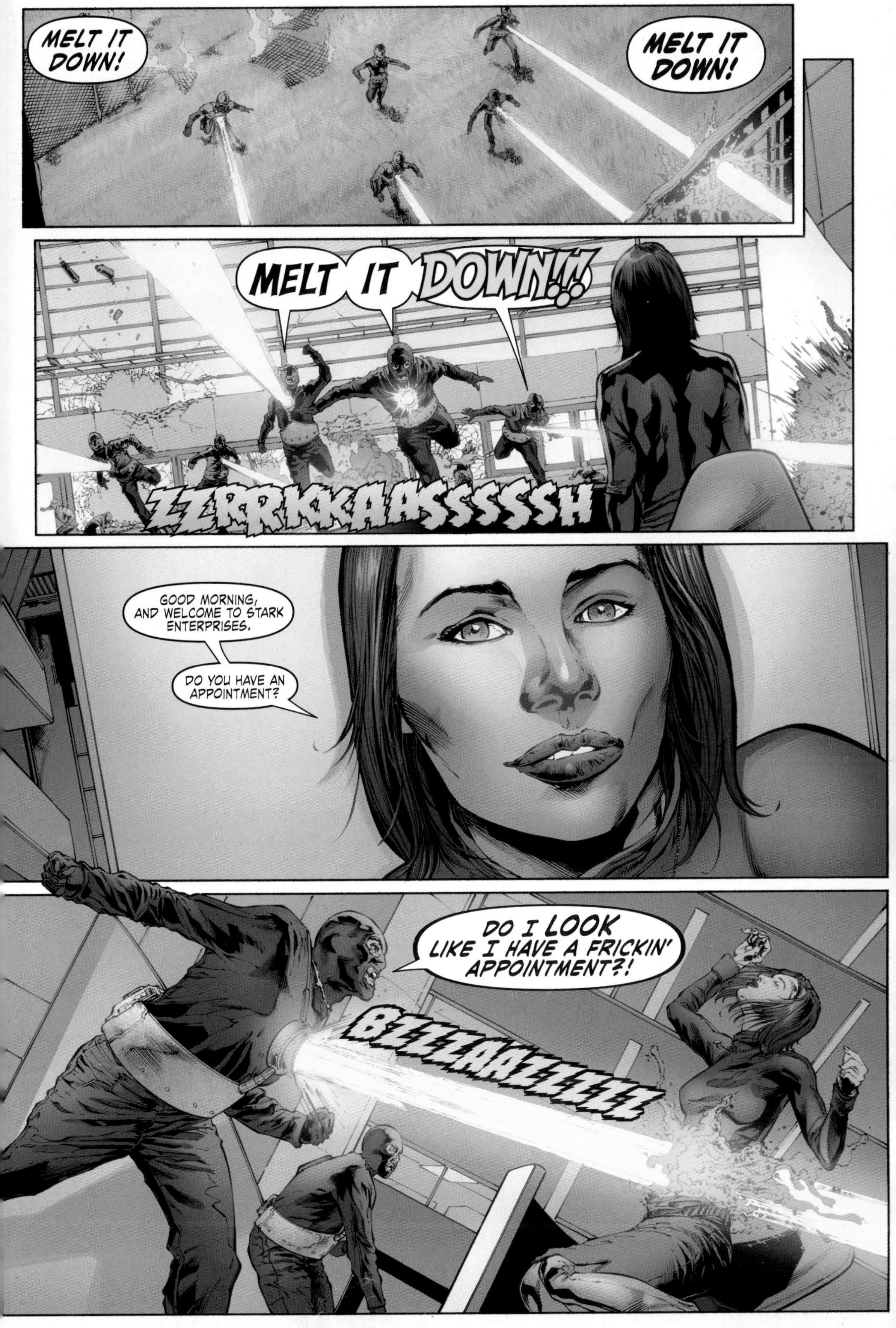
MELT IT DOWN!
MELT IT DOWN!
MELT IT DOWN!!
ZZRRKKAASSSSSH
GOOD MORNING, AND WELCOME TO STARK ENTERPRISES.
DO YOU HAVE AN APPOINTMENT?
DO I LOOK LIKE I HAVE A FRICKIN' APPOINTMENT?!
BZZZZAAZZZZZZ

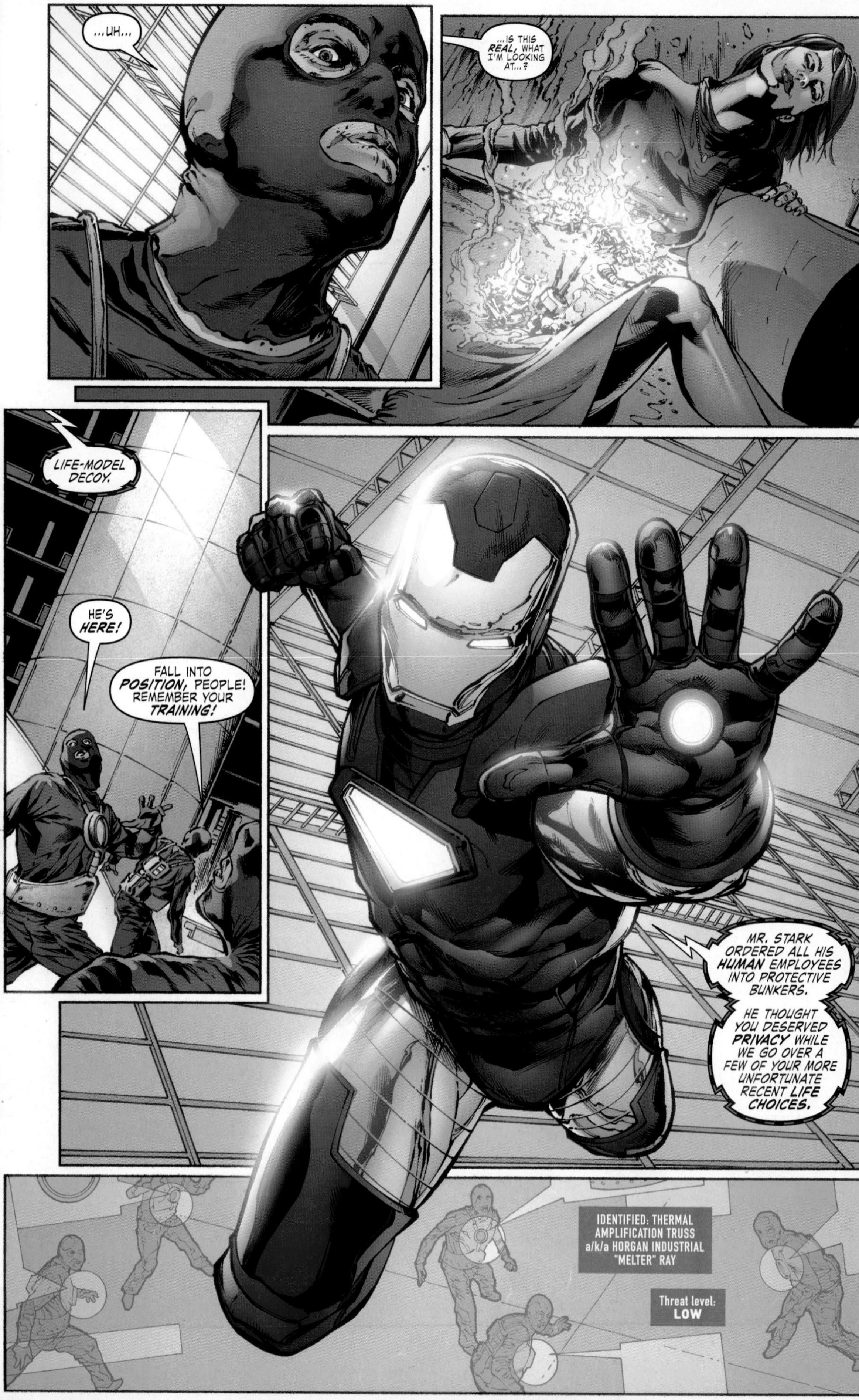
...UH...
...IS THIS REAL, WHAT I'M LOOKING AT...?
LIFE-MODEL DECOY.
HE'S HERE!
FALL INTO POSITION, PEOPLE! REMEMBER YOUR TRAINING!
MR. STARK ORDERED ALL HIS HUMAN EMPLOYEES INTO PROTECTIVE BUNKERS.
HE THOUGHT YOU DESERVED PRIVACY WHILE WE GO OVER A FEW OF YOUR MORE UNFORTUNATE RECENT LIFE CHOICES.
IDENTIFIED: THERMAL AMPLIFICATION TRUSS a/k/a HORGAN INDUSTRIAL "MELTER" RAY
Threat level: LOW

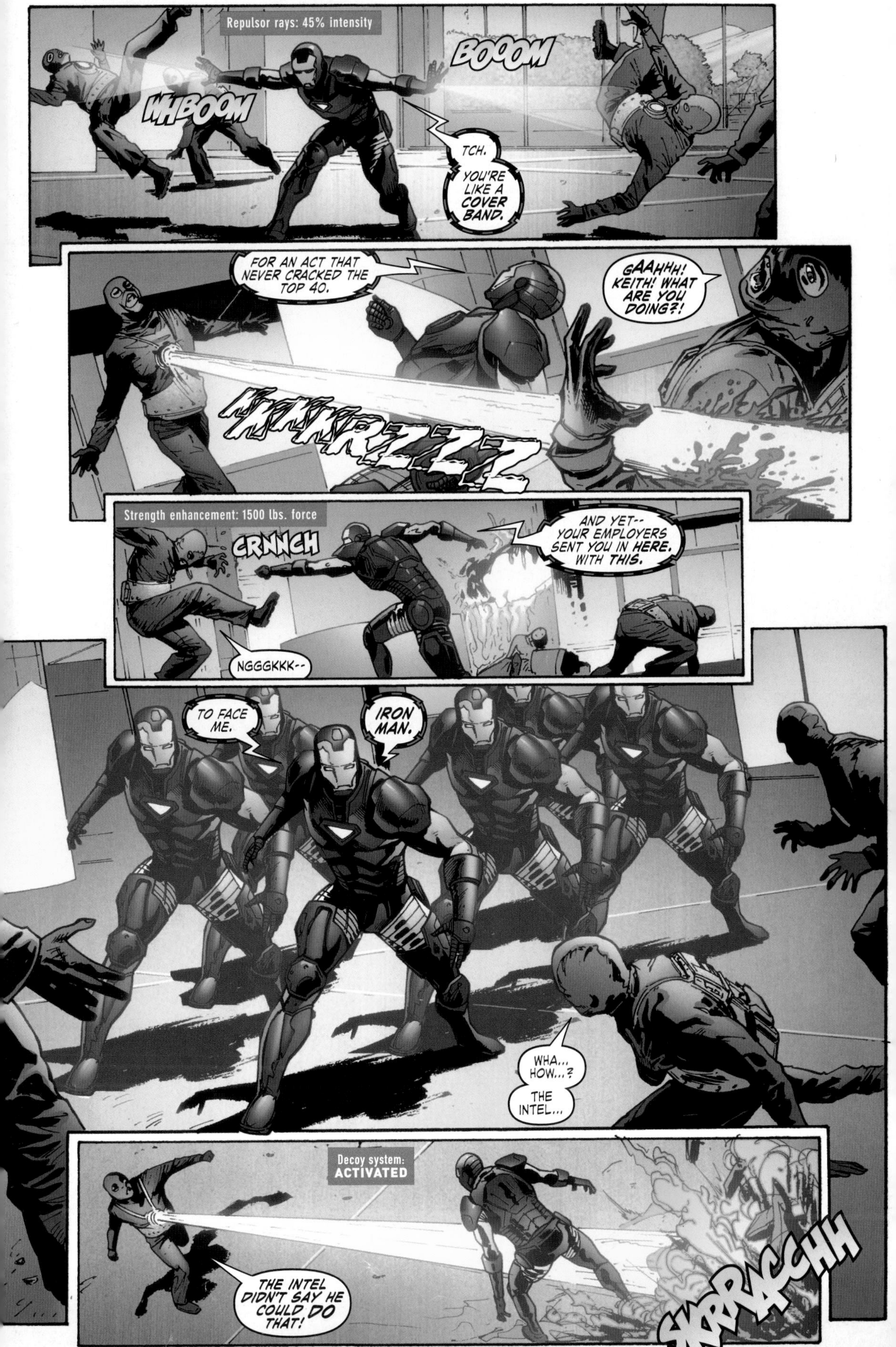
Repulsor rays: 45% intensity
WHBOOM
BOOOM
TCH.
YOU'RE LIKE A COVER BAND.
FOR AN ACT THAT NEVER CRACKED THE TOP 40.
GAAHHH! KEITH! WHAT ARE YOU DOING?!
KKKKRZZZ
Strength enhancement: 1500 lbs. force
CRNNCH
AND YET-- YOUR EMPLOYERS SENT YOU IN HERE. WITH THIS.
NGGGKKK--
TO FACE ME.
IRON MAN.
WHA... HOW...?
THE INTEL...
Decoy system: ACTIVATED
THE INTEL DIDN'T SAY HE COULD DO THAT!
SKRRACCHH

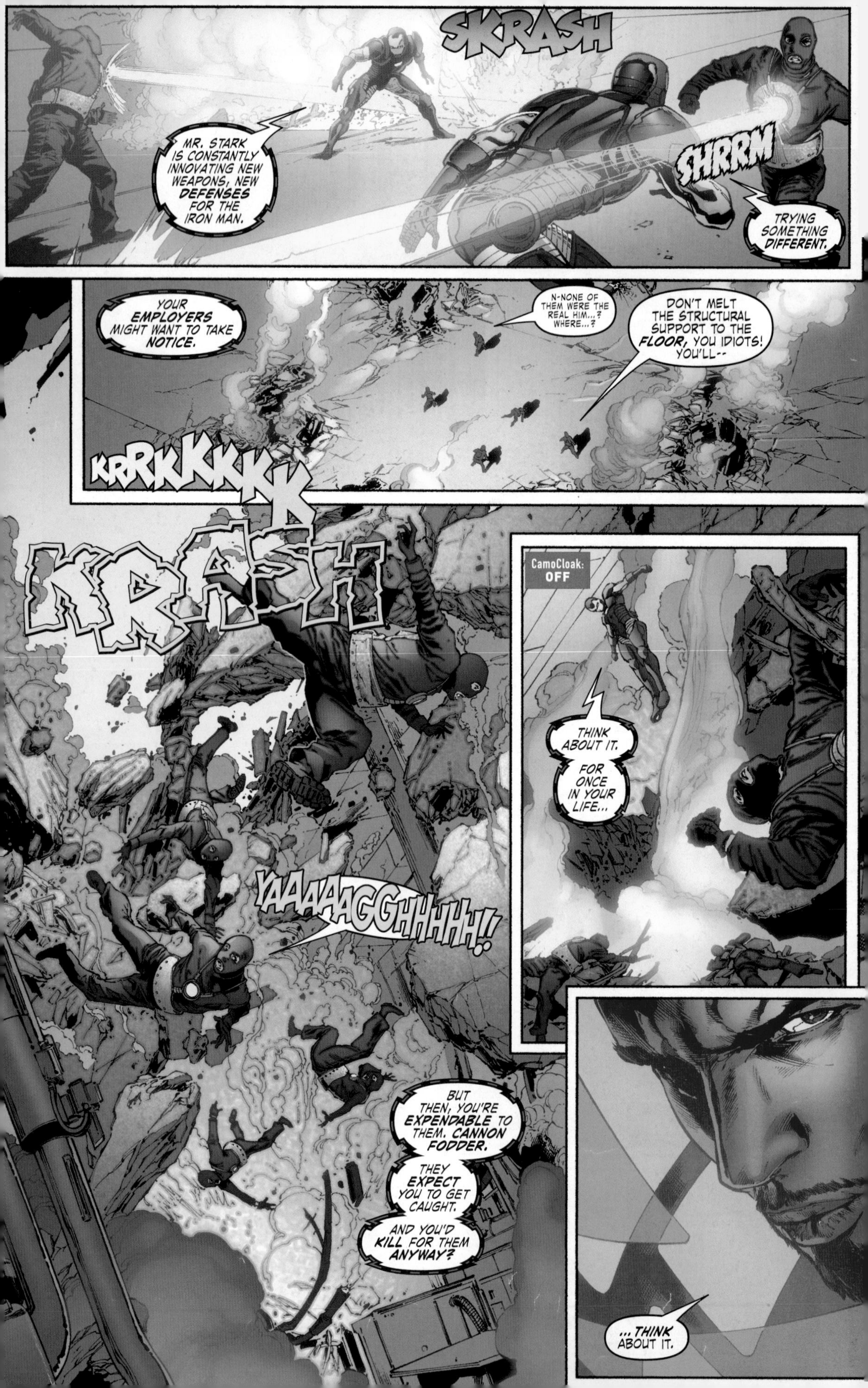
SKRASH
MR. STARK IS CONSTANTLY INNOVATING NEW WEAPONS, NEW DEFENSES FOR THE IRON MAN.
SHRRM
TRYING SOMETHING DIFFERENT.
YOUR EMPLOYERS MIGHT WANT TO TAKE NOTICE.
N-NONE OF THEM WERE THE REAL HIM...? WHERE...?
DON'T MELT THE STRUCTURAL SUPPORT TO THE FLOOR, YOU IDIOTS! YOU'LL--
KRRKKKKKK
KRASH
YAAAAAGGHHHHH!!
CamoCloak: OFF
THINK ABOUT IT.
FOR ONCE IN YOUR LIFE...
BUT THEN, YOU'RE EXPENDABLE TO THEM. CANNON FODDER.
THEY EXPECT YOU TO GET CAUGHT.
AND YOU'D KILL FOR THEM ANYWAY?
...THINK ABOUT IT.

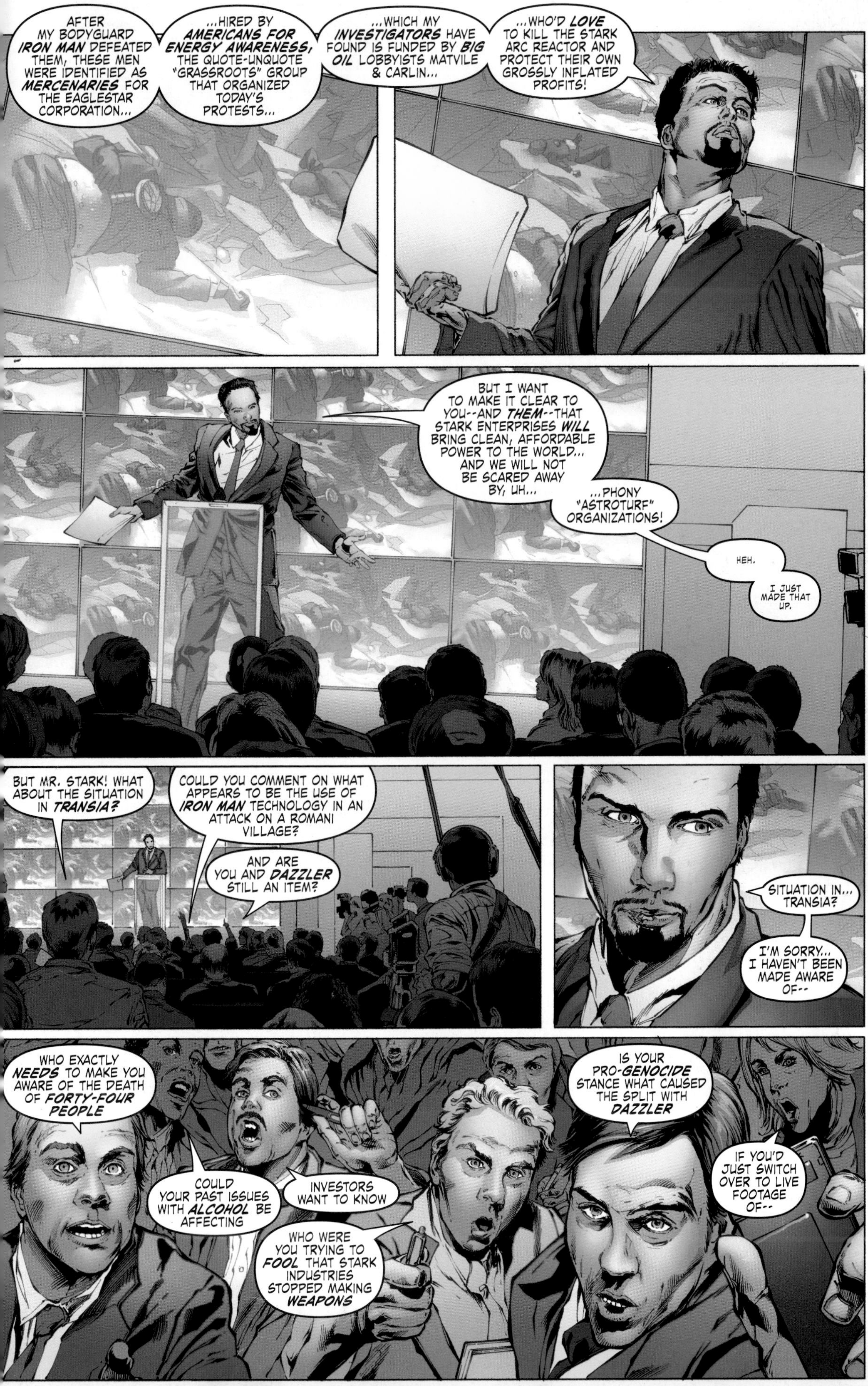
AFTER MY BODYGUARD IRON MAN DEFEATED THEM, THESE MEN WERE IDENTIFIED AS MERCENARIES FOR THE EAGLESTAR CORPORATION...
...HIRED BY AMERICANS FOR ENERGY AWARENESS, THE QUOTE-UNQUOTE "GRASSROOTS" GROUP THAT ORGANIZED TODAY'S PROTESTS...
...WHICH MY INVESTIGATORS HAVE FOUND IS FUNDED BY BIG OIL LOBBYISTS MATVILE & CARLIN...
...WHO'D LOVE TO KILL THE STARK ARC REACTOR AND PROTECT THEIR OWN GROSSLY INFLATED PROFITS!
BUT I WANT TO MAKE IT CLEAR TO YOU--AND THEM--THAT STARK ENTERPRISES WILL BRING CLEAN, AFFORDABLE POWER TO THE WORLD... AND WE WILL NOT BE SCARED AWAY BY, UH...
...PHONY "ASTROTURF" ORGANIZATIONS!
HEH.
I JUST MADE THAT UP.
BUT MR. STARK! WHAT ABOUT THE SITUATION IN TRANSIA?
COULD YOU COMMENT ON WHAT APPEARS TO BE THE USE OF IRON MAN TECHNOLOGY IN AN ATTACK ON A ROMANI VILLAGE?
AND ARE YOU AND DAZZLER STILL AN ITEM?
SITUATION IN... TRANSIA?
I'M SORRY... I HAVEN'T BEEN MADE AWARE OF--
WHO EXACTLY NEEDS TO MAKE YOU AWARE OF THE DEATH OF FORTY-FOUR PEOPLE
COULD YOUR PAST ISSUES WITH ALCOHOL BE AFFECTING
INVESTORS WANT TO KNOW
WHO WERE YOU TRYING TO FOOL THAT STARK INDUSTRIES STOPPED MAKING WEAPONS
IS YOUR PRO-GENOCIDE STANCE WHAT CAUSED THE SPLIT WITH DAZZLER
IF YOU'D JUST SWITCH OVER TO LIVE FOOTAGE OF--

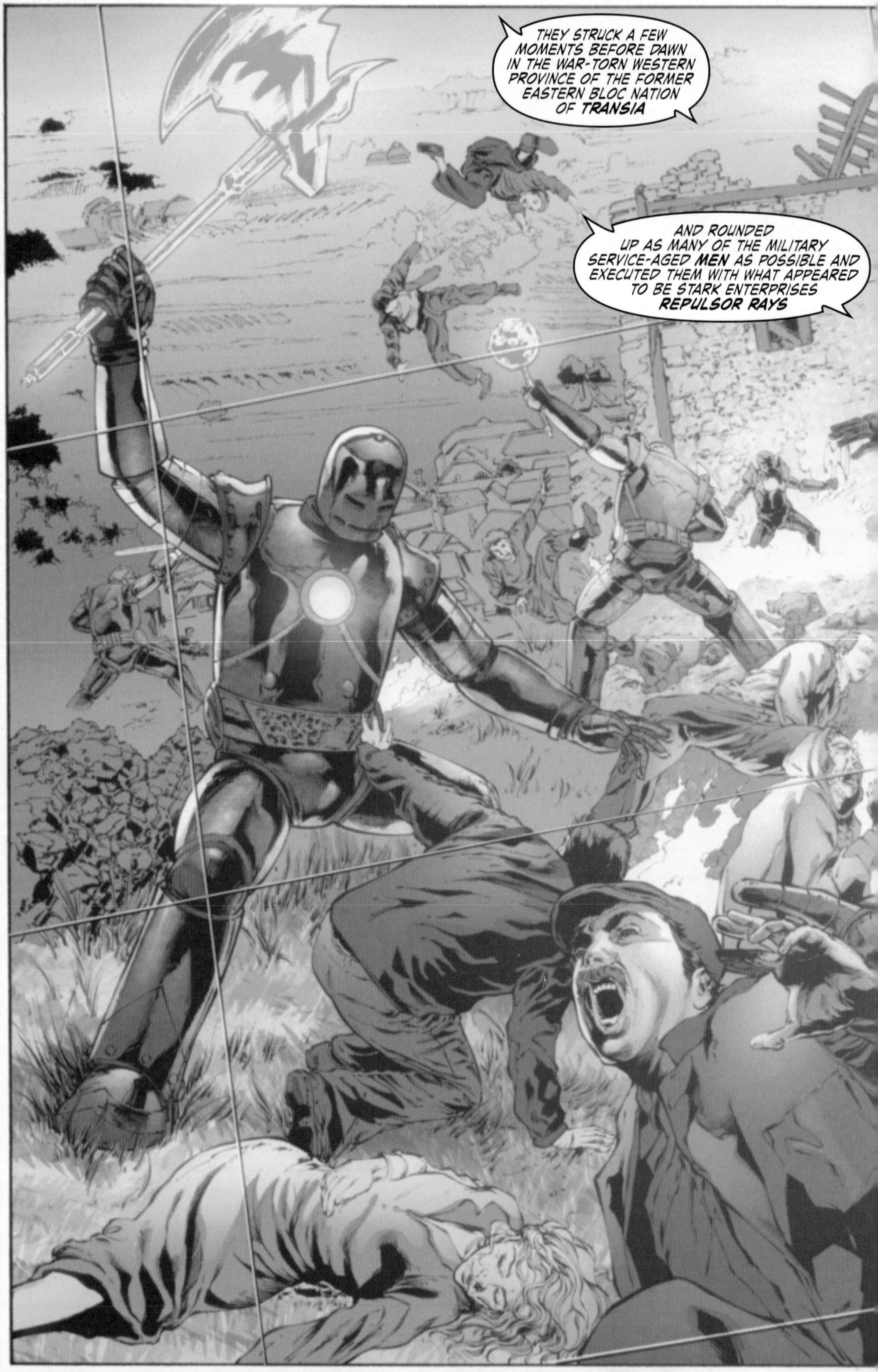
THEY STRUCK A FEW MOMENTS BEFORE DAWN IN THE WAR-TORN WESTERN PROVINCE OF THE FORMER EASTERN BLOC NATION OF TRANSIA
AND ROUNDED UP AS MANY OF THE MILITARY SERVICE-AGED MEN AS POSSIBLE AND EXECUTED THEM WITH WHAT APPEARED TO BE STARK ENTERPRISES REPULSOR RAYS

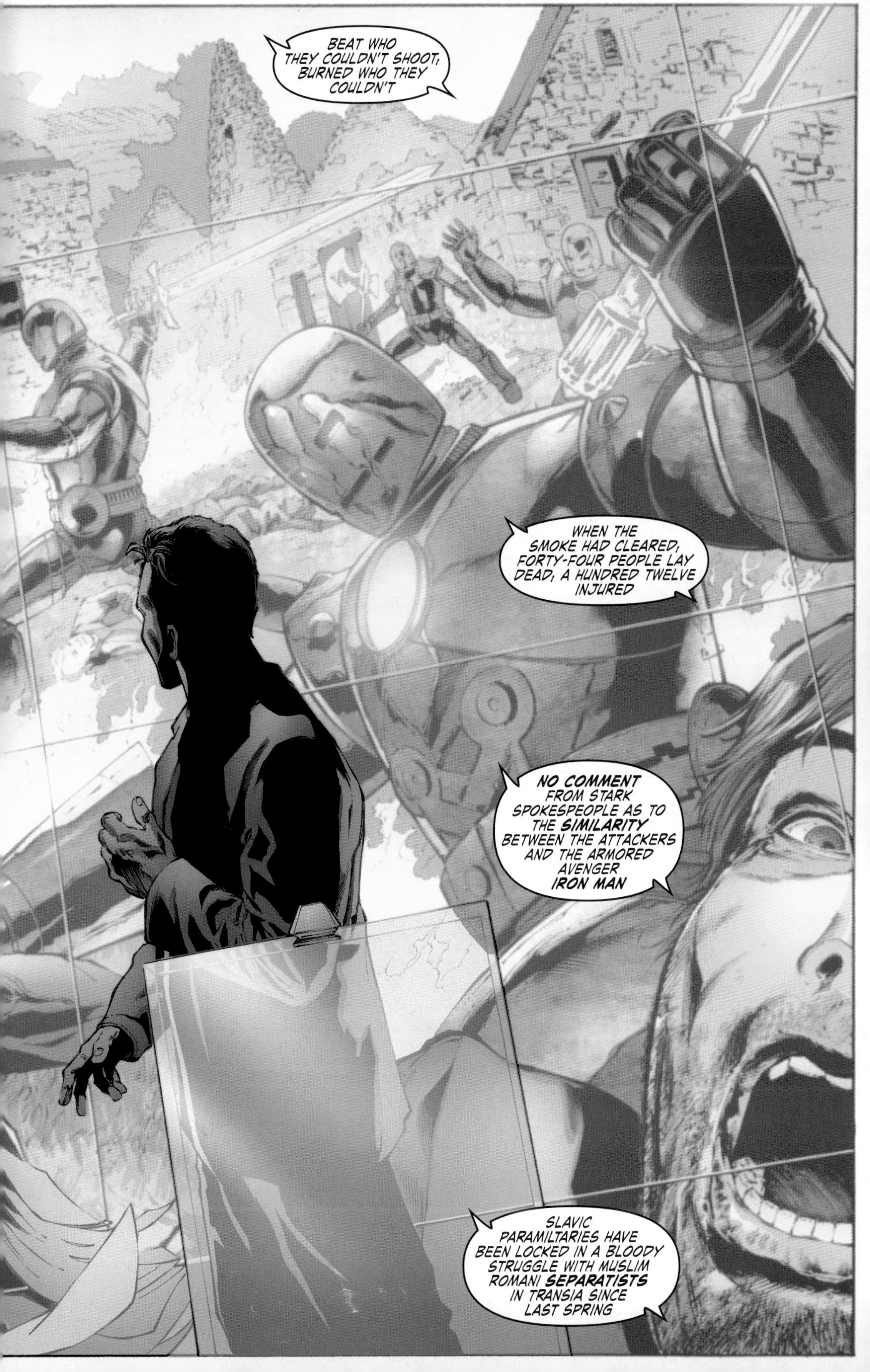
BEAT WHO THEY COULDN'T SHOOT, BURNED WHO THEY COULDN'T
WHEN THE SMOKE HAD CLEARED, FORTY-FOUR PEOPLE LAY DEAD, A HUNDRED TWELVE INJURED
NO COMMENT FROM STARK SPOKESPEOPLE AS TO THE SIMILARITY BETWEEN THE ATTACKERS AND THE ARMORED AVENGER IRON MAN
SLAVIC PARAMILTARIES HAVE BEEN LOCKED IN A BLOODY STRUGGLE WITH MUSLIM ROMANI SEPARATISTS IN TRANSIA SINCE LAST SPRING

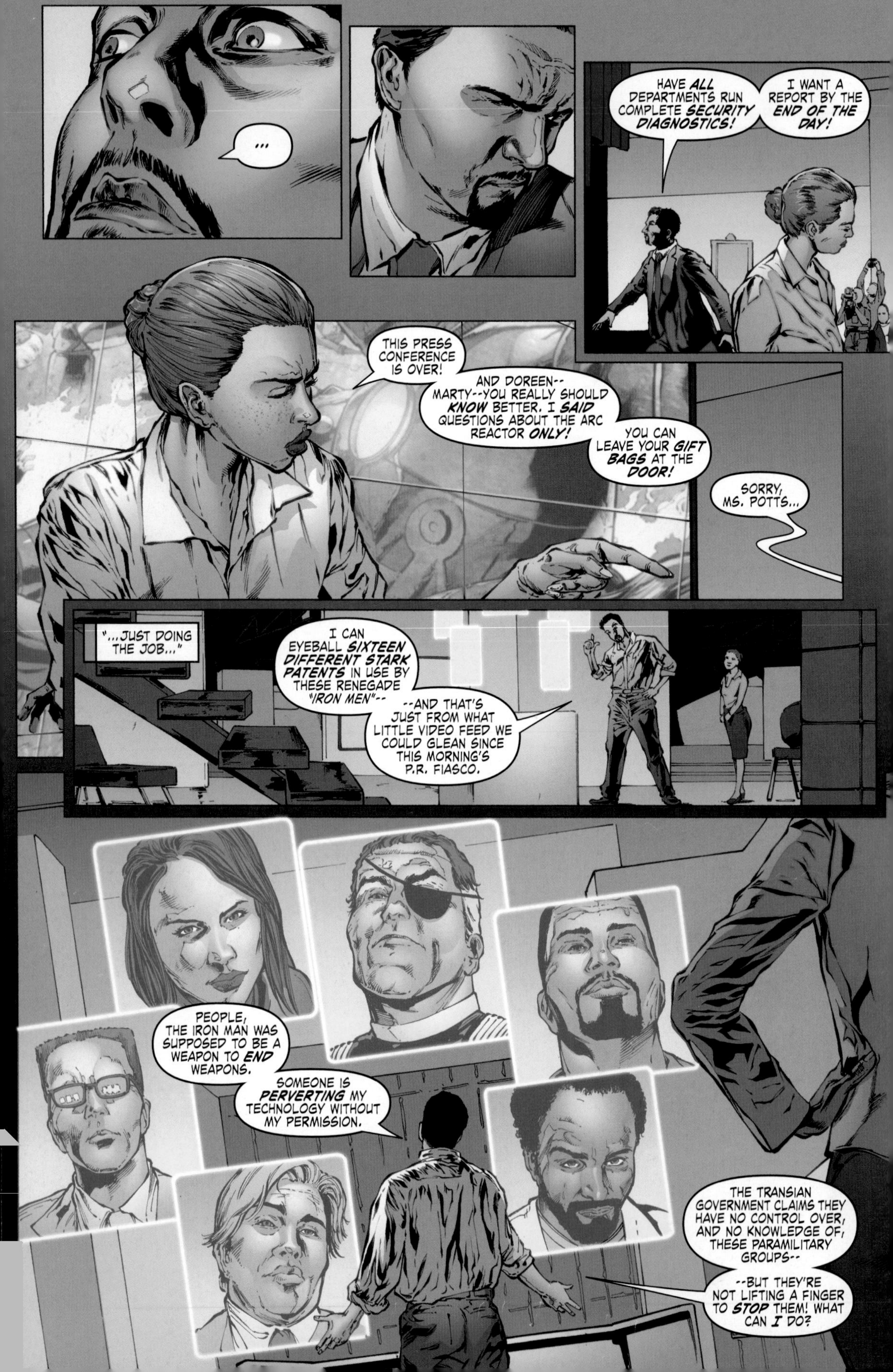
...
HAVE ALL DEPARTMENTS RUN COMPLETE SECURITY DIAGNOSTICS!
I WANT A REPORT BY THE END OF THE DAY!
THIS PRESS CONFERENCE IS OVER!
AND DOREEN-- MARTY--YOU REALLY SHOULD KNOW BETTER. I SAID QUESTIONS ABOUT THE ARC REACTOR ONLY!
YOU CAN LEAVE YOUR GIFT BAGS AT THE DOOR!
SORRY, MS. POTTS...
"...JUST DOING THE JOB..."
I CAN EYEBALL SIXTEEN DIFFERENT STARK PATENTS IN USE BY THESE RENEGADE "IRON MEN"--
--AND THAT'S JUST FROM WHAT LITTLE VIDEO FEED WE COULD GLEAN SINCE THIS MORNING'S P.R. FIASCO.
PEOPLE, THE IRON MAN WAS SUPPOSED TO BE A WEAPON TO END WEAPONS.
SOMEONE IS PERVERTING MY TECHNOLOGY WITHOUT MY PERMISSION.
THE TRANSIAN GOVERNMENT CLAIMS THEY HAVE NO CONTROL OVER, AND NO KNOWLEDGE OF, THESE PARAMILITARY GROUPS--
--BUT THEY'RE NOT LIFTING A FINGER TO STOP THEM! WHAT CAN I DO?

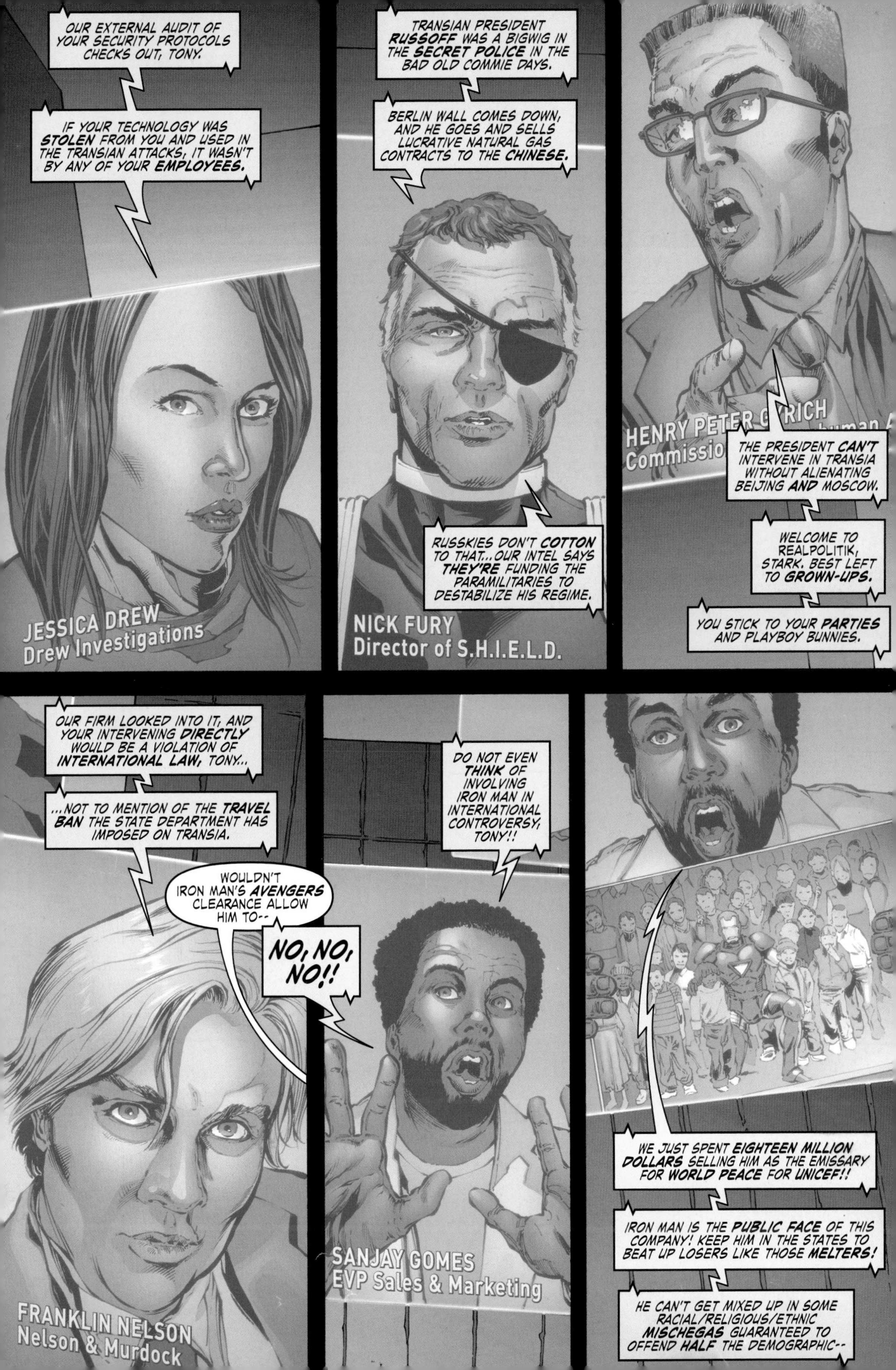
OUR EXTERNAL AUDIT OF YOUR SECURITY PROTOCOLS CHECKS OUT, TONY.
IF YOUR TECHNOLOGY WAS STOLEN FROM YOU AND USED IN THE TRANSIAN ATTACKS, IT WASN'T BY ANY OF YOUR EMPLOYEES.
JESSICA DREW
Drew Investigations
TRANSIAN PRESIDENT RUSSOFF WAS A BIGWIG IN THE SECRET POLICE IN THE BAD OLD COMMIE DAYS.
BERLIN WALL COMES DOWN, AND HE GOES AND SELLS LUCRATIVE NATURAL GAS CONTRACTS TO THE CHINESE.
RUSSKIES DON'T COTTON TO THAT...OUR INTEL SAYS THEY'RE FUNDING THE PARAMILITARIES TO DESTABILIZE HIS REGIME.
NICK FURY
Director of S.H.I.E.L.D.
THE PRESIDENT CAN'T INTERVENE IN TRANSIA WITHOUT ALIENATING BEIJING AND MOSCOW.
WELCOME TO REALPOLITIK, STARK. BEST LEFT TO GROWN-UPS.
YOU STICK TO YOUR PARTIES AND PLAYBOY BUNNIES.
OUR FIRM LOOKED INTO IT, AND YOUR INTERVENING DIRECTLY WOULD BE A VIOLATION OF INTERNATIONAL LAW, TONY...
...NOT TO MENTION OF THE TRAVEL BAN THE STATE DEPARTMENT HAS IMPOSED ON TRANSIA.
WOULDN'T IRON MAN'S AVENGERS CLEARANCE ALLOW HIM TO--
FRANKLIN NELSON
Nelson & Murdock
DO NOT EVEN THINK OF INVOLVING IRON MAN IN INTERNATIONAL CONTROVERSY, TONY!!
NO, NO, NO!!
SANJAY GOMES
EVP Sales & Marketing
WE JUST SPENT EIGHTEEN MILLION DOLLARS SELLING HIM AS THE EMISSARY FOR WORLD PEACE FOR UNICEF!!
IRON MAN IS THE PUBLIC FACE OF THIS COMPANY! KEEP HIM IN THE STATES TO BEAT UP LOSERS LIKE THOSE MELTERS!
HE CAN'T GET MIXED UP IN SOME RACIAL/RELIGIOUS/ETHNIC MISCHEGAS GUARANTEED TO OFFEND HALF THE DEMOGRAPHIC--

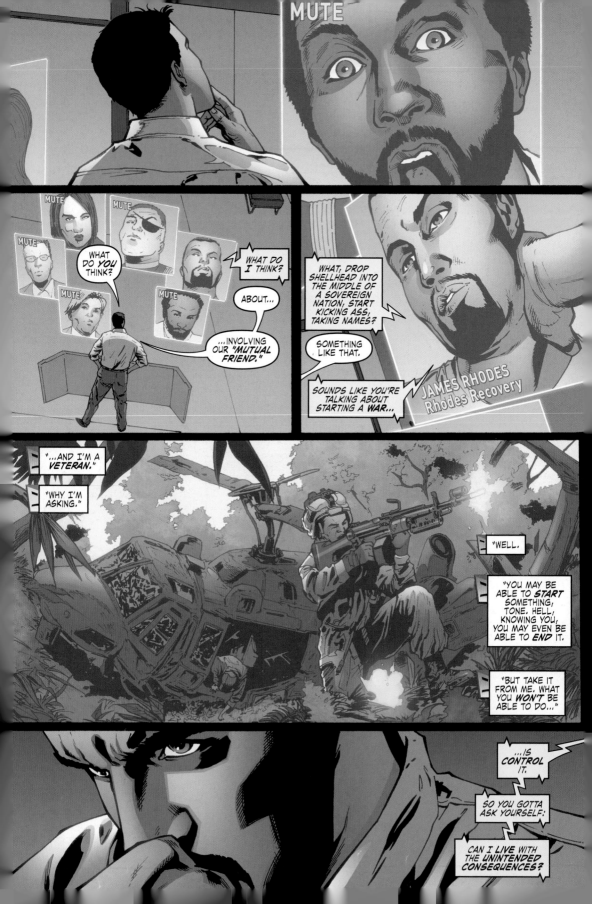

MUTE

MUTE

MUTE

MUTE

MUTE

WHAT DO *YOU* THINK?

ABOUT...

...INVOLVING OUR *"MUTUAL FRIEND."*

WHAT DO I THINK?

WHAT, DROP SHELLHEAD INTO THE MIDDLE OF A SOVEREIGN NATION, START KICKING ASS, TAKING NAMES?

SOMETHING LIKE THAT.

SOUNDS LIKE YOU'RE TALKING ABOUT STARTING A *WAR...*

JAMES RHODES
Rhodes Recovery

"...AND I'M A *VETERAN.*"

"WHY I'M ASKING."

"WELL."

"YOU MAY BE ABLE TO *START* SOMETHING, TONE. HELL, KNOWING YOU, YOU MAY EVEN BE ABLE TO *END* IT."

"BUT TAKE IT FROM ME. WHAT YOU *WON'T* BE ABLE TO DO..."

...IS *CONTROL* IT.

SO YOU GOTTA ASK YOURSELF:

CAN I *LIVE* WITH THE *UNINTENDED CONSEQUENCES?*

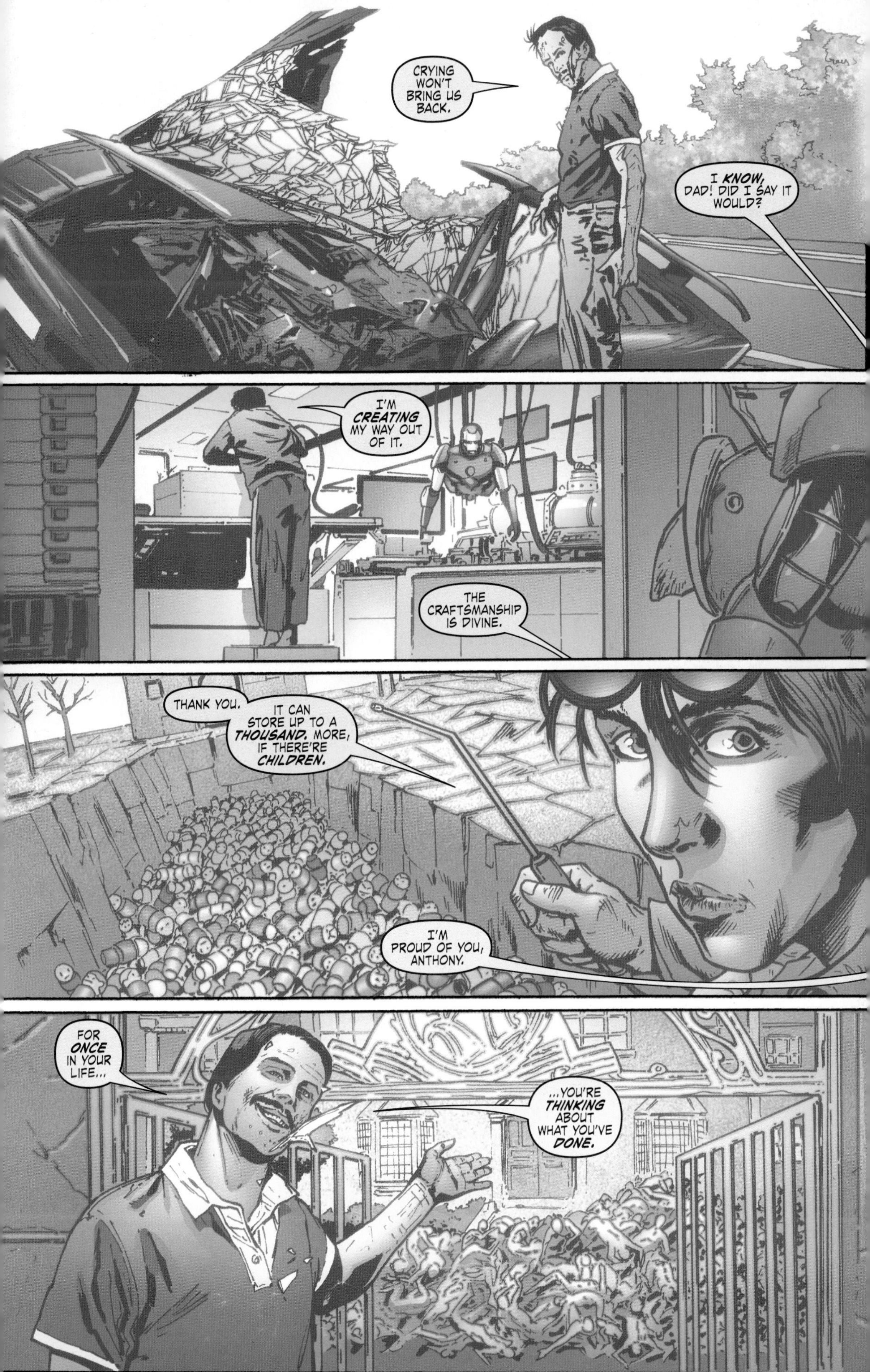
CRYING WON'T BRING US BACK.
I KNOW, DAD! DID I SAY IT WOULD?
I'M CREATING MY WAY OUT OF IT.
THE CRAFTSMANSHIP IS DIVINE.
THANK YOU.
IT CAN STORE UP TO A THOUSAND. MORE, IF THERE'RE CHILDREN.
I'M PROUD OF YOU, ANTHONY.
FOR ONCE IN YOUR LIFE...
...YOU'RE THINKING ABOUT WHAT YOU'VE DONE.

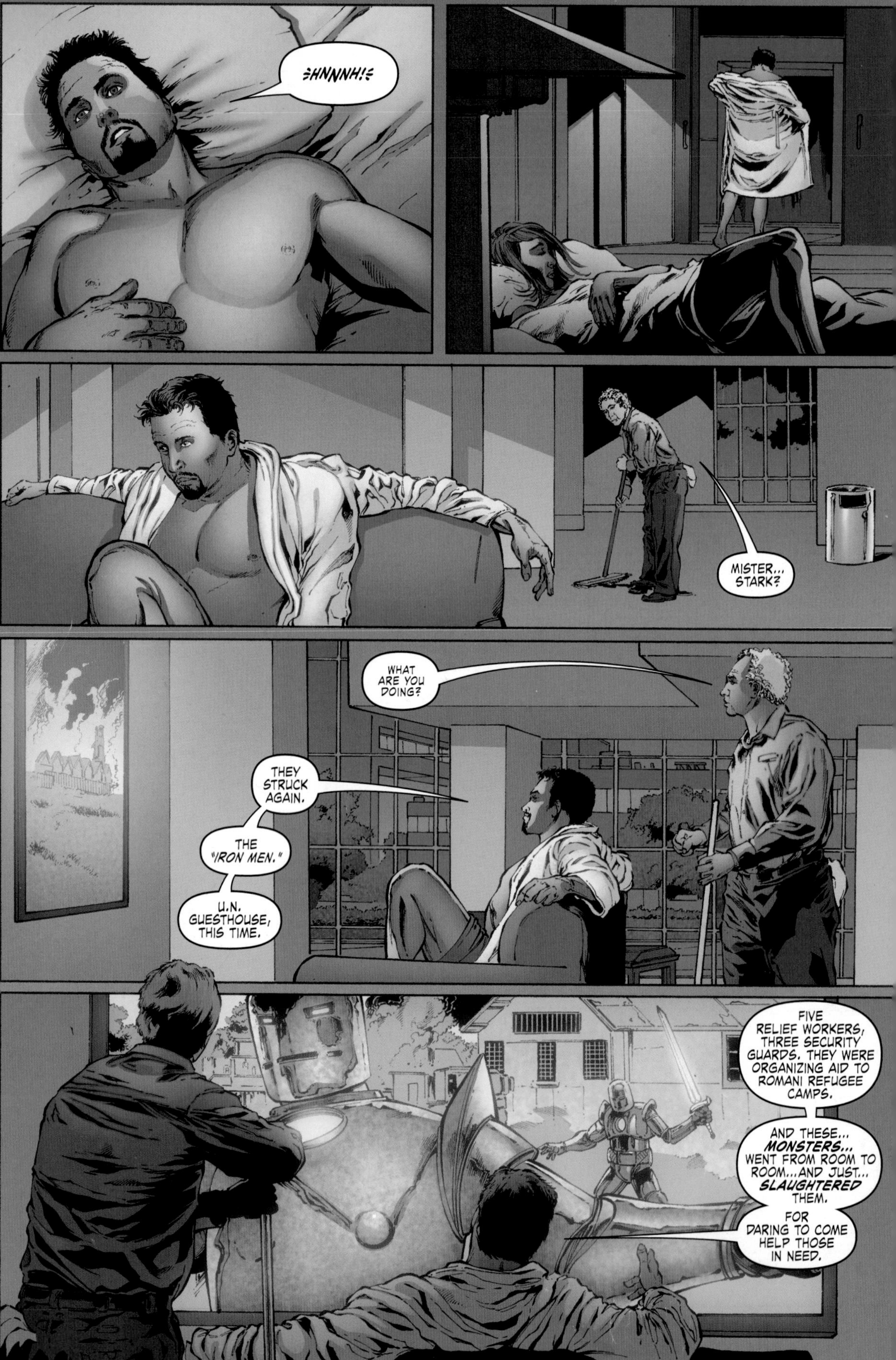

≶HNNNH!≶
MISTER... STARK?
WHAT ARE YOU DOING?
THEY STRUCK AGAIN.
THE "IRON MEN."
U.N. GUESTHOUSE, THIS TIME.
FIVE RELIEF WORKERS, THREE SECURITY GUARDS. THEY WERE ORGANIZING AID TO ROMANI REFUGEE CAMPS.
AND THESE... ***MONSTERS...*** WENT FROM ROOM TO ROOM...AND JUST... ***SLAUGHTERED*** THEM.
FOR DARING TO COME HELP THOSE IN NEED.

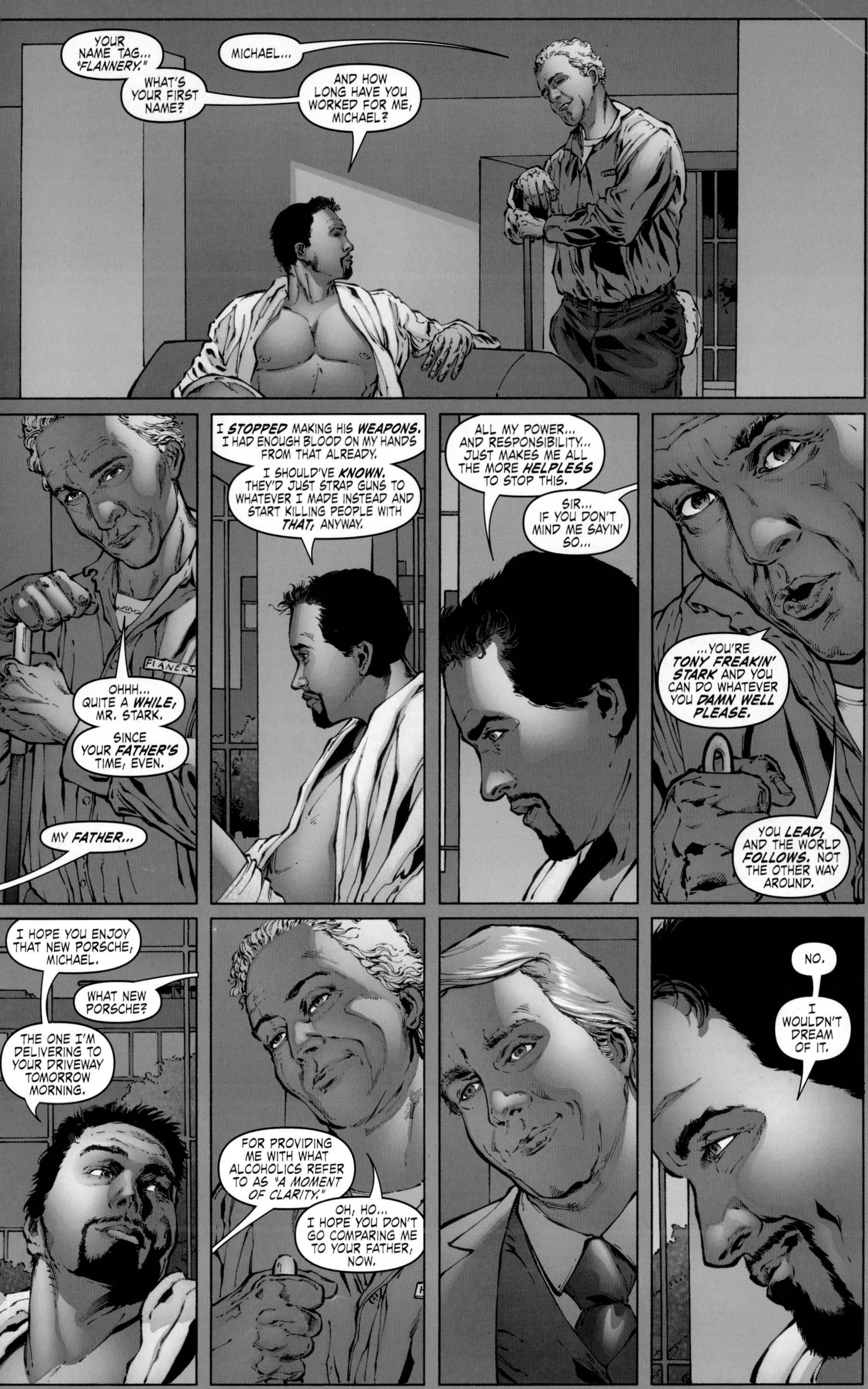
YOUR NAME TAG... "FLANNERY."
WHAT'S YOUR FIRST NAME?
MICHAEL...
AND HOW LONG HAVE YOU WORKED FOR ME, MICHAEL?
FLANERY
OHHH... QUITE A WHILE, MR. STARK.
SINCE YOUR FATHER'S TIME, EVEN.
MY FATHER...
I STOPPED MAKING HIS WEAPONS. I HAD ENOUGH BLOOD ON MY HANDS FROM THAT ALREADY.
I SHOULD'VE KNOWN. THEY'D JUST STRAP GUNS TO WHATEVER I MADE INSTEAD AND START KILLING PEOPLE WITH THAT, ANYWAY.
ALL MY POWER... AND RESPONSIBILITY... JUST MAKES ME ALL THE MORE HELPLESS TO STOP THIS.
SIR... IF YOU DON'T MIND ME SAYIN' SO...
...YOU'RE TONY FREAKIN' STARK AND YOU CAN DO WHATEVER YOU DAMN WELL PLEASE.
YOU LEAD, AND THE WORLD FOLLOWS. NOT THE OTHER WAY AROUND.
I HOPE YOU ENJOY THAT NEW PORSCHE, MICHAEL.
WHAT NEW PORSCHE?
THE ONE I'M DELIVERING TO YOUR DRIVEWAY TOMORROW MORNING.
FOR PROVIDING ME WITH WHAT ALCOHOLICS REFER TO AS "A MOMENT OF CLARITY."
OH, HO... I HOPE YOU DON'T GO COMPARING ME TO YOUR FATHER, NOW.
NO.
I WOULDN'T DREAM OF IT.

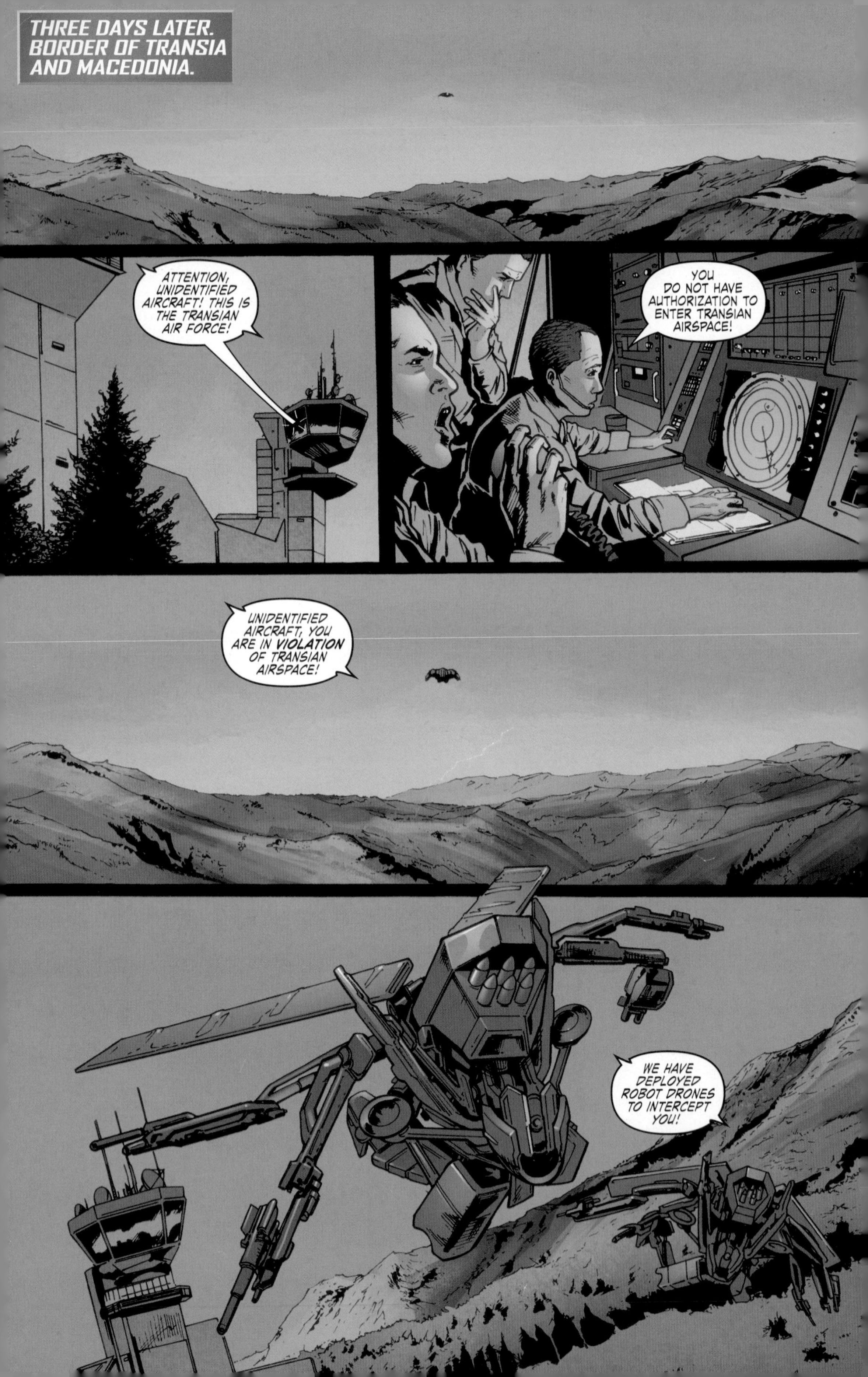
THREE DAYS LATER. BORDER OF TRANSIA AND MACEDONIA.
ATTENTION, UNIDENTIFIED AIRCRAFT! THIS IS THE TRANSIAN AIR FORCE!
YOU DO NOT HAVE AUTHORIZATION TO ENTER TRANSIAN AIRSPACE!
UNIDENTIFIED AIRCRAFT, YOU ARE IN **VIOLATION** OF TRANSIAN AIRSPACE!
WE HAVE DEPLOYED ROBOT DRONES TO INTERCEPT YOU!

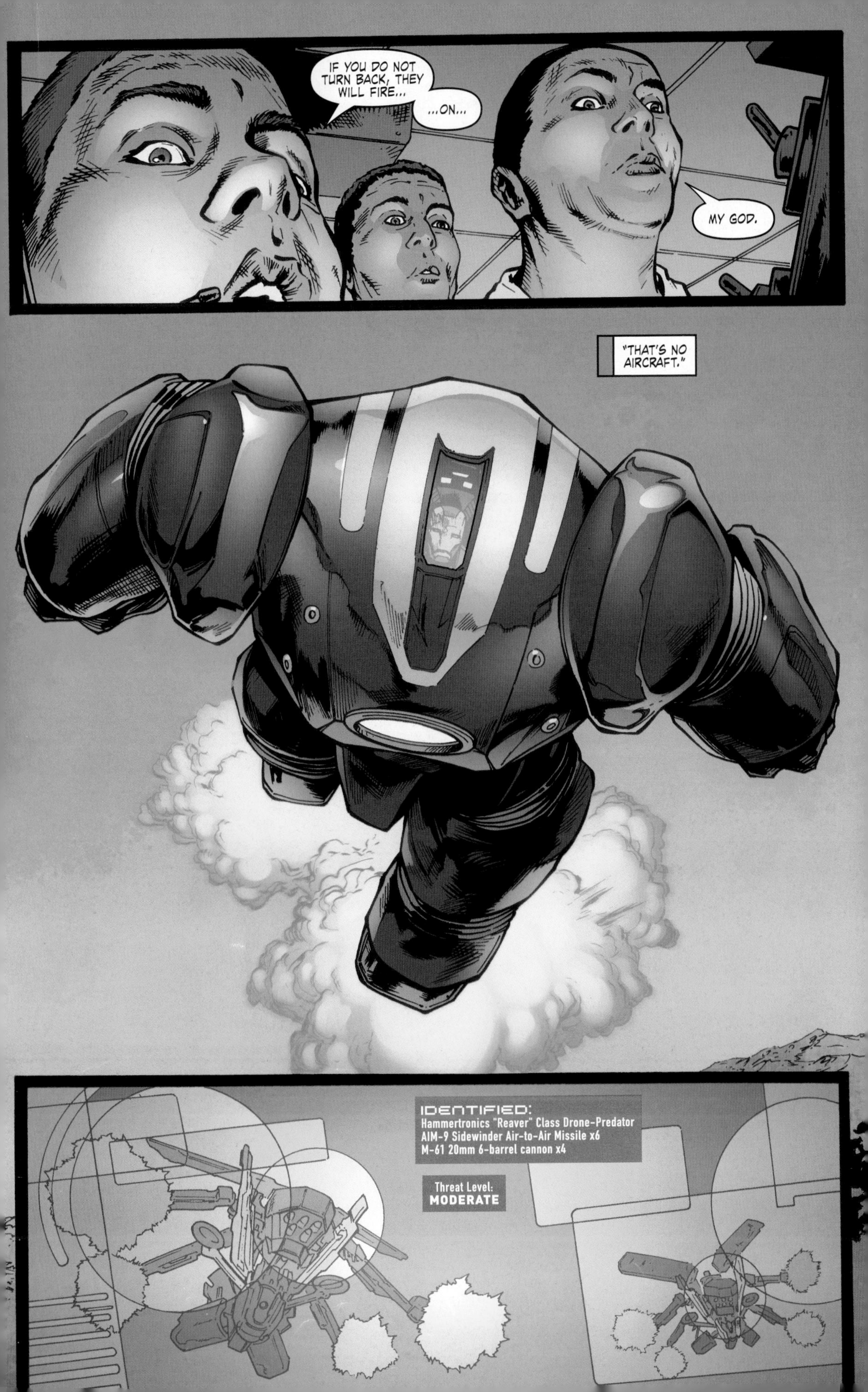
IF YOU DO NOT TURN BACK, THEY WILL FIRE...
...ON...
MY GOD.
"THAT'S NO AIRCRAFT."
IDENTIFIED:
Hammertronics "Reaver" Class Drone-Predator
AIM-9 Sidewinder Air-to-Air Missile x6
M-61 20mm 6-barrel cannon x4
Threat Level:
MODERATE

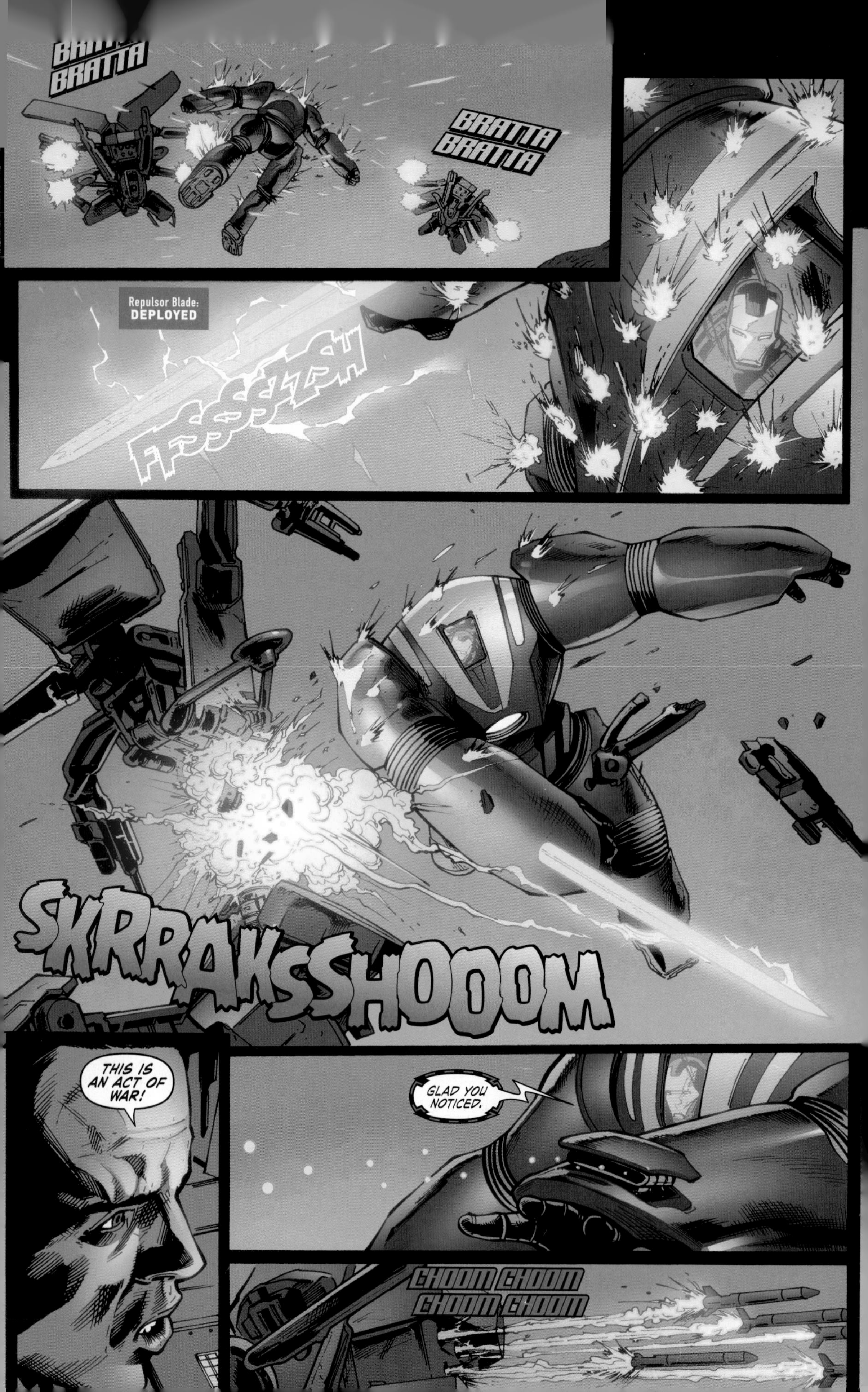
BRATTA
BRATTA
BRATTA
Repulsor Blade: DEPLOYED
FSSSZZSH
SKRRAKSSHOOOM
THIS IS AN ACT OF WAR!
GLAD YOU NOTICED.
CHOOM CHOOM
CHOOM CHOOM

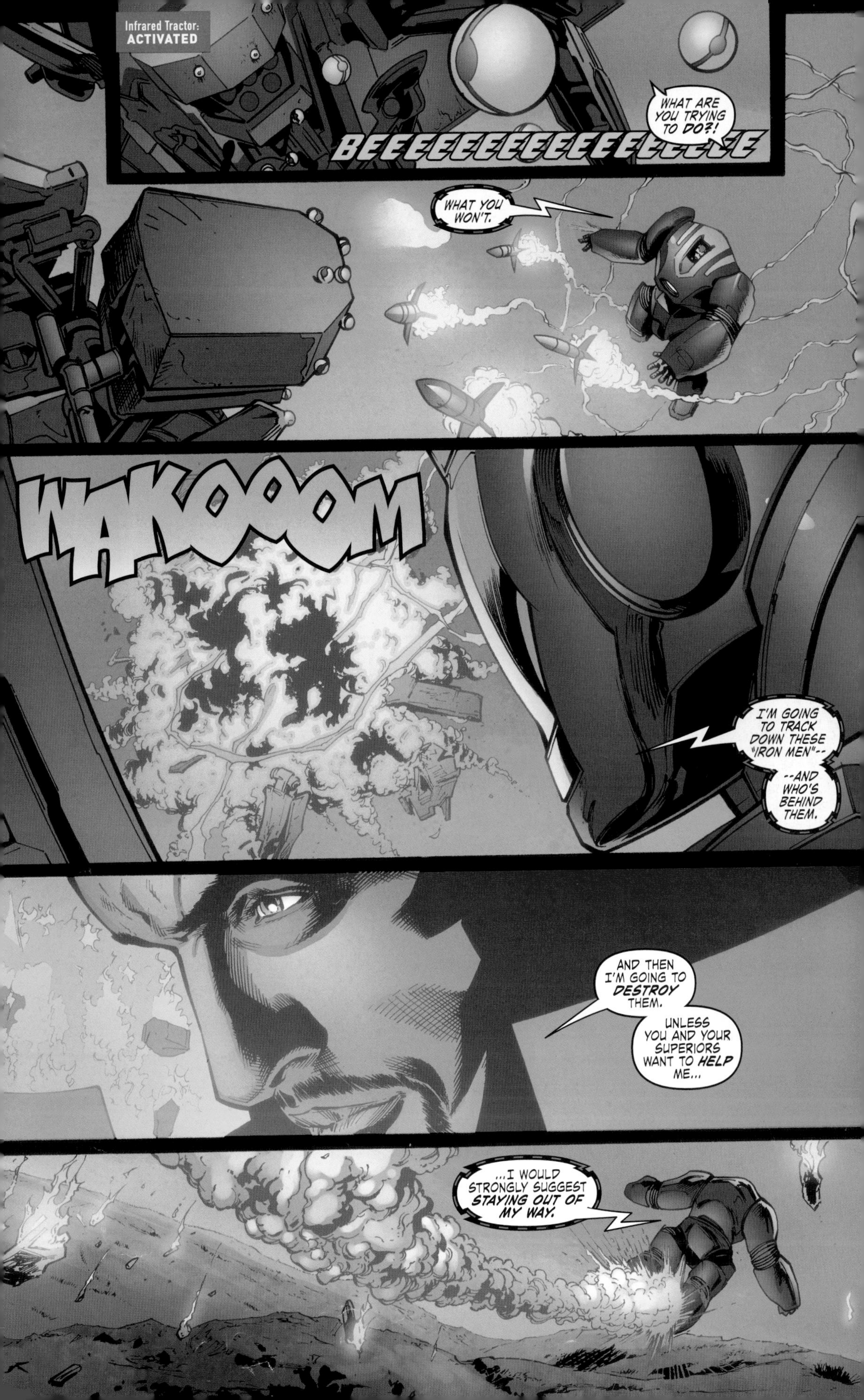
Infrared Tractor: ACTIVATED
WHAT ARE YOU TRYING TO DO?!
BEEEEEEEEEEEEEEEEEE
WHAT YOU WON'T.
WAKOOOM
I'M GOING TO TRACK DOWN THESE "IRON MEN"--
--AND WHO'S BEHIND THEM.
AND THEN I'M GOING TO DESTROY THEM.
UNLESS YOU AND YOUR SUPERIORS WANT TO HELP ME...
...I WOULD STRONGLY SUGGEST STAYING OUT OF MY WAY.

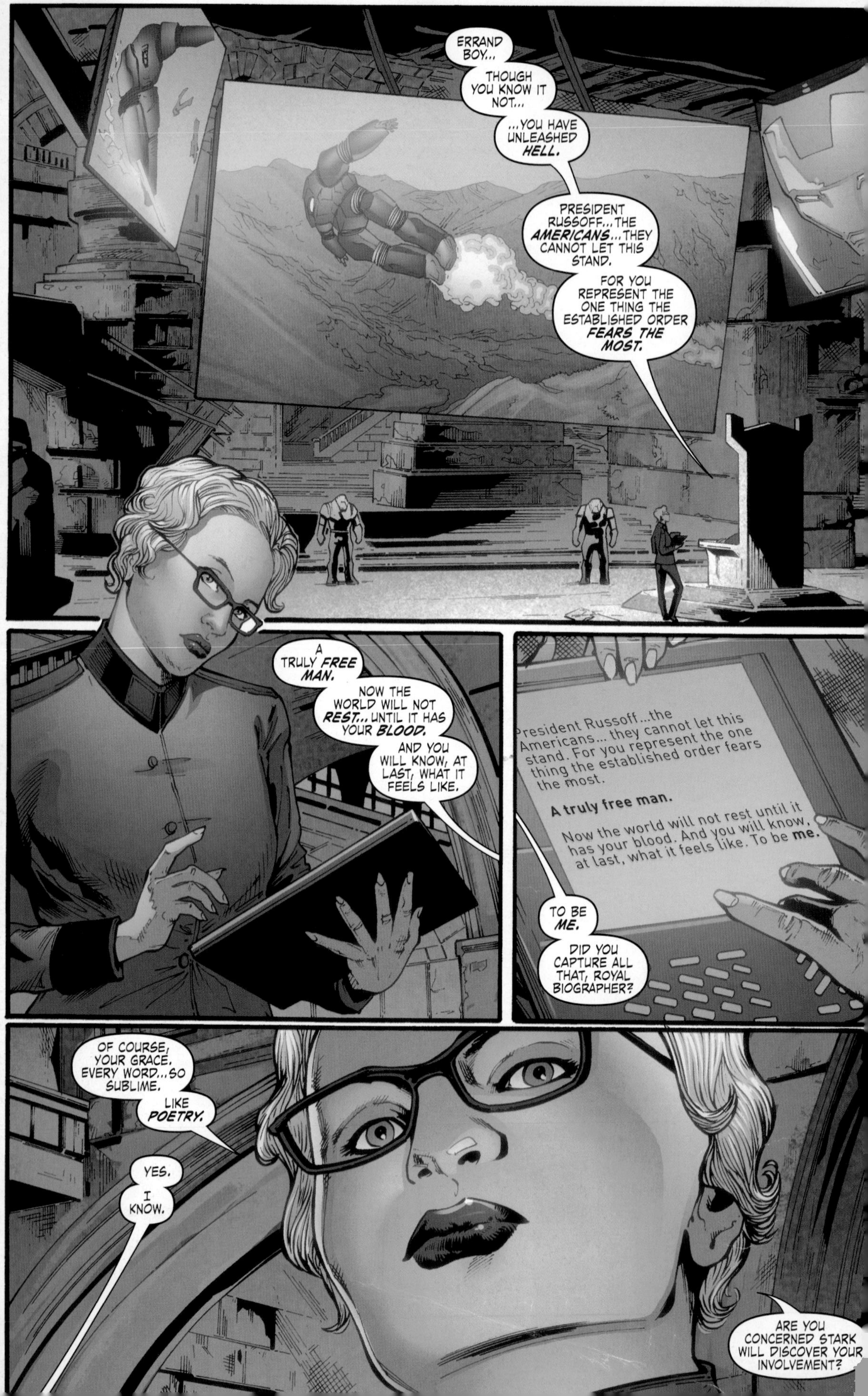
ERRAND BOY...
THOUGH YOU KNOW IT NOT...
...YOU HAVE UNLEASHED *HELL.*
PRESIDENT RUSSOFF...THE *AMERICANS*...THEY CANNOT LET THIS STAND.
FOR YOU REPRESENT THE ONE THING THE ESTABLISHED ORDER *FEARS THE MOST.*
A TRULY *FREE MAN.*
NOW THE WORLD WILL NOT *REST...* UNTIL IT HAS YOUR *BLOOD.*
AND YOU WILL KNOW, AT LAST, WHAT IT FEELS LIKE.
President Russoff...the Americans... they cannot let this stand. For you represent the one thing the established order fears the most.
A truly free man.
Now the world will not rest until it has your blood. And you will know, at last, what it feels like. To be **me.**
TO BE *ME.*
DID YOU CAPTURE ALL THAT, ROYAL BIOGRAPHER?
OF COURSE, YOUR GRACE. EVERY WORD...SO SUBLIME.
LIKE *POETRY.*
YES.
I KNOW.
ARE YOU CONCERNED STARK WILL DISCOVER YOUR INVOLVEMENT?

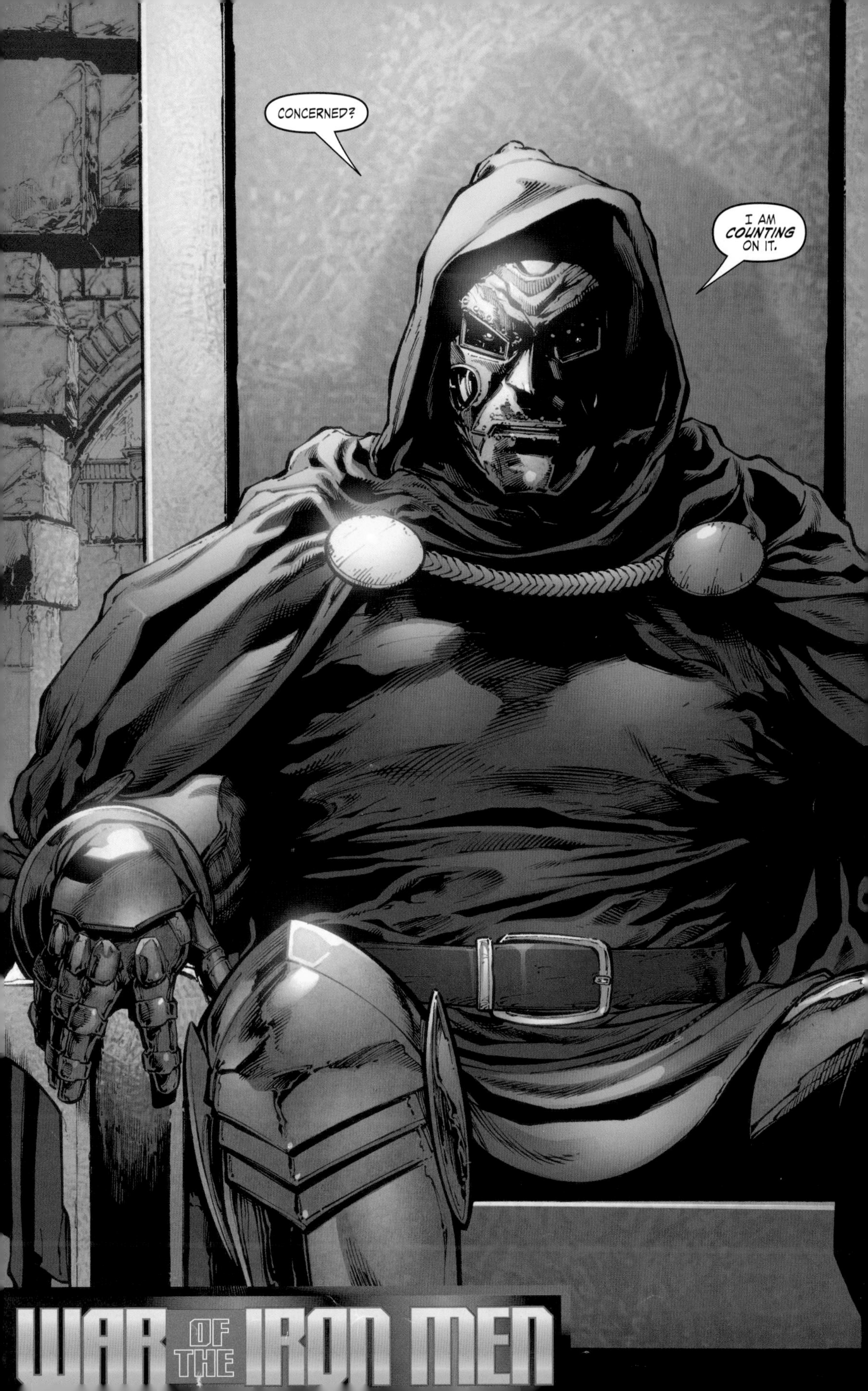
CONCERNED?
I AM COUNTING ON IT.
WAR OF THE IRON MEN

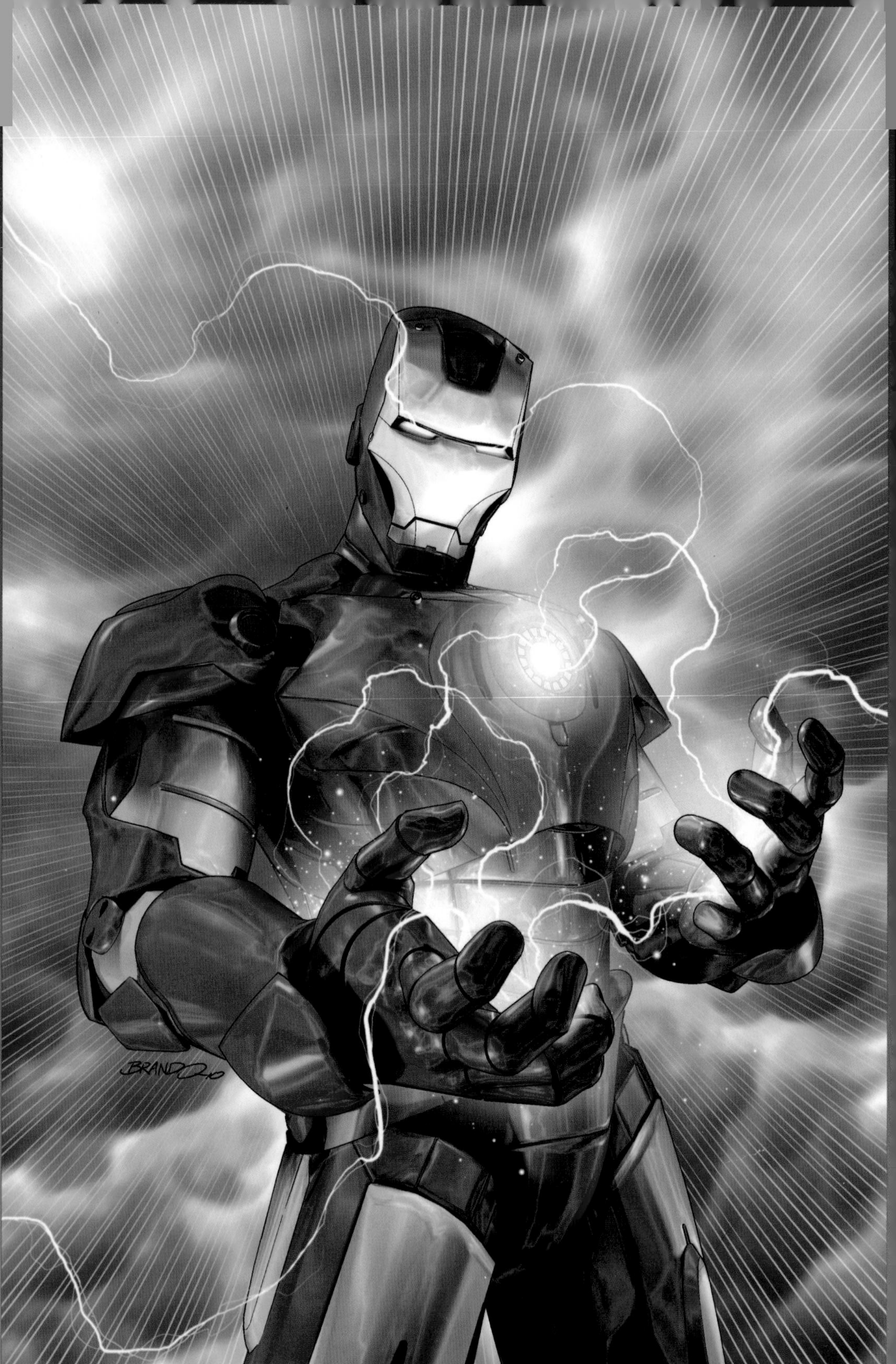

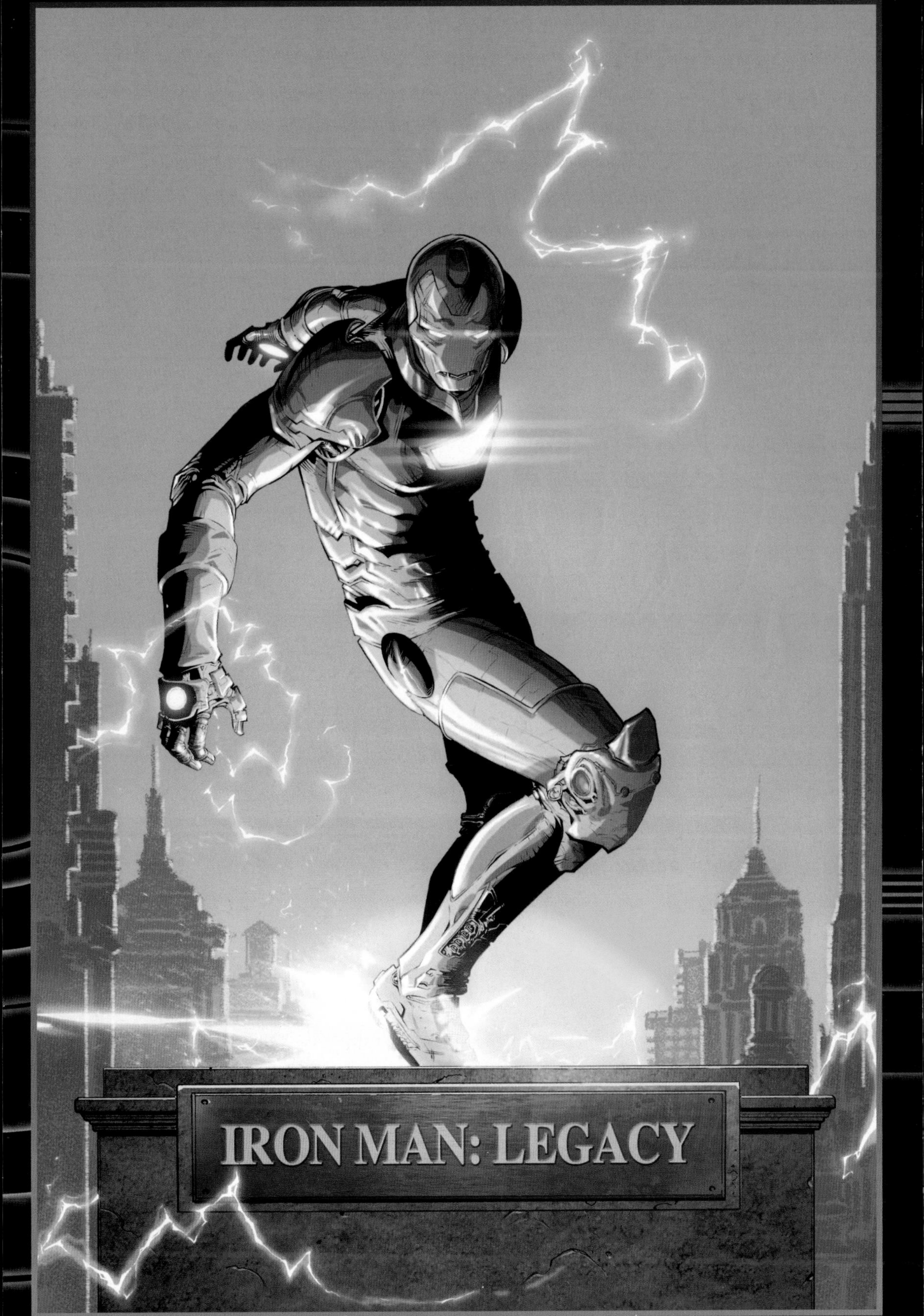
IRON MAN: LEGACY

#2 HEROIC AGE VARIANT
BY PASCAL ALIXE

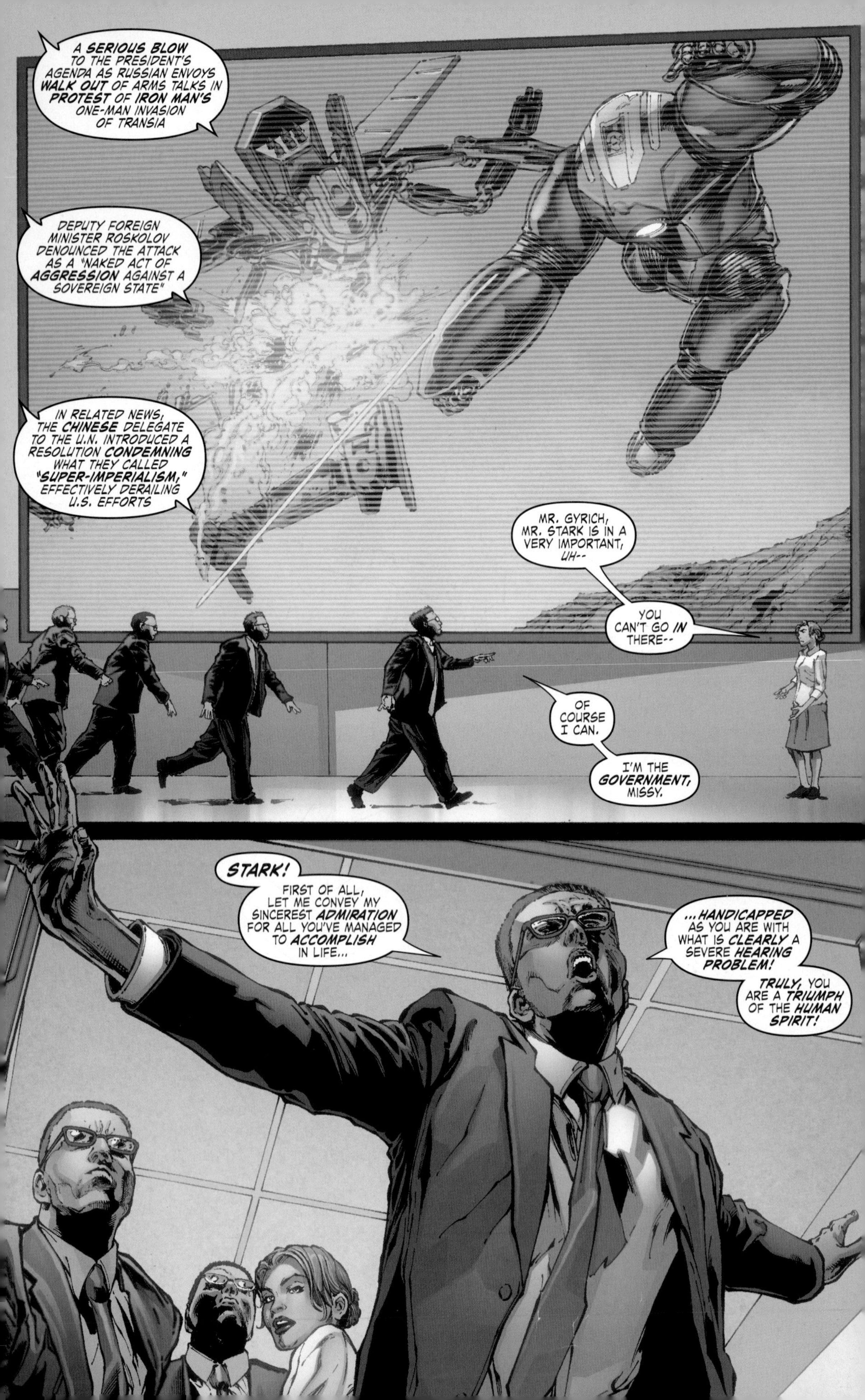
A SERIOUS BLOW TO THE PRESIDENT'S AGENDA AS RUSSIAN ENVOYS WALK OUT OF ARMS TALKS IN PROTEST OF IRON MAN'S ONE-MAN INVASION OF TRANSIA
DEPUTY FOREIGN MINISTER ROSKOLOV DENOUNCED THE ATTACK AS A "NAKED ACT OF AGGRESSION AGAINST A SOVEREIGN STATE"
IN RELATED NEWS, THE CHINESE DELEGATE TO THE U.N. INTRODUCED A RESOLUTION CONDEMNING WHAT THEY CALLED "SUPER-IMPERIALISM," EFFECTIVELY DERAILING U.S. EFFORTS
MR. GYRICH, MR. STARK IS IN A VERY IMPORTANT, UH--
YOU CAN'T GO IN THERE--
OF COURSE I CAN.
I'M THE GOVERNMENT, MISSY.
STARK!
FIRST OF ALL, LET ME CONVEY MY SINCEREST ADMIRATION FOR ALL YOU'VE MANAGED TO ACCOMPLISH IN LIFE...
...HANDICAPPED AS YOU ARE WITH WHAT IS CLEARLY A SEVERE HEARING PROBLEM!
TRULY, YOU ARE A TRIUMPH OF THE HUMAN SPIRIT!

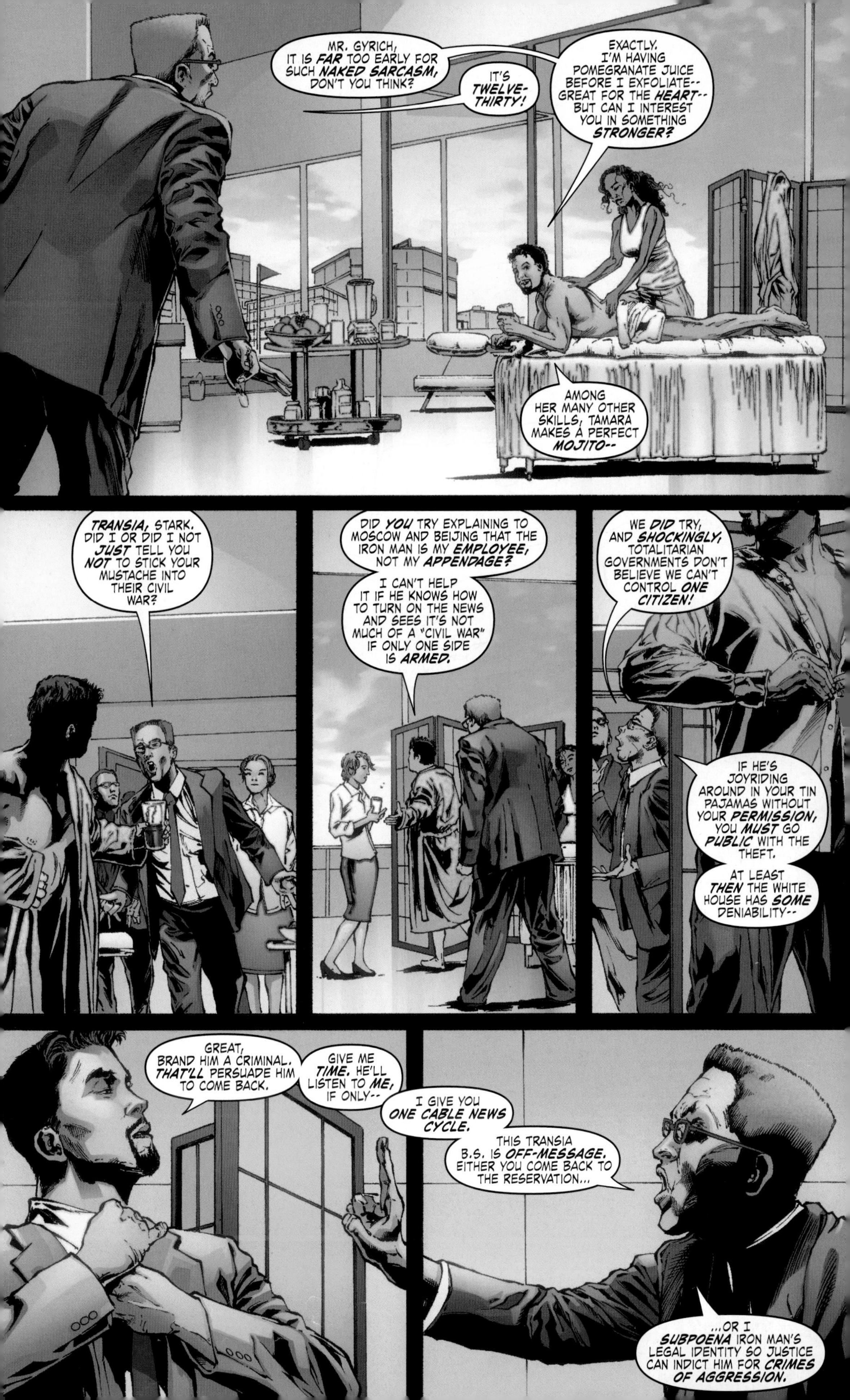
MR. GYRICH, IT IS FAR TOO EARLY FOR SUCH NAKED SARCASM, DON'T YOU THINK?
IT'S TWELVE-THIRTY!
EXACTLY. I'M HAVING POMEGRANATE JUICE BEFORE I EXFOLIATE-- GREAT FOR THE HEART-- BUT CAN I INTEREST YOU IN SOMETHING STRONGER?
AMONG HER MANY OTHER SKILLS, TAMARA MAKES A PERFECT MOJITO--
TRANSIA, STARK. DID I OR DID I NOT JUST TELL YOU NOT TO STICK YOUR MUSTACHE INTO THEIR CIVIL WAR?
DID YOU TRY EXPLAINING TO MOSCOW AND BEIJING THAT THE IRON MAN IS MY EMPLOYEE, NOT MY APPENDAGE?
I CAN'T HELP IT IF HE KNOWS HOW TO TURN ON THE NEWS AND SEES IT'S NOT MUCH OF A "CIVIL WAR" IF ONLY ONE SIDE IS ARMED.
WE DID TRY, AND SHOCKINGLY, TOTALITARIAN GOVERNMENTS DON'T BELIEVE WE CAN'T CONTROL ONE CITIZEN!
IF HE'S JOYRIDING AROUND IN YOUR TIN PAJAMAS WITHOUT YOUR PERMISSION, YOU MUST GO PUBLIC WITH THE THEFT.
AT LEAST THEN THE WHITE HOUSE HAS SOME DENIABILITY--
GREAT, BRAND HIM A CRIMINAL. THAT'LL PERSUADE HIM TO COME BACK.
GIVE ME TIME. HE'LL LISTEN TO ME, IF ONLY--
I GIVE YOU ONE CABLE NEWS CYCLE.
THIS TRANSIA B.S. IS OFF-MESSAGE. EITHER YOU COME BACK TO THE RESERVATION...
...OR I SUBPOENA IRON MAN'S LEGAL IDENTITY SO JUSTICE CAN INDICT HIM FOR CRIMES OF AGGRESSION.

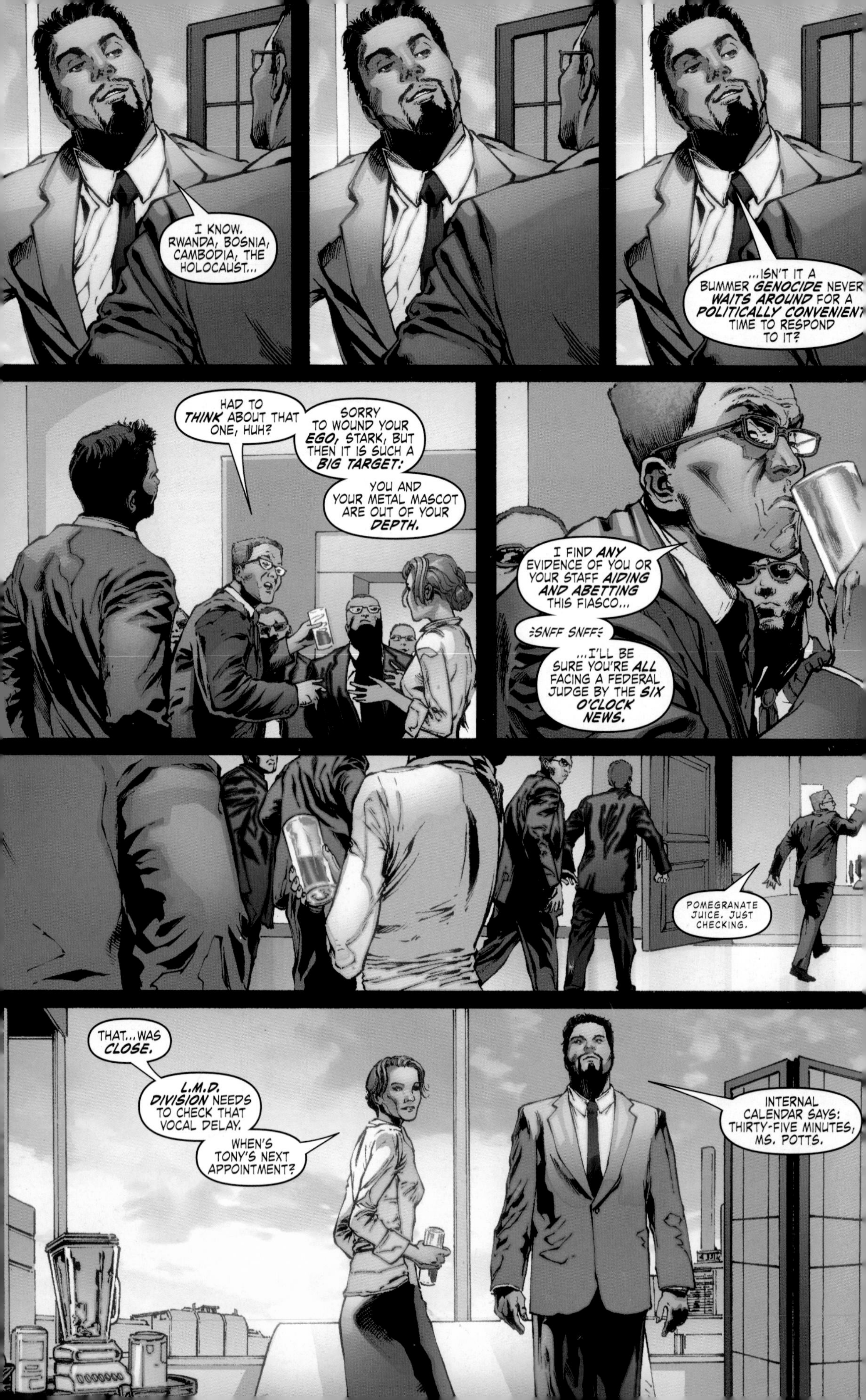
I KNOW. RWANDA, BOSNIA, CAMBODIA, THE HOLOCAUST...
...ISN'T IT A BUMMER GENOCIDE NEVER WAITS AROUND FOR A POLITICALLY CONVENIENT TIME TO RESPOND TO IT?
HAD TO THINK ABOUT THAT ONE, HUH?
SORRY TO WOUND YOUR EGO, STARK, BUT THEN IT IS SUCH A BIG TARGET:
YOU AND YOUR METAL MASCOT ARE OUT OF YOUR DEPTH.
I FIND ANY EVIDENCE OF YOU OR YOUR STAFF AIDING AND ABETTING THIS FIASCO...
SNFF SNFF
...I'LL BE SURE YOU'RE ALL FACING A FEDERAL JUDGE BY THE SIX O'CLOCK NEWS.
POMEGRANATE JUICE. JUST CHECKING.
THAT...WAS CLOSE.
L.M.D. DIVISION NEEDS TO CHECK THAT VOCAL DELAY.
WHEN'S TONY'S NEXT APPOINTMENT?
INTERNAL CALENDAR SAYS: THIRTY-FIVE MINUTES, MS. POTTS.

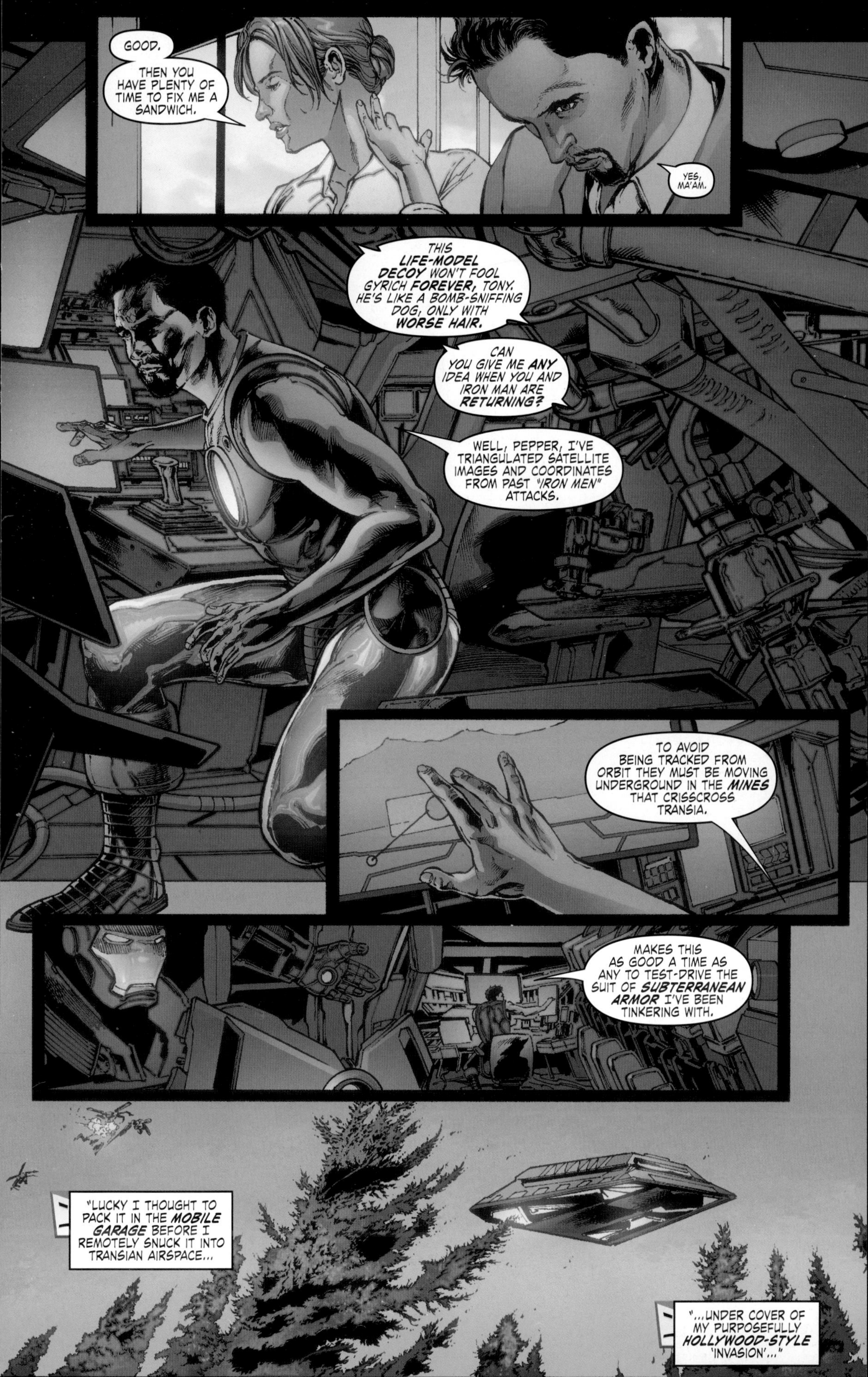
GOOD.
THEN YOU HAVE PLENTY OF TIME TO FIX ME A SANDWICH.
YES, MA'AM.
THIS LIFE-MODEL DECOY WON'T FOOL GYRICH FOREVER, TONY. HE'S LIKE A BOMB-SNIFFING DOG, ONLY WITH WORSE HAIR.
CAN YOU GIVE ME ANY IDEA WHEN YOU AND IRON MAN ARE RETURNING?
WELL, PEPPER, I'VE TRIANGULATED SATELLITE IMAGES AND COORDINATES FROM PAST "IRON MEN" ATTACKS.
TO AVOID BEING TRACKED FROM ORBIT THEY MUST BE MOVING UNDERGROUND IN THE MINES THAT CRISSCROSS TRANSIA.
MAKES THIS AS GOOD A TIME AS ANY TO TEST-DRIVE THE SUIT OF SUBTERRANEAN ARMOR I'VE BEEN TINKERING WITH.
"LUCKY I THOUGHT TO PACK IT IN THE MOBILE GARAGE BEFORE I REMOTELY SNUCK IT INTO TRANSIAN AIRSPACE...
"...UNDER COVER OF MY PURPOSEFULLY HOLLYWOOD-STYLE 'INVASION'..."

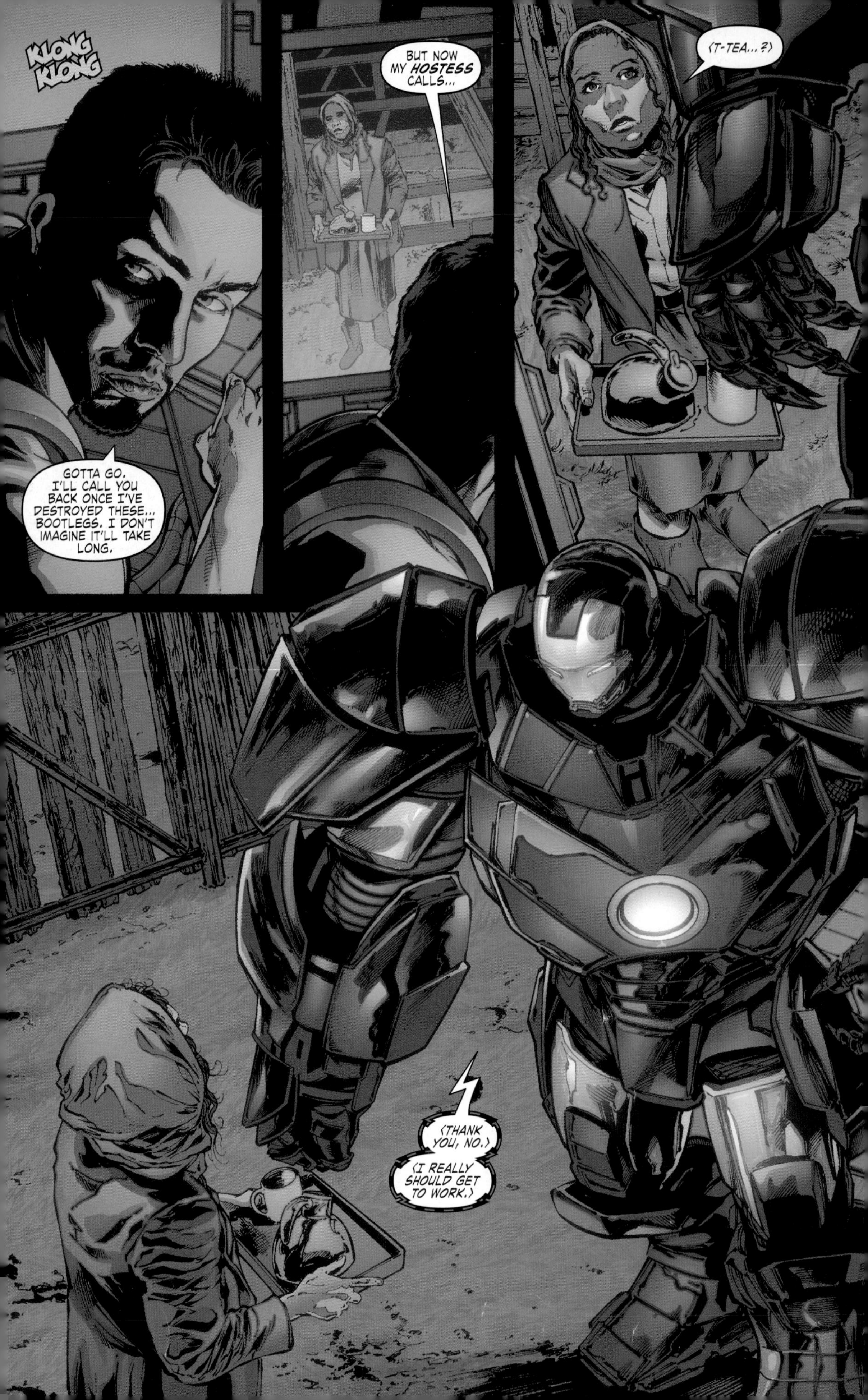
KLONG KLONG
GOTTA GO. I'LL CALL YOU BACK ONCE I'VE DESTROYED THESE... BOOTLEGS. I DON'T IMAGINE IT'LL TAKE LONG.
BUT NOW MY HOSTESS CALLS...
⟨T-TEA...?⟩
⟨THANK YOU, NO.⟩
⟨I REALLY SHOULD GET TO WORK.⟩

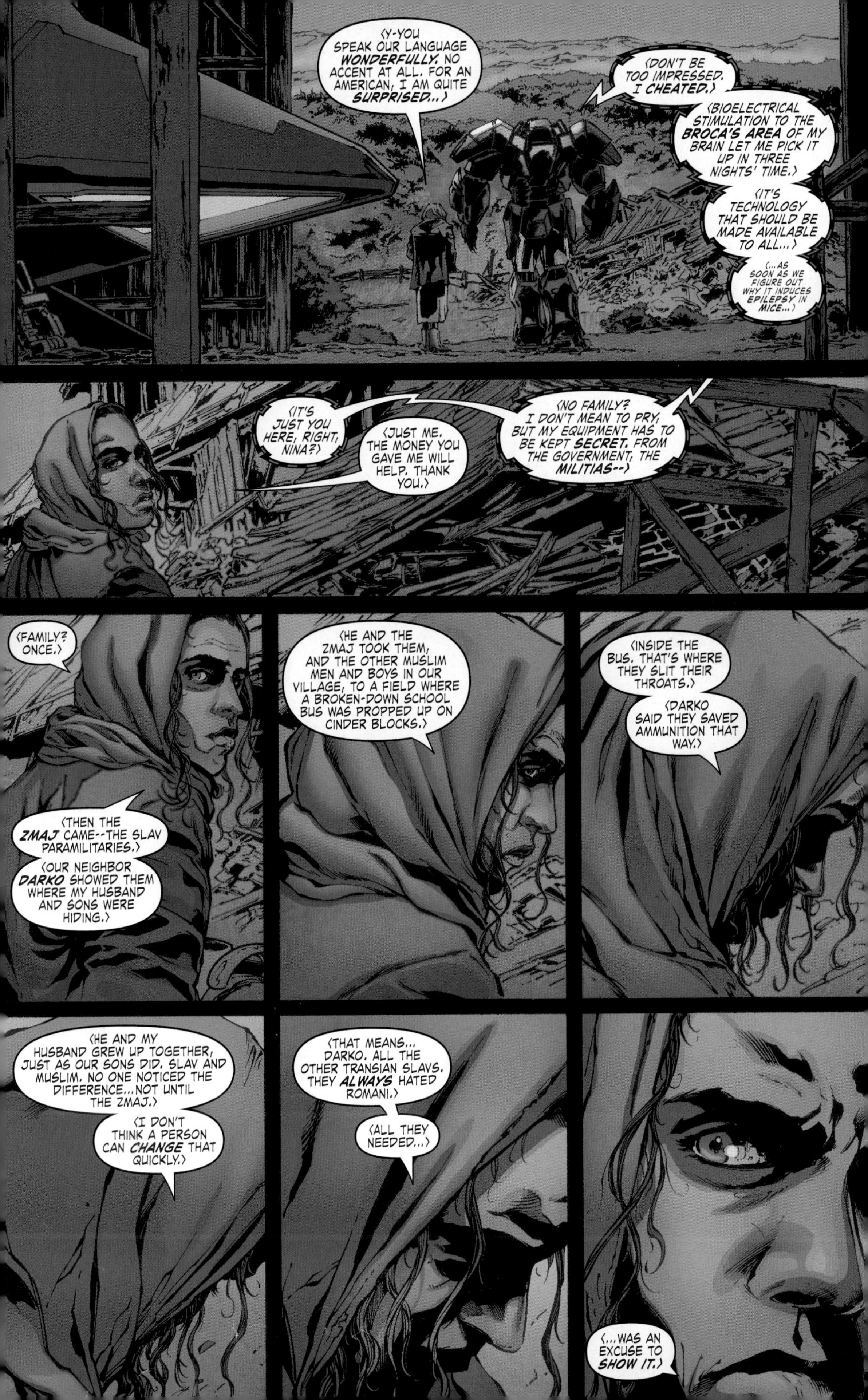
〈Y-YOU SPEAK OUR LANGUAGE WONDERFULLY. NO ACCENT AT ALL. FOR AN AMERICAN, I AM QUITE SURPRISED...〉
〈DON'T BE TOO IMPRESSED. I CHEATED.〉
〈BIOELECTRICAL STIMULATION TO THE BROCA'S AREA OF MY BRAIN LET ME PICK IT UP IN THREE NIGHTS' TIME.〉
〈IT'S TECHNOLOGY THAT SHOULD BE MADE AVAILABLE TO ALL...〉
〈...AS SOON AS WE FIGURE OUT WHY IT INDUCES EPILEPSY IN MICE...〉
〈IT'S JUST YOU HERE, RIGHT, NINA?〉
〈JUST ME. THE MONEY YOU GAVE ME WILL HELP. THANK YOU.〉
〈NO FAMILY? I DON'T MEAN TO PRY, BUT MY EQUIPMENT HAS TO BE KEPT SECRET. FROM THE GOVERNMENT, THE MILITIAS--〉
〈FAMILY? ONCE.〉
〈THEN THE ZMAJ CAME--THE SLAV PARAMILITARIES.〉
〈OUR NEIGHBOR DARKO SHOWED THEM WHERE MY HUSBAND AND SONS WERE HIDING.〉
〈HE AND THE ZMAJ TOOK THEM, AND THE OTHER MUSLIM MEN AND BOYS IN OUR VILLAGE, TO A FIELD WHERE A BROKEN-DOWN SCHOOL BUS WAS PROPPED UP ON CINDER BLOCKS.〉
〈INSIDE THE BUS. THAT'S WHERE THEY SLIT THEIR THROATS.〉
〈DARKO SAID THEY SAVED AMMUNITION THAT WAY.〉
〈HE AND MY HUSBAND GREW UP TOGETHER, JUST AS OUR SONS DID. SLAV AND MUSLIM. NO ONE NOTICED THE DIFFERENCE...NOT UNTIL THE ZMAJ.〉
〈I DON'T THINK A PERSON CAN CHANGE THAT QUICKLY.〉
〈THAT MEANS... DARKO. ALL THE OTHER TRANSIAN SLAVS. THEY ALWAYS HATED ROMANI.〉
〈ALL THEY NEEDED...〉
〈...WAS AN EXCUSE TO SHOW IT.〉

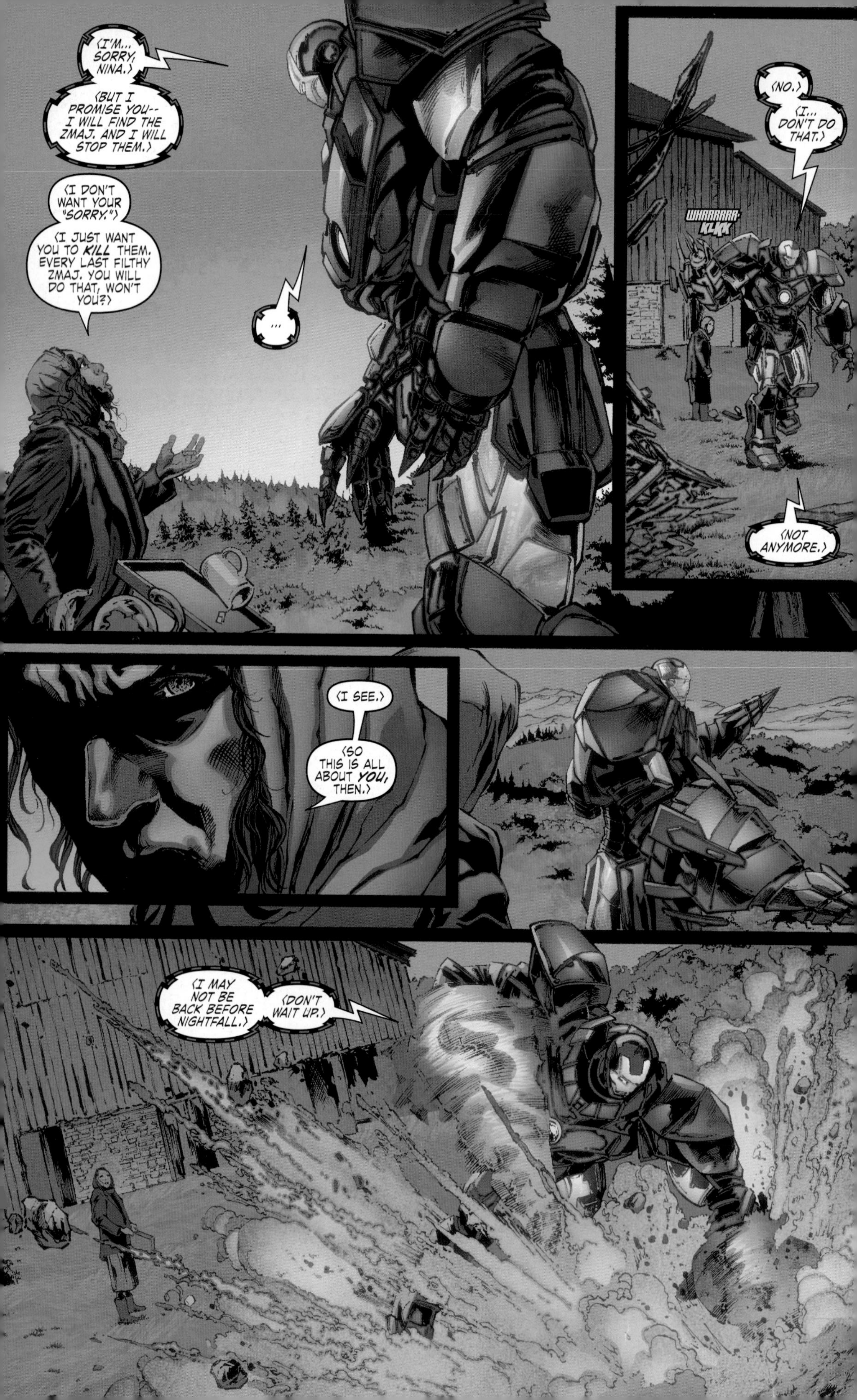
⟨I'M... SORRY, NINA.⟩
⟨BUT I PROMISE YOU-- I WILL FIND THE ZMAJ. AND I WILL STOP THEM.⟩
⟨I DON'T WANT YOUR "SORRY."⟩
⟨I JUST WANT YOU TO KILL THEM. EVERY LAST FILTHY ZMAJ. YOU WILL DO THAT, WON'T YOU?⟩
⟨...⟩
⟨NO.⟩
⟨I... DON'T DO THAT.⟩
WHRRRRRR-KLKK
⟨NOT ANYMORE.⟩
⟨I SEE.⟩
⟨SO THIS IS ALL ABOUT YOU, THEN.⟩
⟨I MAY NOT BE BACK BEFORE NIGHTFALL.⟩
⟨DON'T WAIT UP.⟩

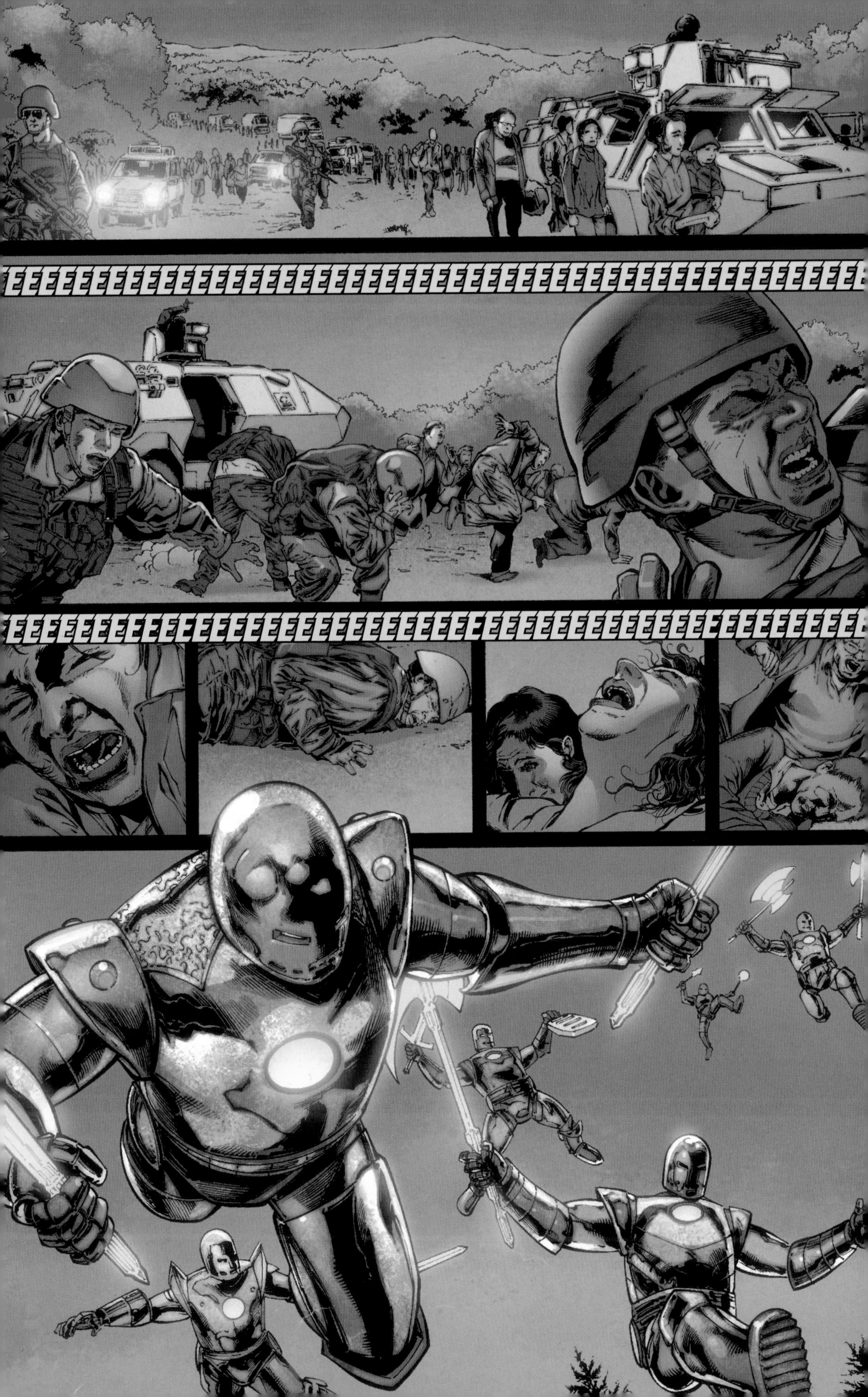
EEEEEEEEEEEEEEEEEEEEEEEEEEEEEEEEEEEEEEEEE
EEEEEEEEEEEEEEEEEEEEEEEEEEEEEEEEEEEEEEEEE

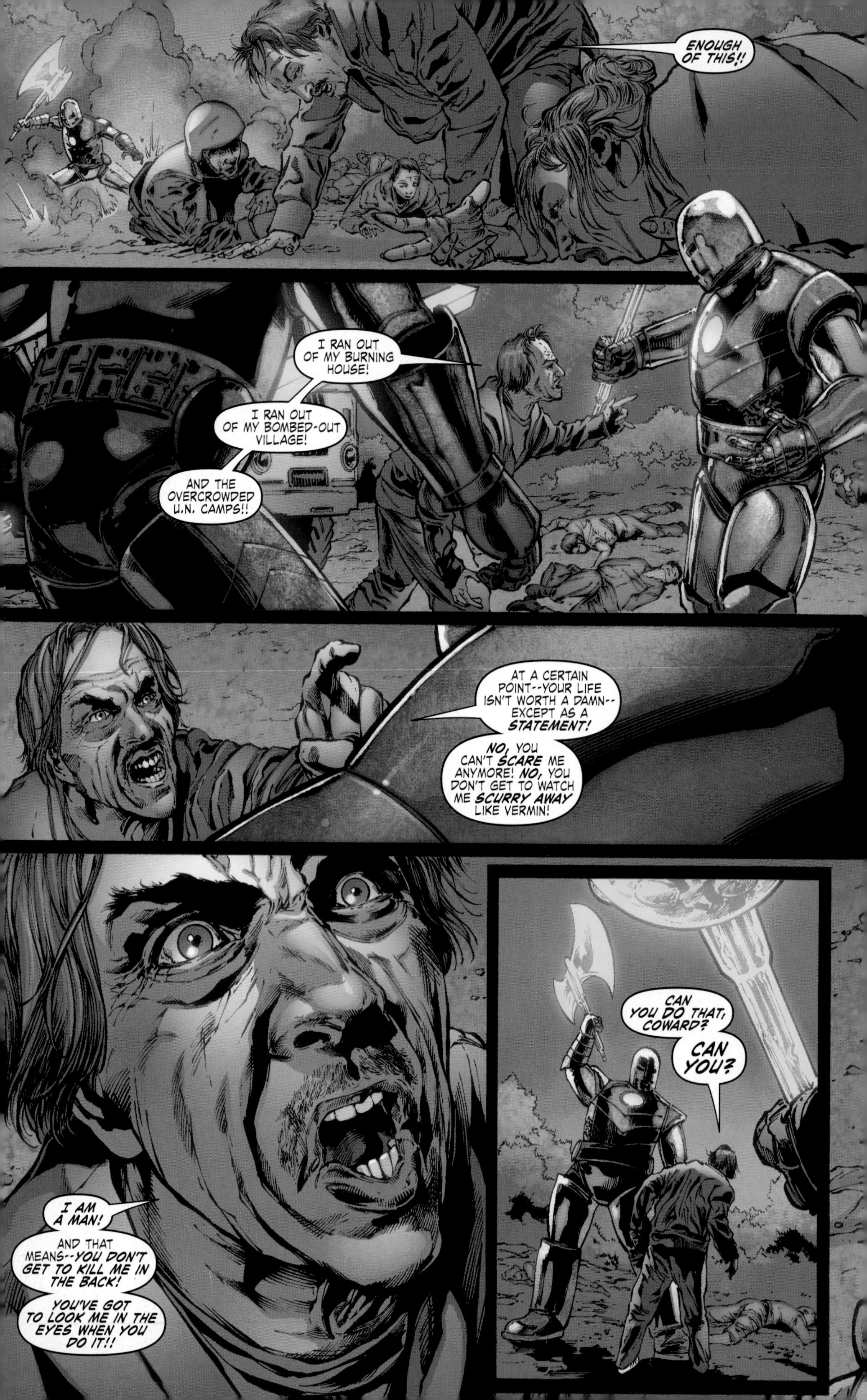

ENOUGH OF THIS!!
I RAN OUT OF MY BURNING HOUSE!
I RAN OUT OF MY BOMBED-OUT VILLAGE!
AND THE OVERCROWDED U.N. CAMPS!!
AT A CERTAIN POINT--YOUR LIFE ISN'T WORTH A DAMN--EXCEPT AS A STATEMENT!
NO, YOU CAN'T SCARE ME ANYMORE! NO, YOU DON'T GET TO WATCH ME SCURRY AWAY LIKE VERMIN!
I AM A MAN!
AND THAT MEANS--YOU DON'T GET TO KILL ME IN THE BACK!
YOU'VE GOT TO LOOK ME IN THE EYES WHEN YOU DO IT!!
CAN YOU DO THAT, COWARD?
CAN YOU?

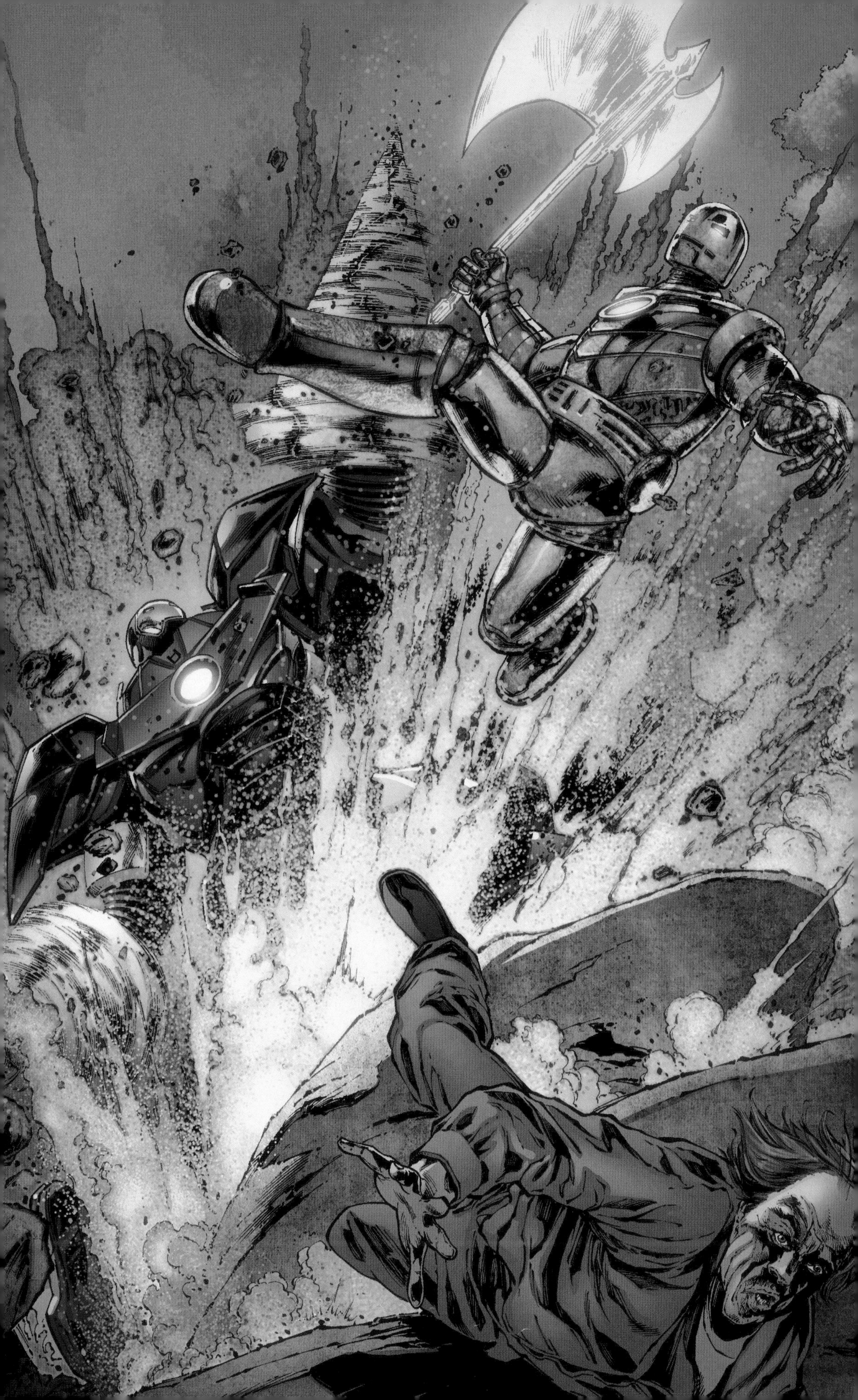

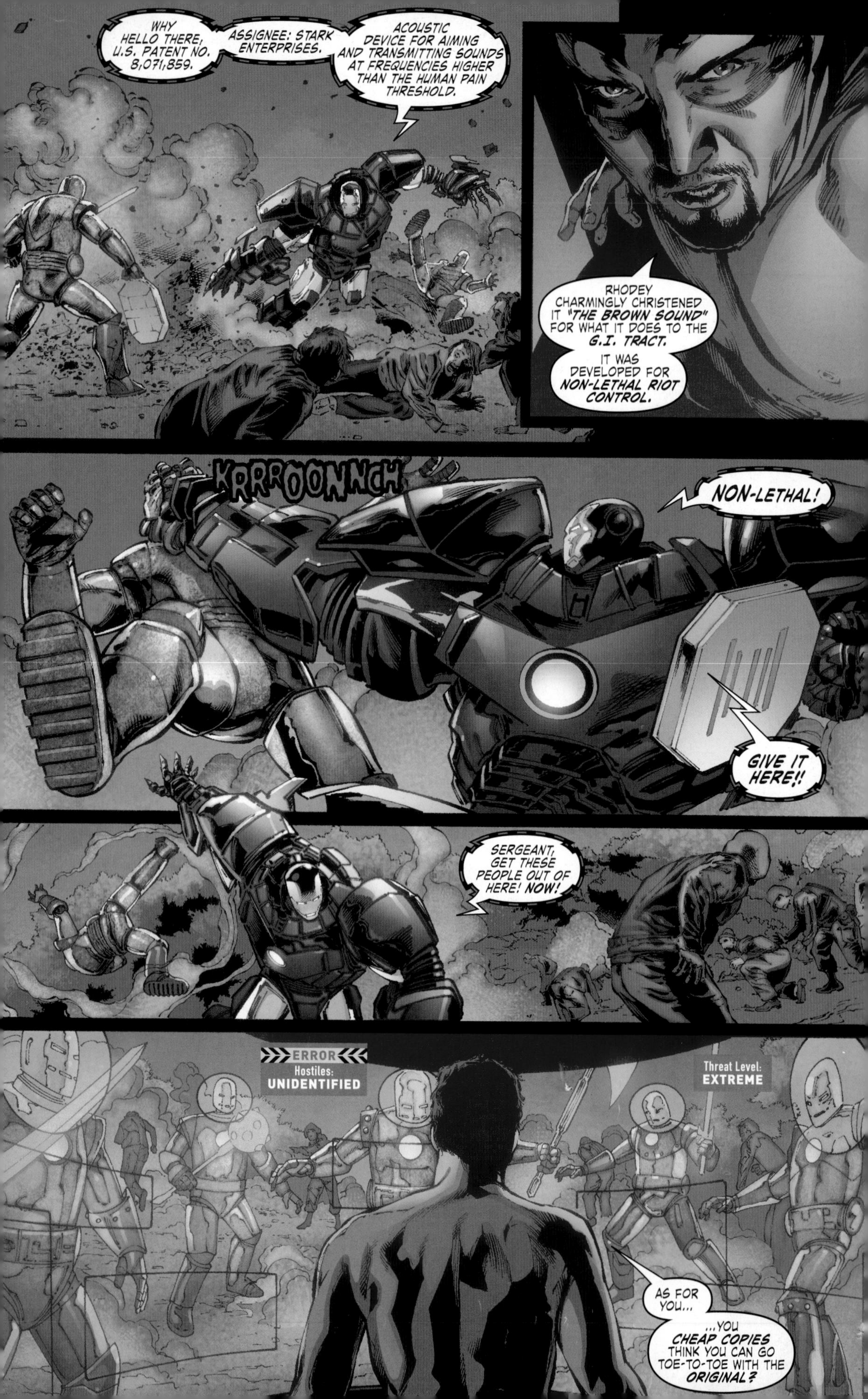
WHY HELLO THERE, U.S. PATENT NO. 8,071,859.
ASSIGNEE: STARK ENTERPRISES.
ACOUSTIC DEVICE FOR AIMING AND TRANSMITTING SOUNDS AT FREQUENCIES HIGHER THAN THE HUMAN PAIN THRESHOLD.
RHODEY CHARMINGLY CHRISTENED IT "THE BROWN SOUND" FOR WHAT IT DOES TO THE G.I. TRACT.
IT WAS DEVELOPED FOR NON-LETHAL RIOT CONTROL.
KRRROONNCH
NON-LETHAL!
GIVE IT HERE!!
SERGEANT, GET THESE PEOPLE OUT OF HERE! NOW!
ERROR
Hostiles: UNIDENTIFIED
Threat Level: EXTREME
AS FOR YOU...
...YOU CHEAP COPIES THINK YOU CAN GO TOE-TO-TOE WITH THE ORIGINAL?

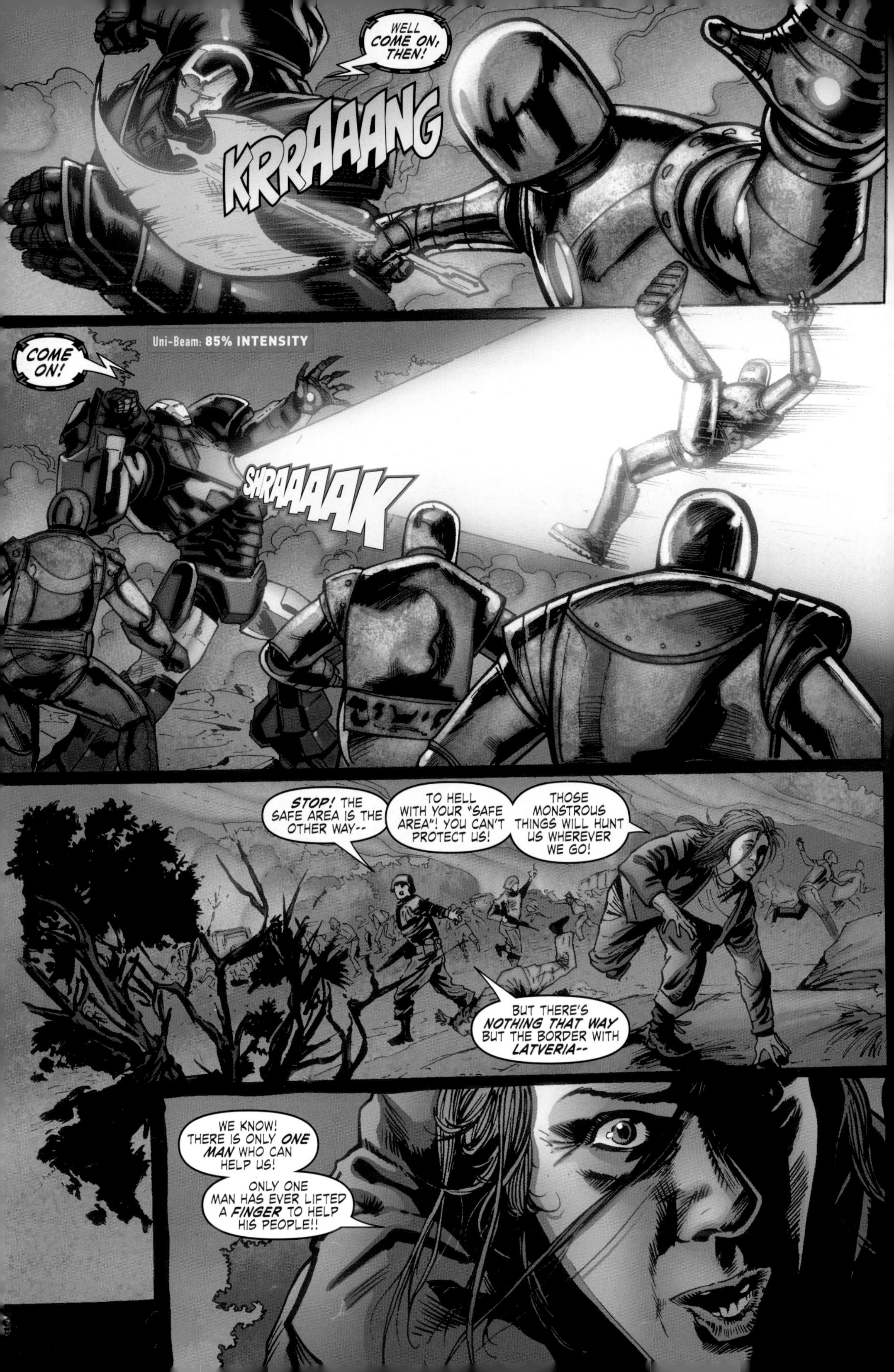
WELL COME ON, THEN!
KRRAAANG
Uni-Beam: 85% INTENSITY
COME ON!
SHRAAAAK
STOP! THE SAFE AREA IS THE OTHER WAY--
TO HELL WITH YOUR "SAFE AREA"! YOU CAN'T PROTECT US!
THOSE MONSTROUS THINGS WILL HUNT US WHEREVER WE GO!
BUT THERE'S NOTHING THAT WAY BUT THE BORDER WITH LATVERIA--
WE KNOW! THERE IS ONLY ONE MAN WHO CAN HELP US!
ONLY ONE MAN HAS EVER LIFTED A FINGER TO HELP HIS PEOPLE!!

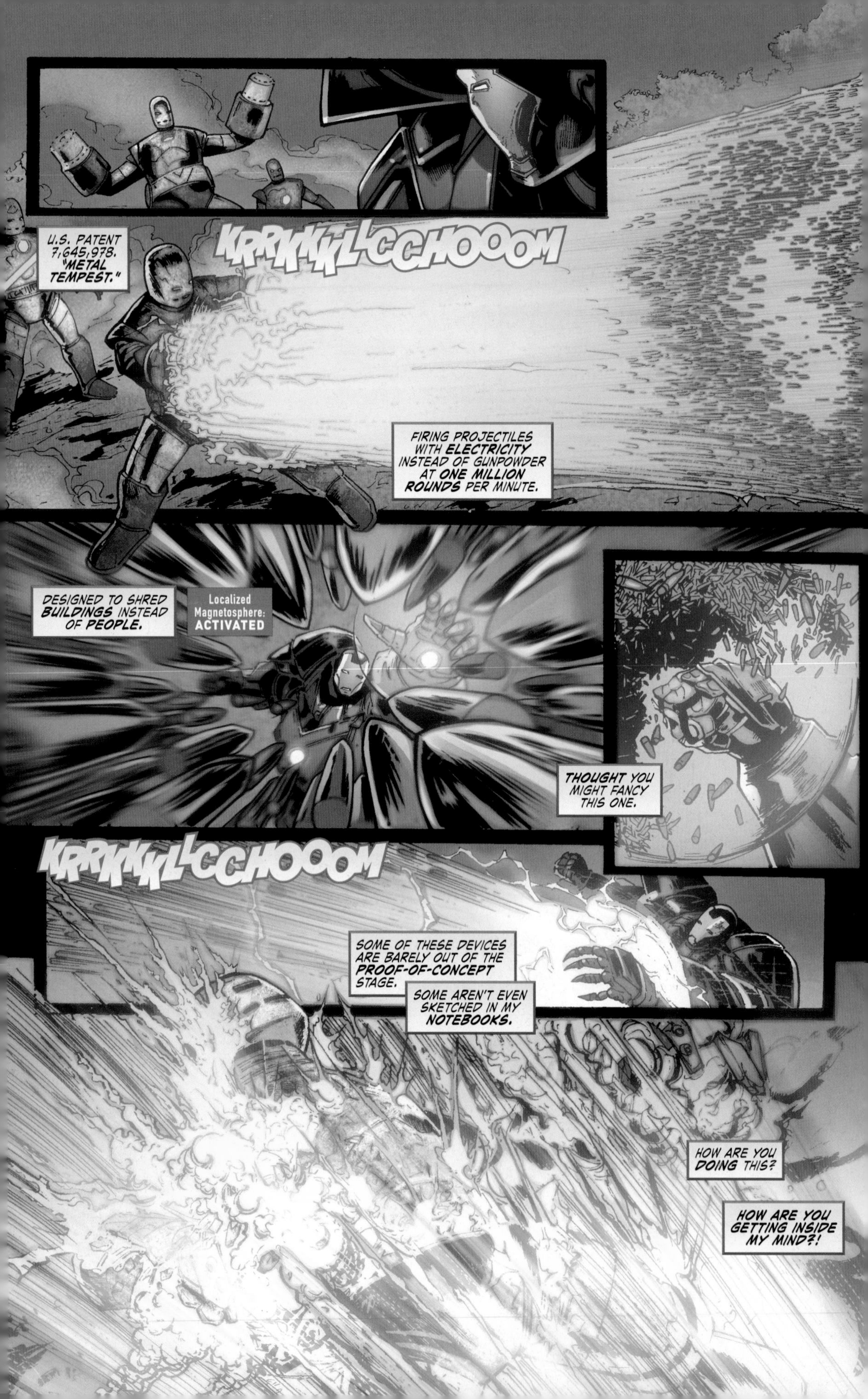
U.S. PATENT 7,645,978. "METAL TEMPEST."
KRRKKKLLCCHOOOOM
FIRING PROJECTILES WITH ELECTRICITY INSTEAD OF GUNPOWDER AT ONE MILLION ROUNDS PER MINUTE.
DESIGNED TO SHRED BUILDINGS INSTEAD OF PEOPLE.
Localized Magnetosphere: ACTIVATED
THOUGHT YOU MIGHT FANCY THIS ONE.
KRRKKKLLCCHOOOOM
SOME OF THESE DEVICES ARE BARELY OUT OF THE PROOF-OF-CONCEPT STAGE.
SOME AREN'T EVEN SKETCHED IN MY NOTEBOOKS.
HOW ARE YOU DOING THIS?
HOW ARE YOU GETTING INSIDE MY MIND?!

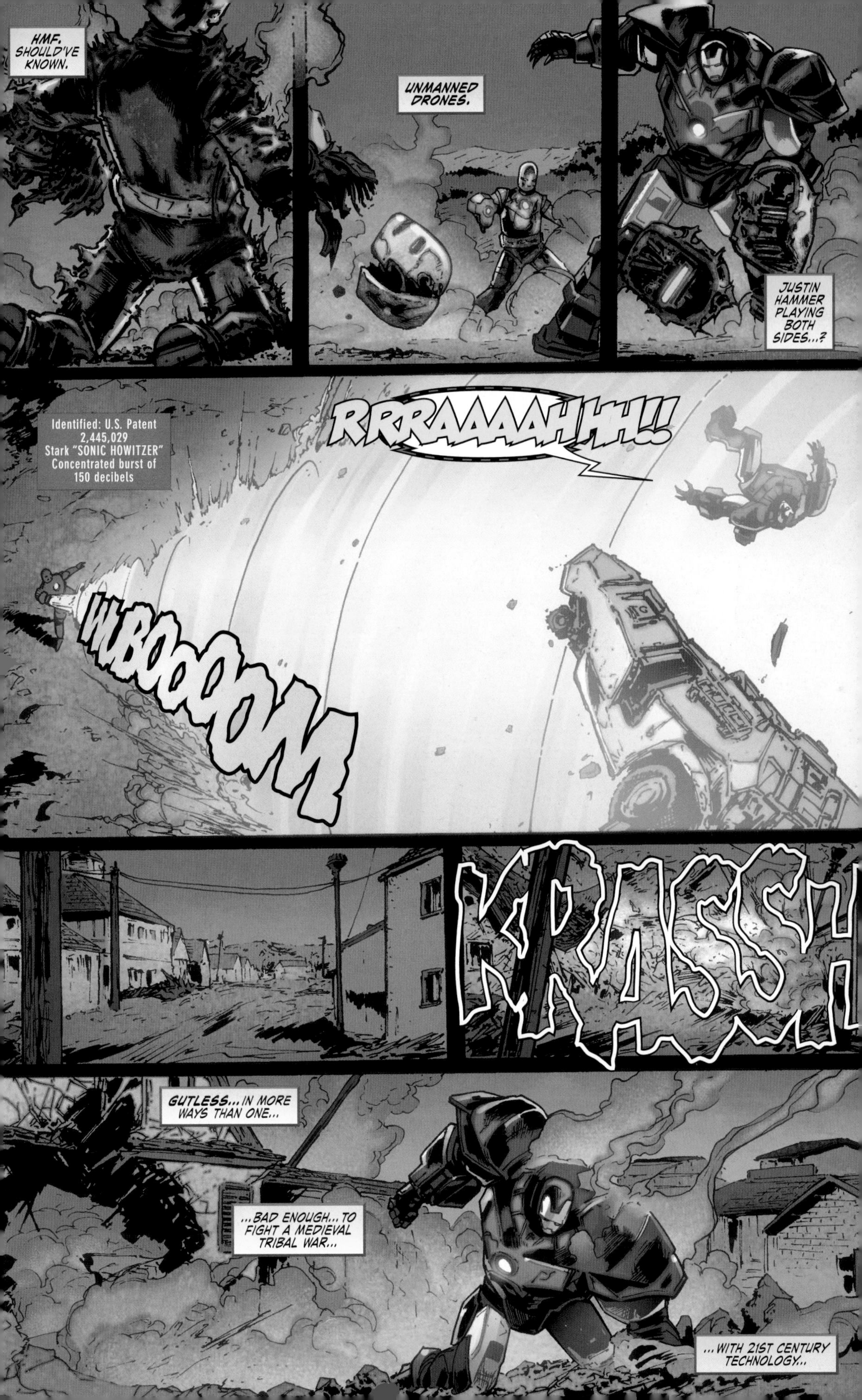
HMF. SHOULD'VE KNOWN.
UNMANNED DRONES.
JUSTIN HAMMER PLAYING BOTH SIDES...?
Identified: U.S. Patent 2,445,029 Stark "SONIC HOWITZER" Concentrated burst of 150 decibels
RRRAAAAHHH!!
WUBOOOOOM
KRASSH
GUTLESS... IN MORE WAYS THAN ONE...
...BAD ENOUGH... TO FIGHT A MEDIEVAL TRIBAL WAR...
...WITH 21ST CENTURY TECHNOLOGY...

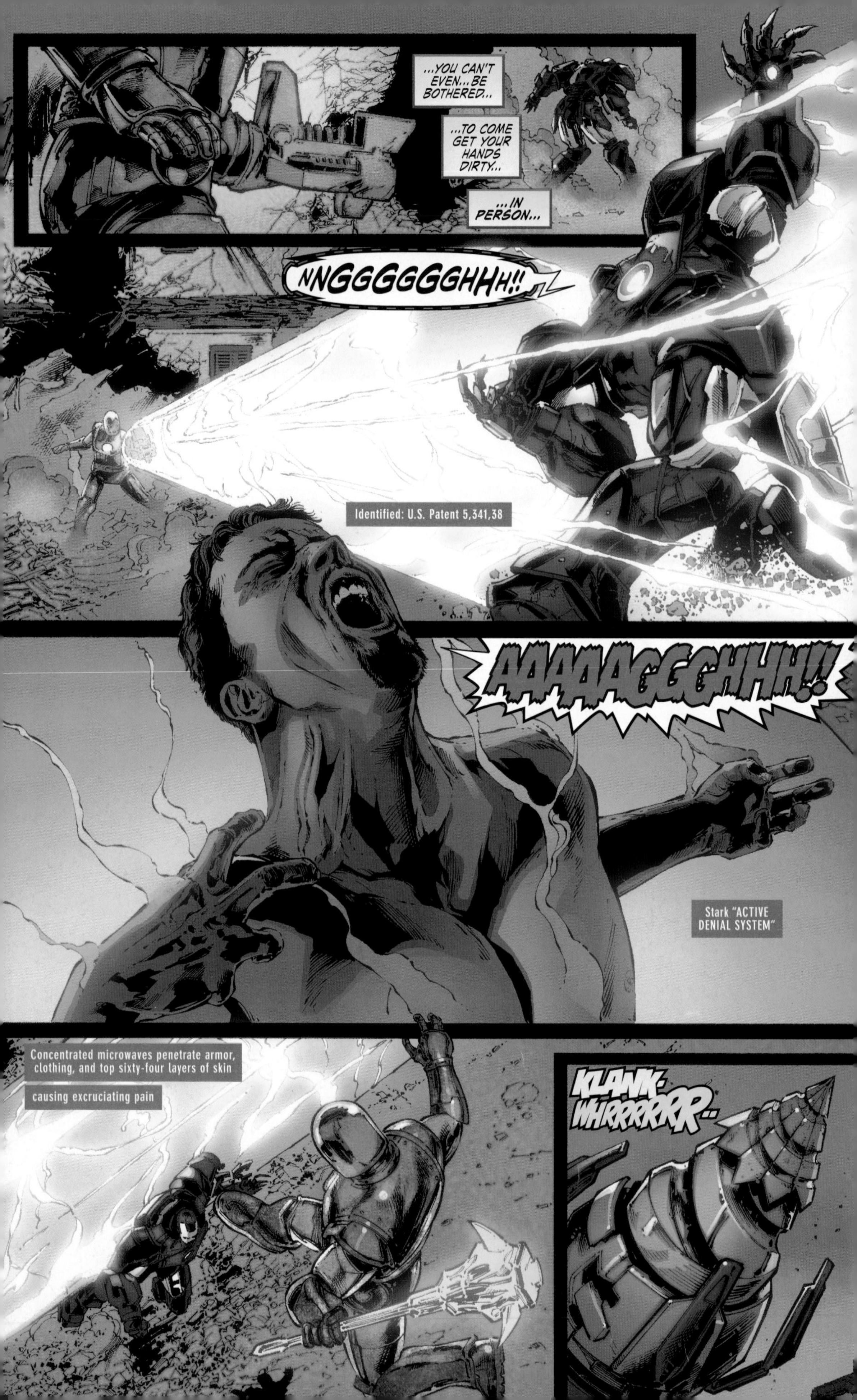
...YOU CAN'T EVEN...BE BOTHERED...
...TO COME GET YOUR HANDS DIRTY...
...IN PERSON...
NNGGGGGGHHH!!
Identified: U.S. Patent 5,341,38
AAAAAGGGHHH!!
Stark "ACTIVE DENIAL SYSTEM"
Concentrated microwaves penetrate armor, clothing, and top sixty-four layers of skin
causing excruciating pain
KLANK-WHRRRRRR..

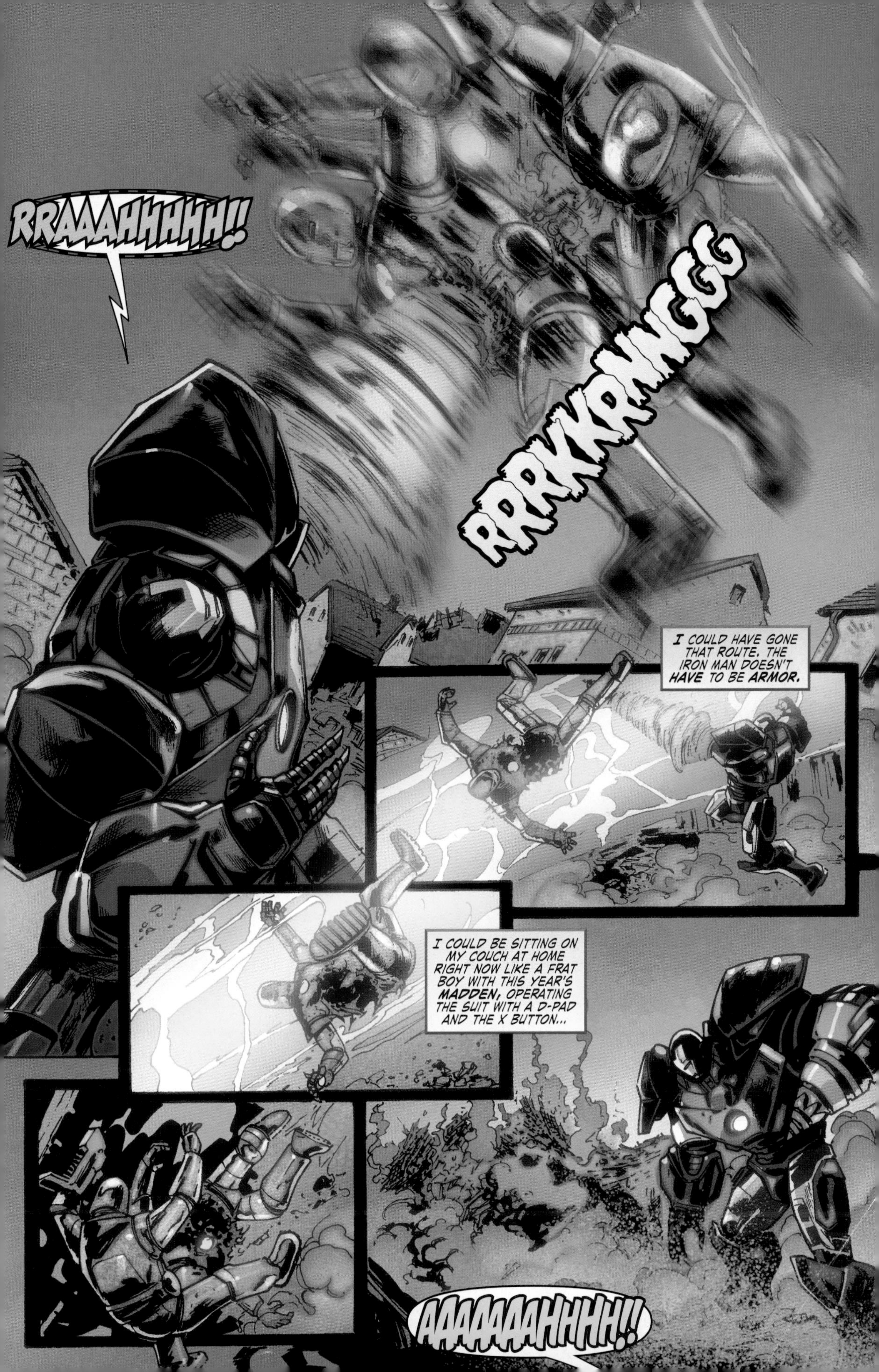
RRAAAHHHHH!!
RRRKRANGG
I COULD HAVE GONE THAT ROUTE. THE IRON MAN DOESN'T HAVE TO BE ARMOR.
I COULD BE SITTING ON MY COUCH AT HOME RIGHT NOW LIKE A FRAT BOY WITH THIS YEAR'S MADDEN, OPERATING THE SUIT WITH A D-PAD AND THE X BUTTON...
AAAAAAHHHH!!

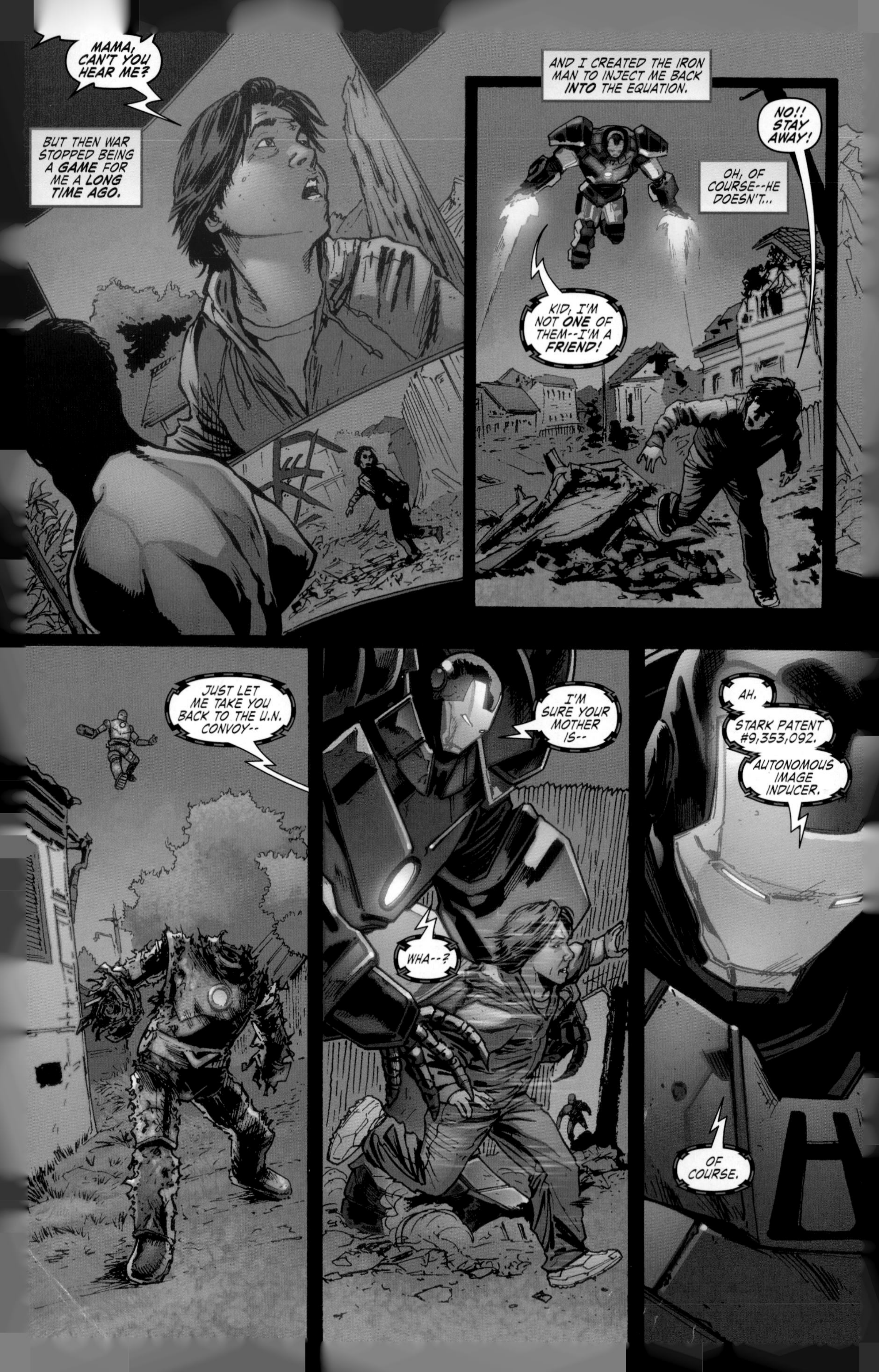
MAMA, CAN'T YOU HEAR ME?
BUT THEN WAR STOPPED BEING A GAME FOR ME A LONG TIME AGO.
AND I CREATED THE IRON MAN TO INJECT ME BACK INTO THE EQUATION.
NO!! STAY AWAY!
OH, OF COURSE--HE DOESN'T...
KID, I'M NOT ONE OF THEM--I'M A FRIEND!
JUST LET ME TAKE YOU BACK TO THE U.N. CONVOY--
I'M SURE YOUR MOTHER IS--
WHA--?
AH.
STARK PATENT #9,353,092.
AUTONOMOUS IMAGE INDUCER.
OF COURSE.

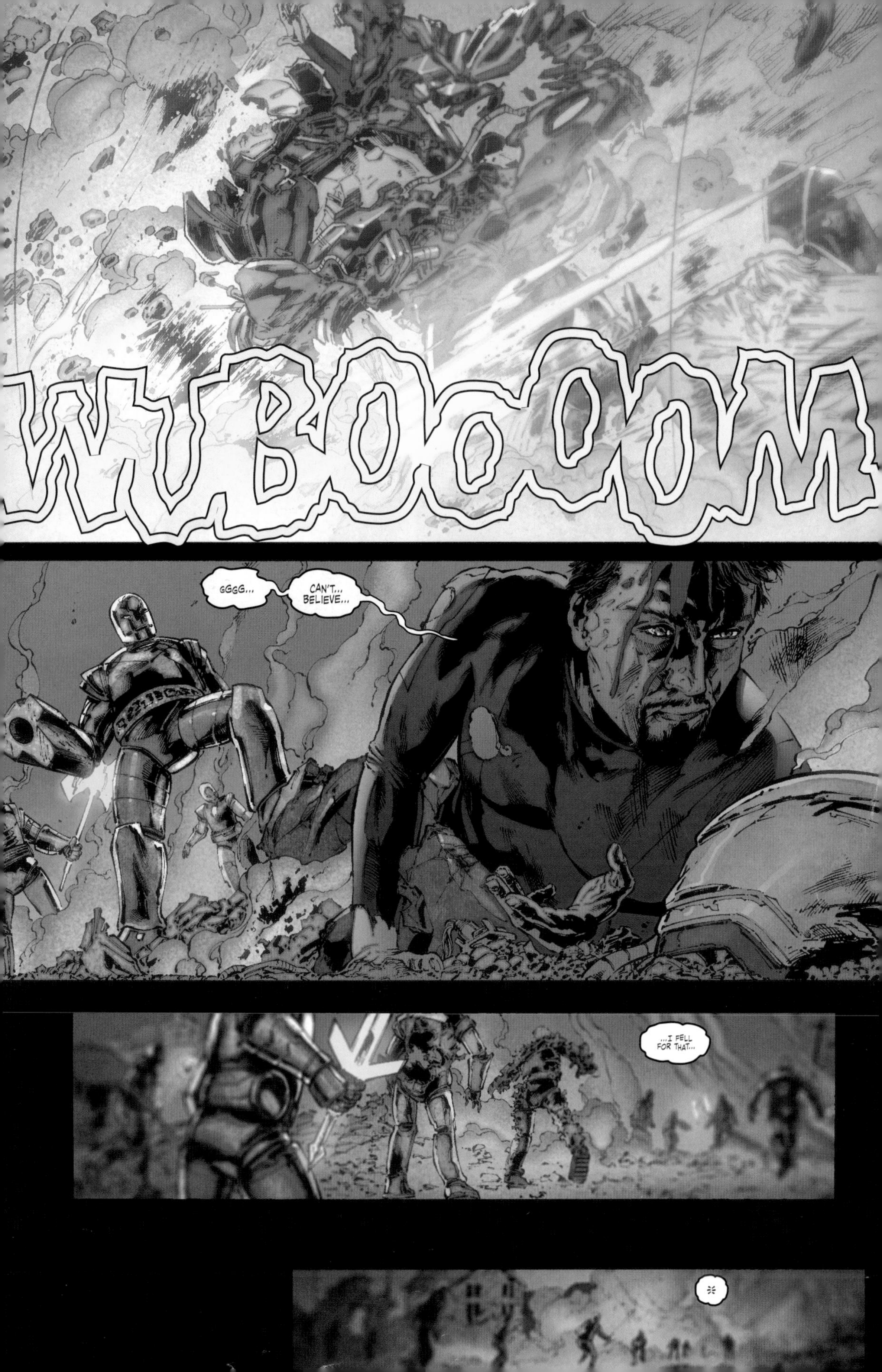
WUBOOOOM
GGGG...
CAN'T... BELIEVE...
...I FELL FOR THAT...

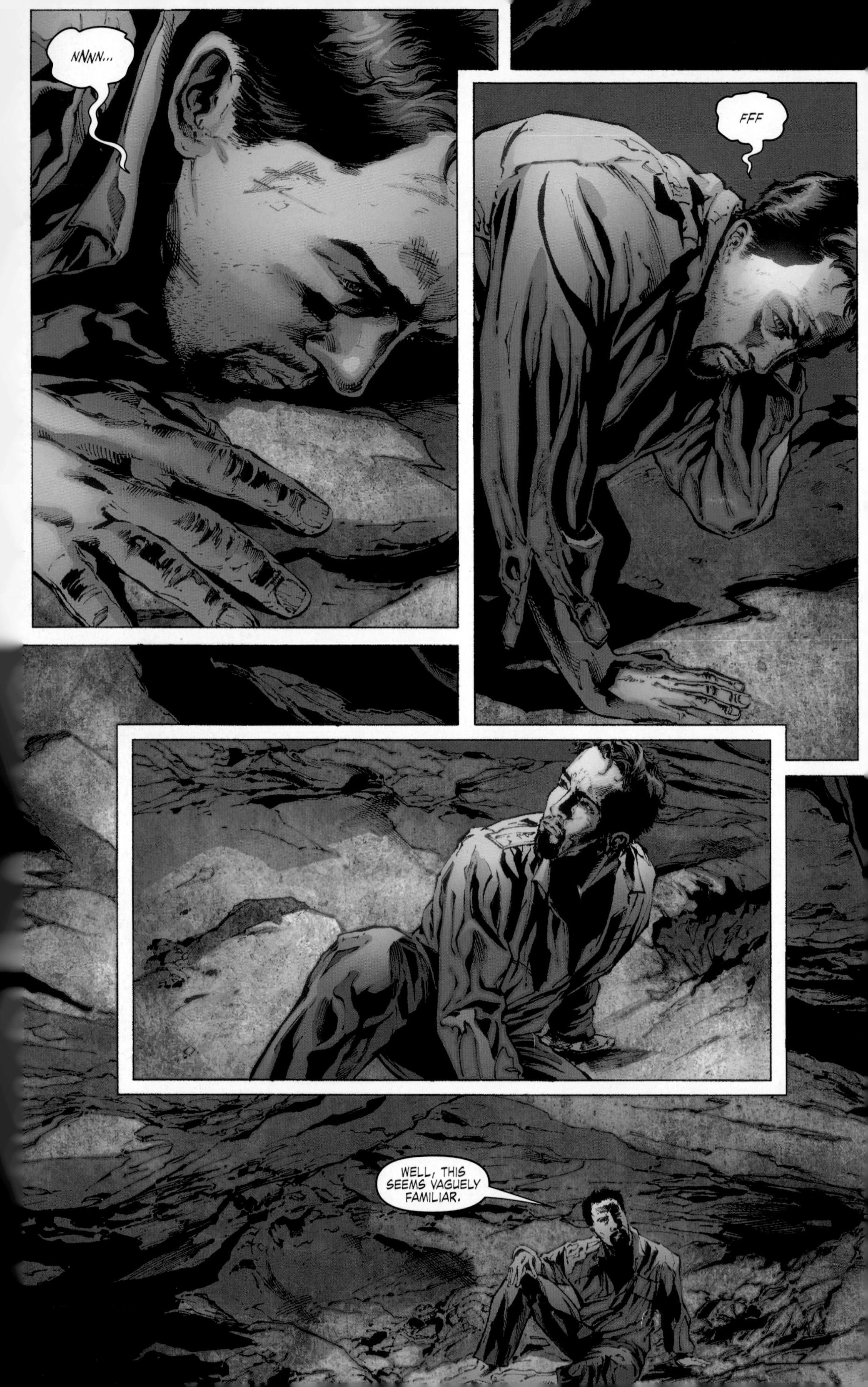
NNNN...
FFF
WELL, THIS SEEMS VAGUELY FAMILIAR.

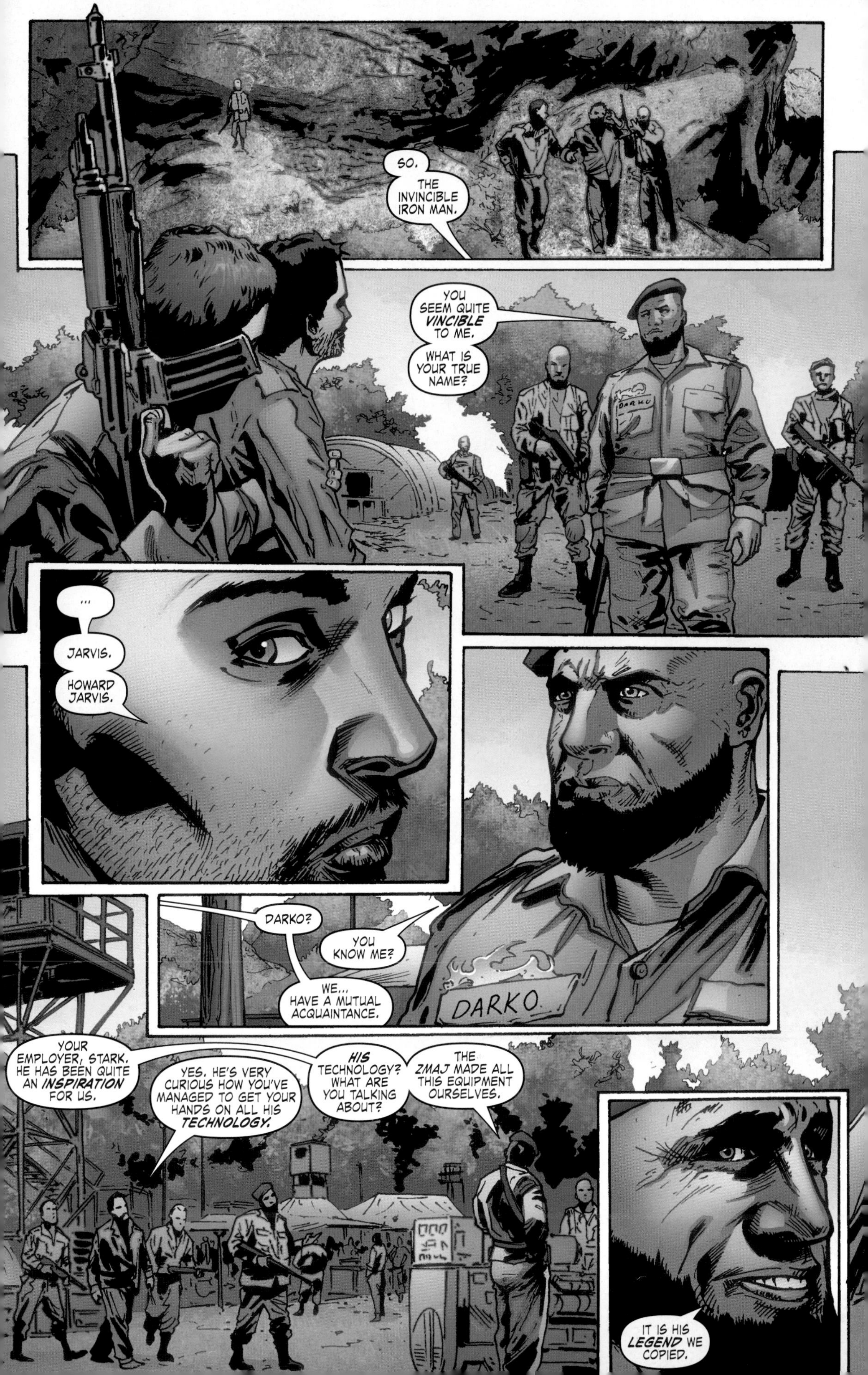
SO.
THE INVINCIBLE IRON MAN.
YOU SEEM QUITE VINCIBLE TO ME.
WHAT IS YOUR TRUE NAME?
DARKO
...
JARVIS.
HOWARD JARVIS.
DARKO?
YOU KNOW ME?
WE... HAVE A MUTUAL ACQUAINTANCE.
DARKO
YOUR EMPLOYER, STARK. HE HAS BEEN QUITE AN INSPIRATION FOR US.
YES, HE'S VERY CURIOUS HOW YOU'VE MANAGED TO GET YOUR HANDS ON ALL HIS TECHNOLOGY.
HIS TECHNOLOGY? WHAT ARE YOU TALKING ABOUT?
THE ZMAJ MADE ALL THIS EQUIPMENT OURSELVES.
IT IS HIS LEGEND WE COPIED.

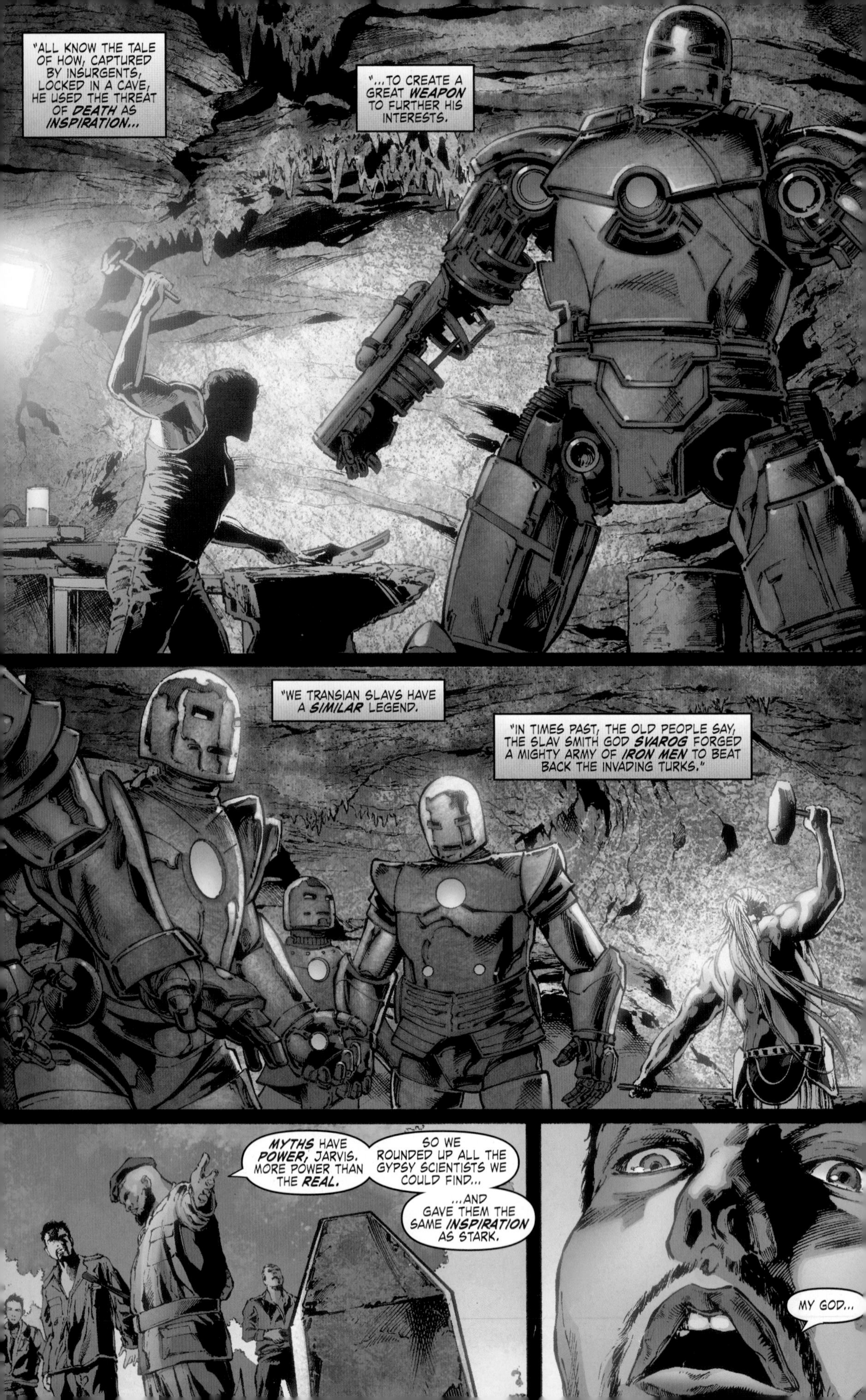
"ALL KNOW THE TALE OF HOW, CAPTURED BY INSURGENTS, LOCKED IN A CAVE, HE USED THE THREAT OF DEATH AS INSPIRATION...
"...TO CREATE A GREAT WEAPON TO FURTHER HIS INTERESTS.
"WE TRANSIAN SLAVS HAVE A SIMILAR LEGEND.
"IN TIMES PAST, THE OLD PEOPLE SAY, THE SLAV SMITH GOD SVAROG FORGED A MIGHTY ARMY OF IRON MEN TO BEAT BACK THE INVADING TURKS."
MYTHS HAVE POWER, JARVIS. MORE POWER THAN THE REAL.
SO WE ROUNDED UP ALL THE GYPSY SCIENTISTS WE COULD FIND...
...AND GAVE THEM THE SAME INSPIRATION AS STARK.
MY GOD...

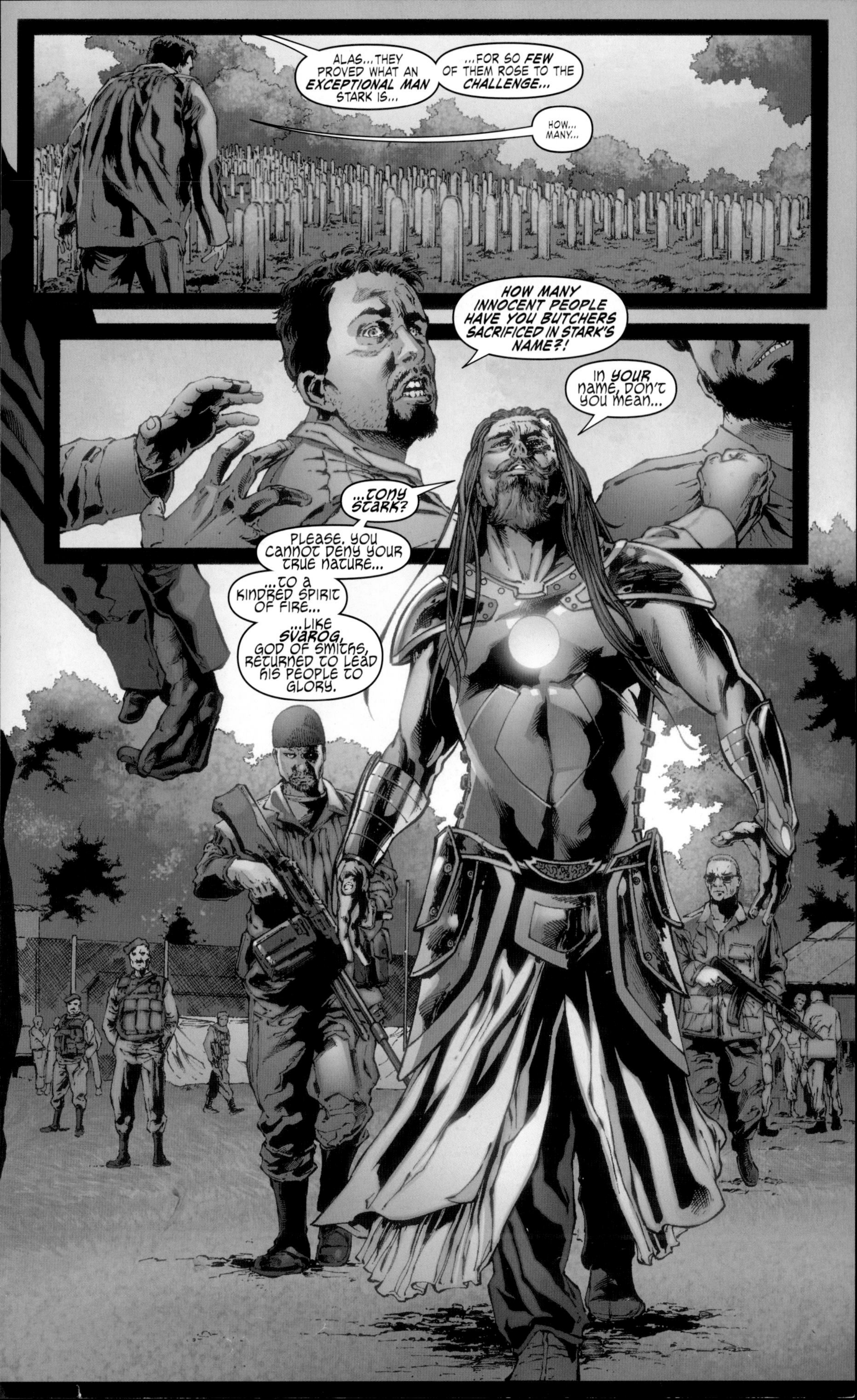
ALAS...THEY PROVED WHAT AN EXCEPTIONAL MAN STARK IS...
...FOR SO FEW OF THEM ROSE TO THE CHALLENGE...
HOW... MANY...
HOW MANY INNOCENT PEOPLE HAVE YOU BUTCHERS SACRIFICED IN STARK'S NAME?!
IN YOUR NAME, DON'T YOU MEAN...
...TONY STARK?
PLEASE. YOU CANNOT DENY YOUR TRUE NATURE...
...TO A KINDRED SPIRIT OF FIRE...
...LIKE SVAROG, GOD OF SMITHS, RETURNED TO LEAD HIS PEOPLE TO GLORY.

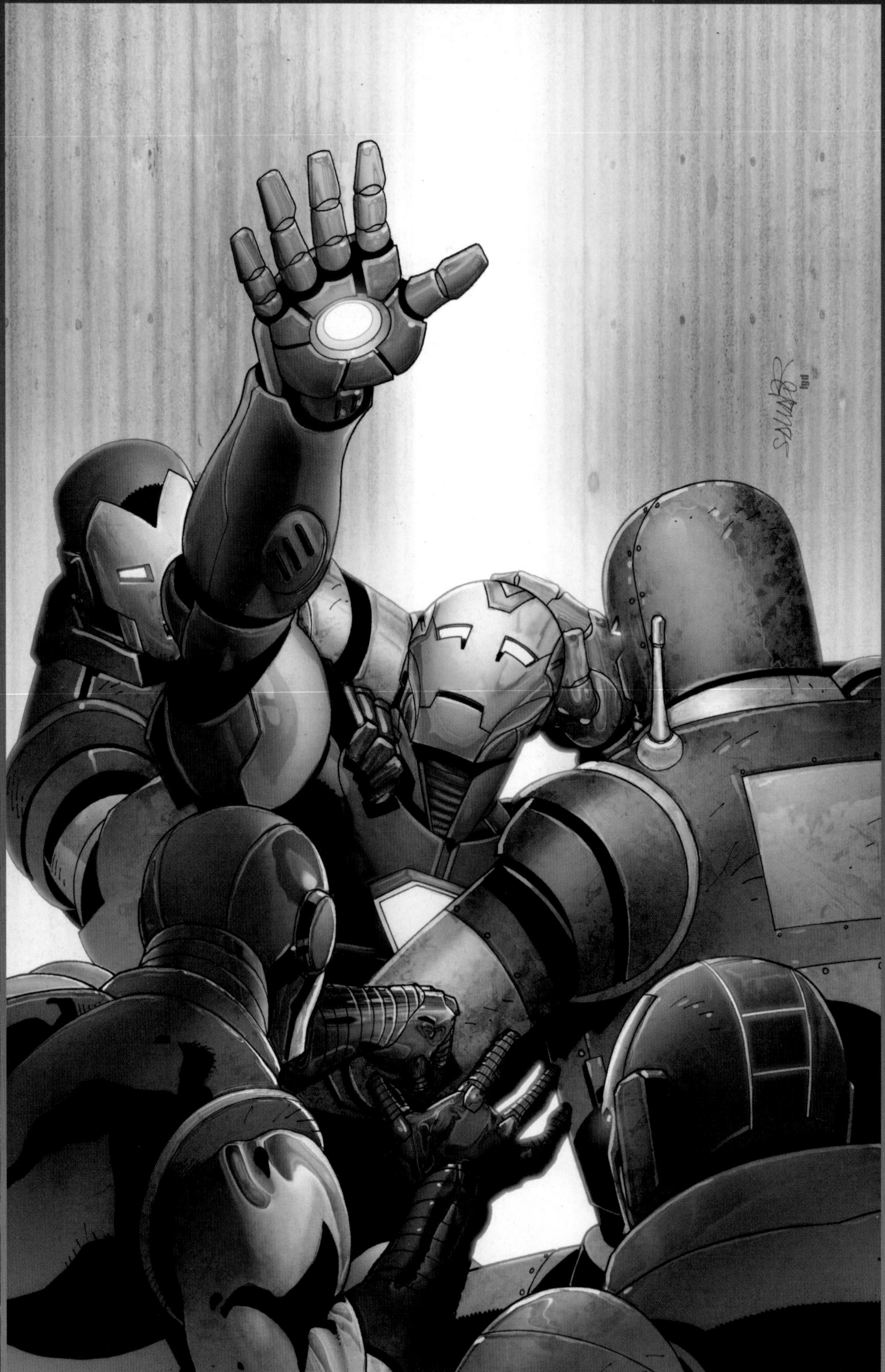

IRON MAN LEGACY 3

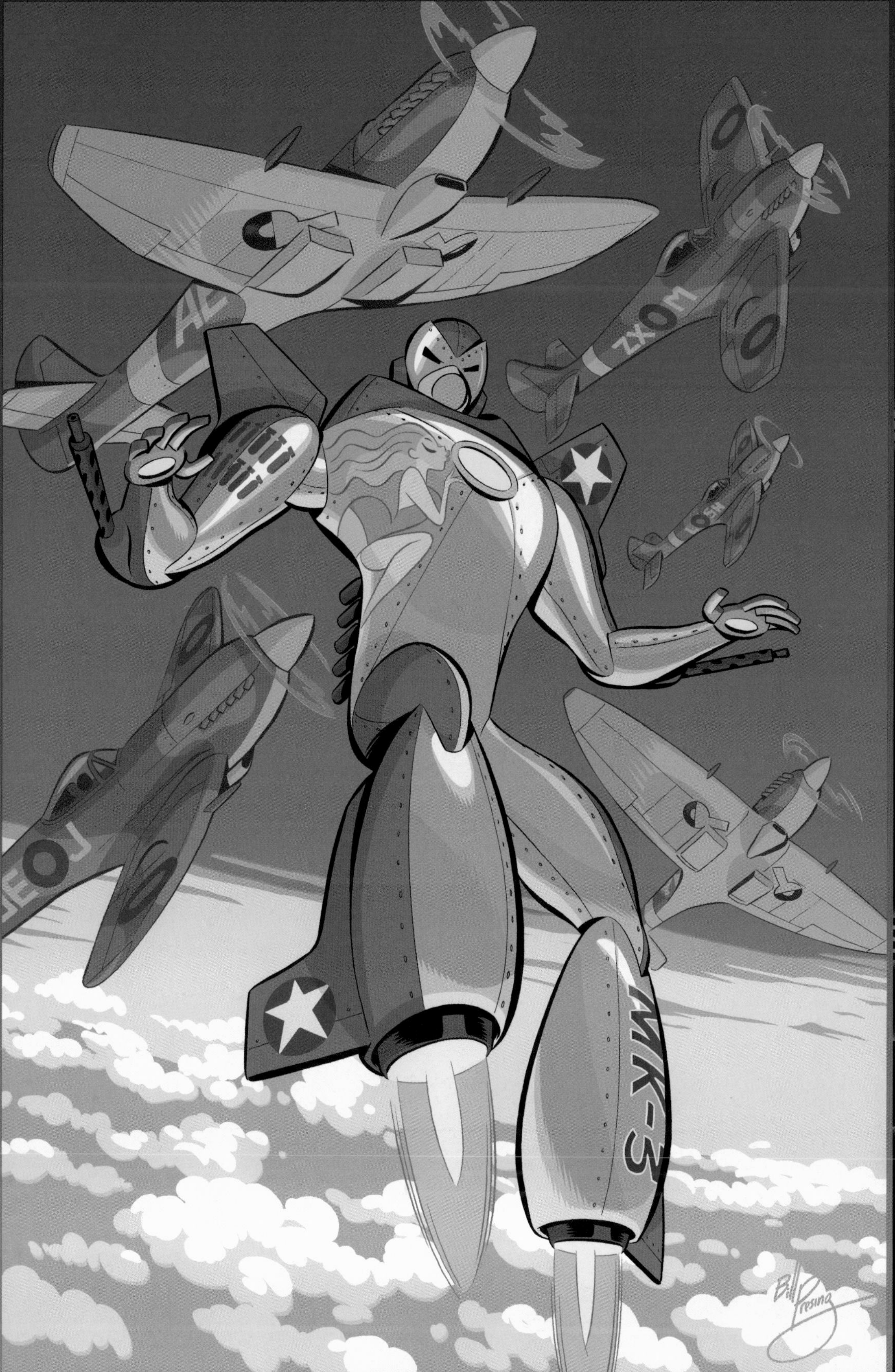
AE
ZXOM
HSOT
JEOJ
MK-3
Bill Presing

#3 IRON MAN BY DESIGN 2.0 VARIANT
BY BILL PRESING

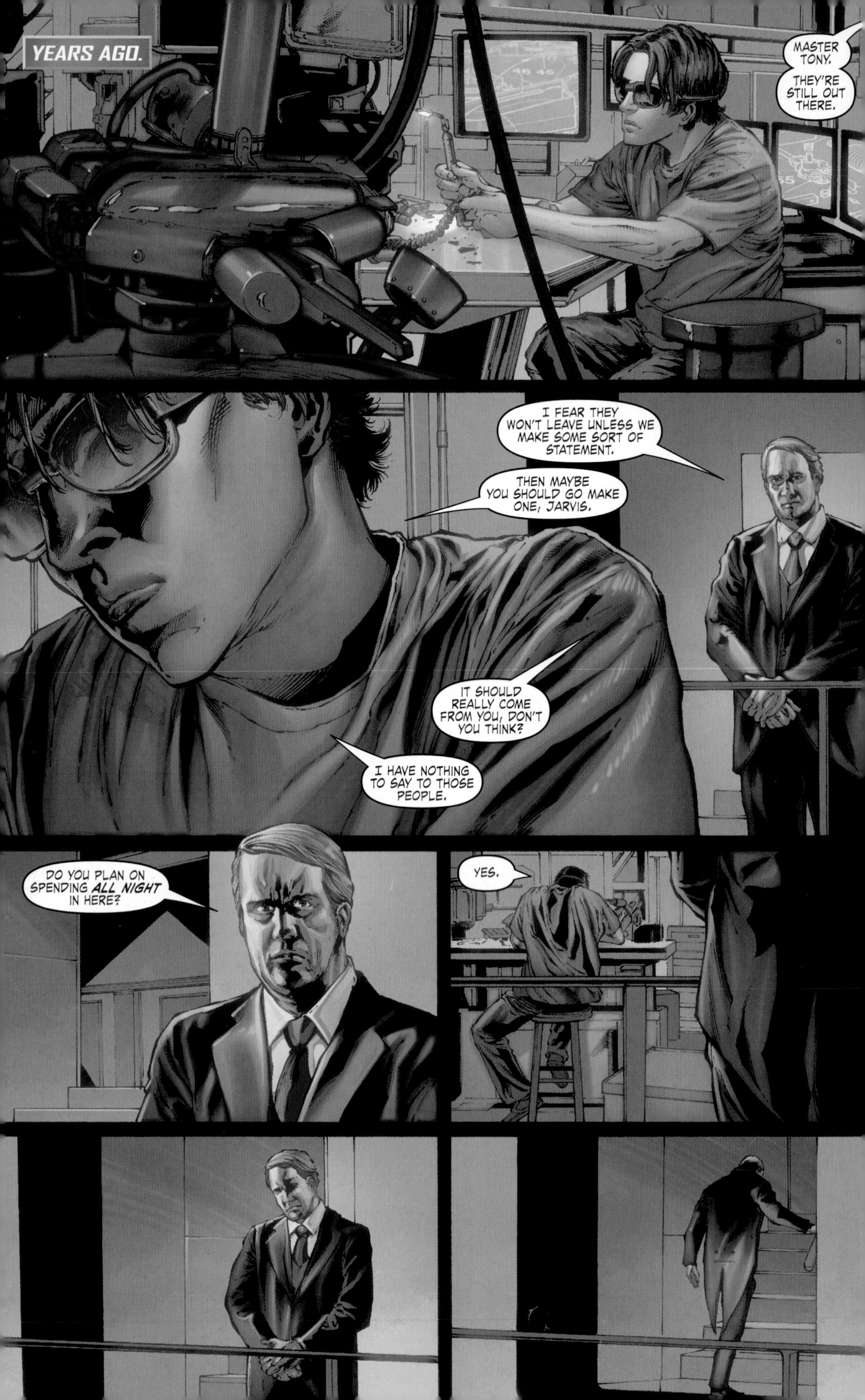
YEARS AGO.
MASTER TONY.
THEY'RE STILL OUT THERE.
I FEAR THEY WON'T LEAVE UNLESS WE MAKE SOME SORT OF STATEMENT.
THEN MAYBE YOU SHOULD GO MAKE ONE, JARVIS.
IT SHOULD REALLY COME FROM YOU, DON'T YOU THINK?
I HAVE NOTHING TO SAY TO THOSE PEOPLE.
DO YOU PLAN ON SPENDING *ALL NIGHT* IN HERE?
YES.

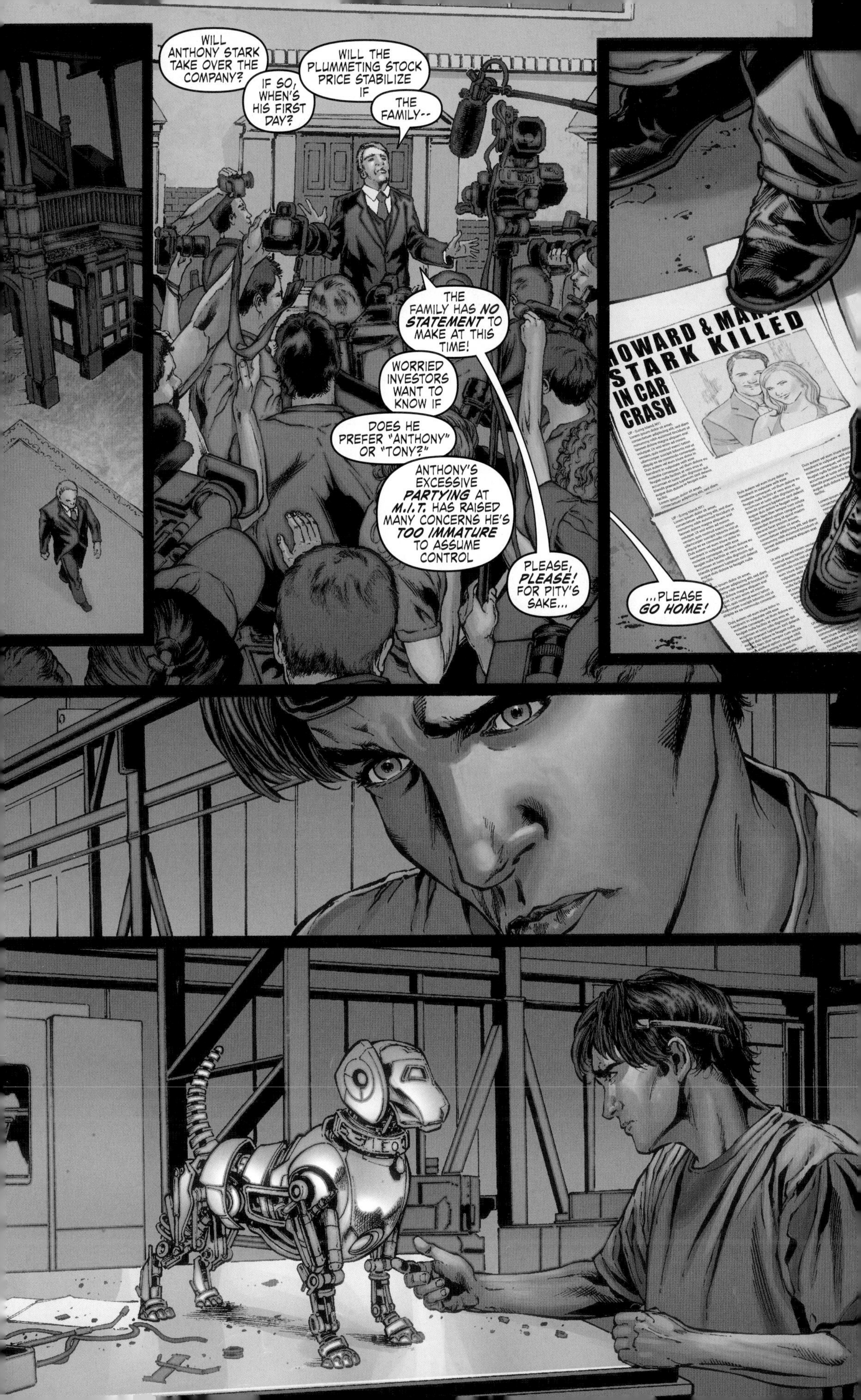
WILL ANTHONY STARK TAKE OVER THE COMPANY?
IF SO, WHEN'S HIS FIRST DAY?
WILL THE PLUMMETING STOCK PRICE STABILIZE IF
THE FAMILY--
THE FAMILY HAS NO STATEMENT TO MAKE AT THIS TIME!
WORRIED INVESTORS WANT TO KNOW IF
DOES HE PREFER "ANTHONY" OR "TONY?"
ANTHONY'S EXCESSIVE PARTYING AT M.I.T. HAS RAISED MANY CONCERNS HE'S TOO IMMATURE TO ASSUME CONTROL
PLEASE, PLEASE! FOR PITY'S SAKE...
...PLEASE GO HOME!
HOWARD & MAR
STARK KILLED
IN CAR CRASH

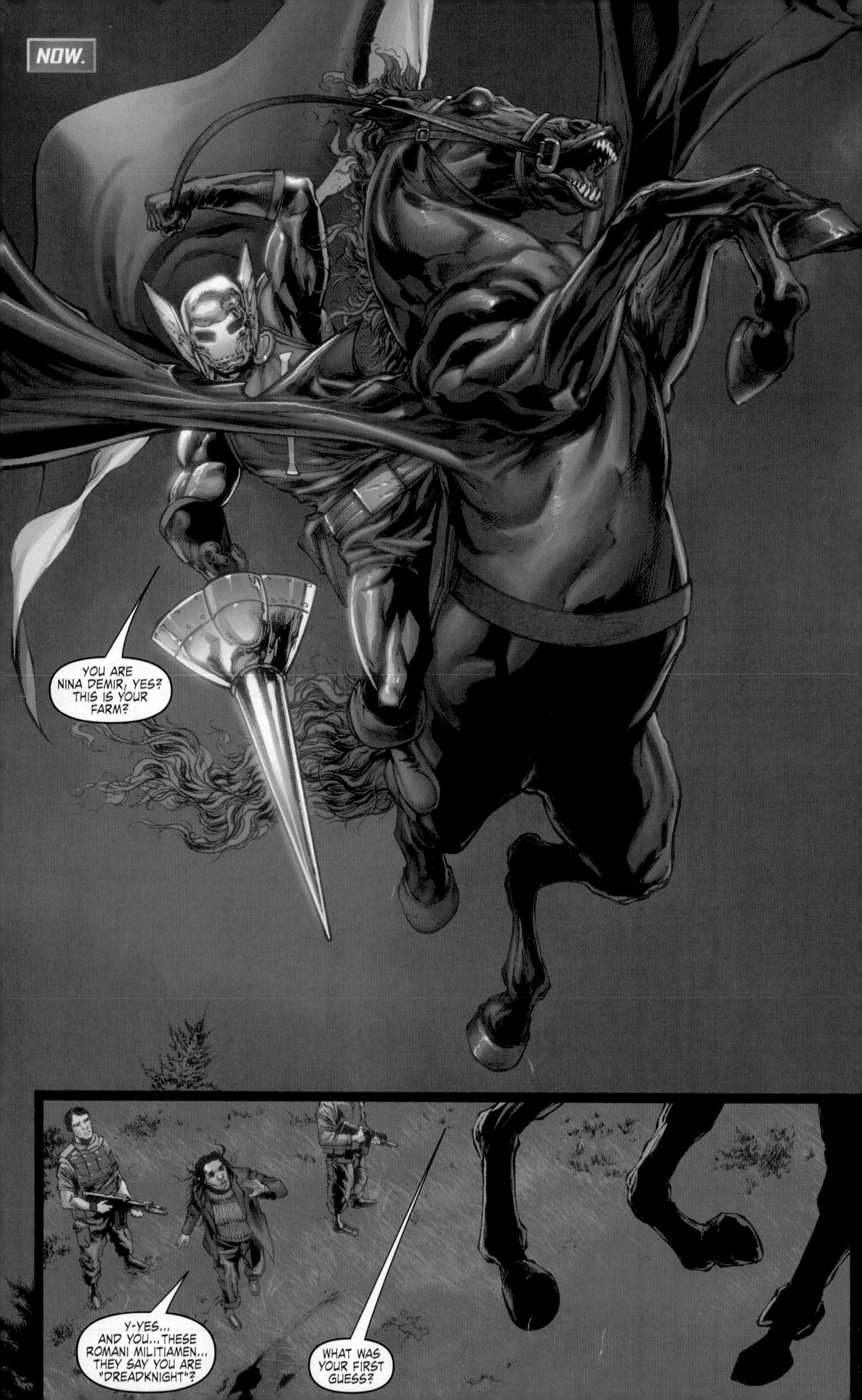
NOW.
YOU ARE NINA DEMIR, YES? THIS IS YOUR FARM?
Y-YES... AND YOU...THESE ROMANI MILITIAMEN... THEY SAY YOU ARE "DREADKNIGHT"?
WHAT WAS YOUR FIRST GUESS?

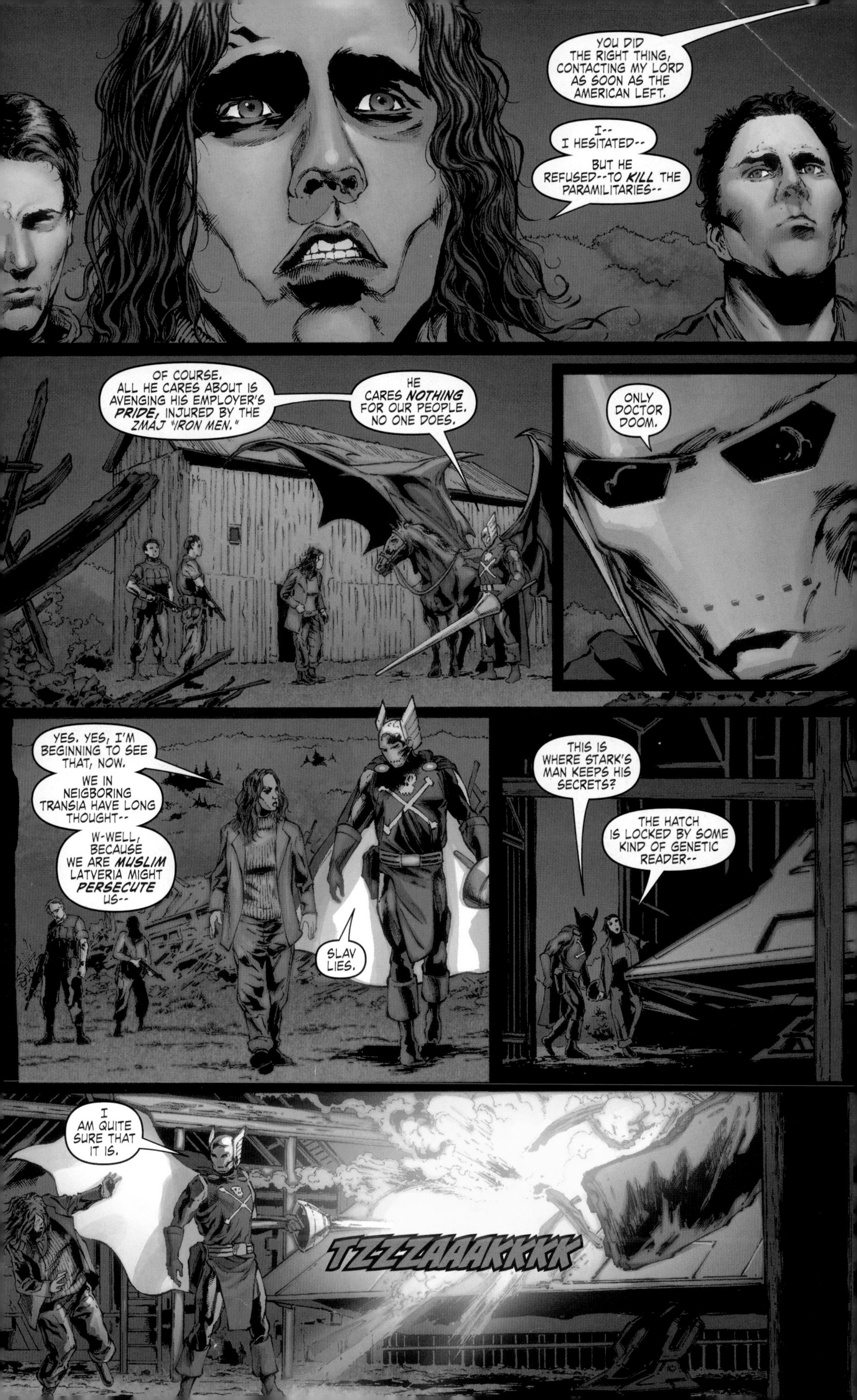
YOU DID THE RIGHT THING, CONTACTING MY LORD AS SOON AS THE AMERICAN LEFT.
I-- I HESITATED--
BUT HE REFUSED--TO KILL THE PARAMILITARIES--
OF COURSE. ALL HE CARES ABOUT IS AVENGING HIS EMPLOYER'S PRIDE, INJURED BY THE ZMAJ "IRON MEN."
HE CARES NOTHING FOR OUR PEOPLE. NO ONE DOES.
ONLY DOCTOR DOOM.
YES. YES, I'M BEGINNING TO SEE THAT, NOW.
WE IN NEIGBORING TRANSIA HAVE LONG THOUGHT--
W-WELL, BECAUSE WE ARE MUSLIM LATVERIA MIGHT PERSECUTE US--
SLAV LIES.
THIS IS WHERE STARK'S MAN KEEPS HIS SECRETS?
THE HATCH IS LOCKED BY SOME KIND OF GENETIC READER--
I AM QUITE SURE THAT IT IS.
TZZZAAAKKKK

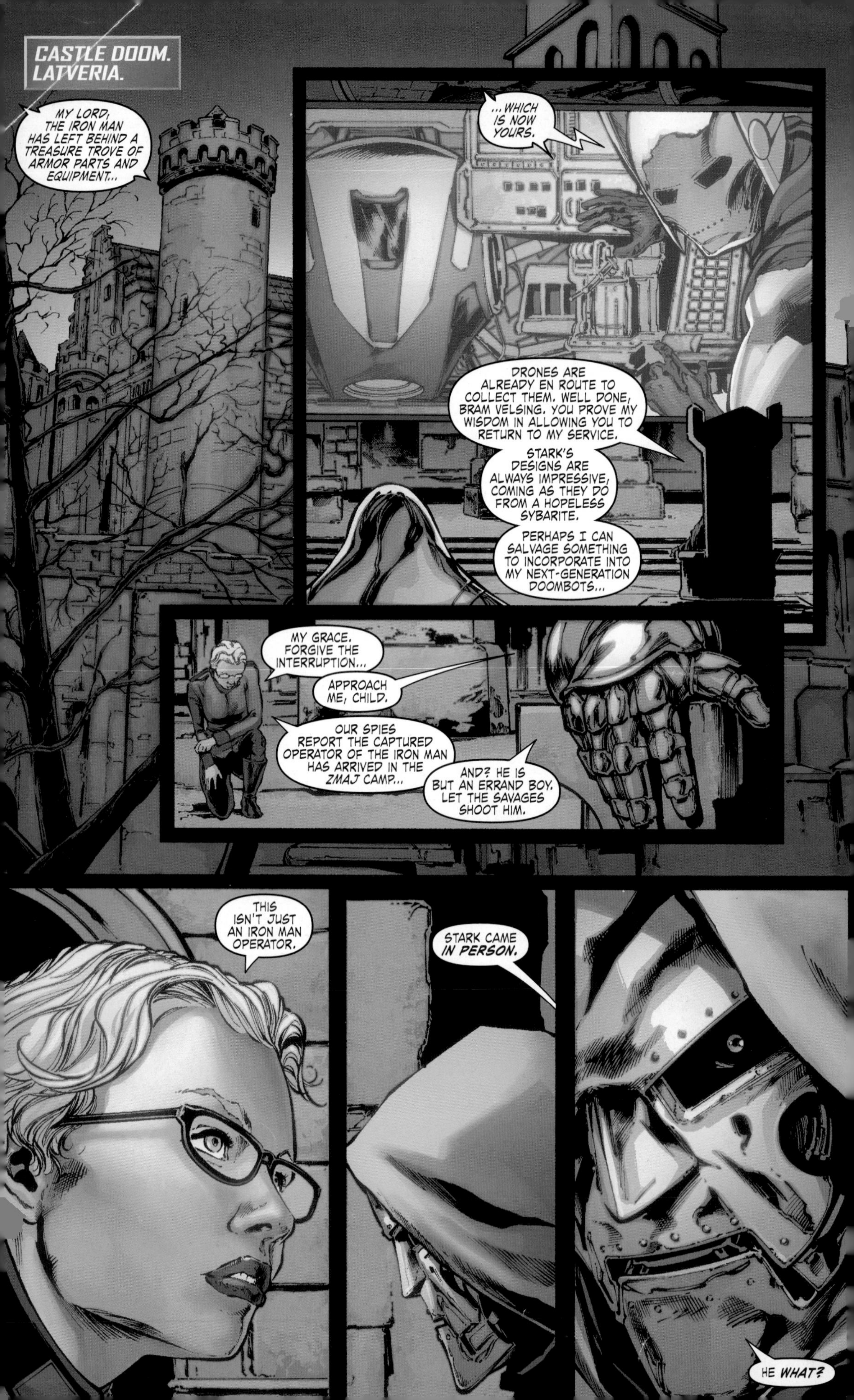

CASTLE DOOM. LATVERIA.
MY LORD, THE IRON MAN HAS LEFT BEHIND A TREASURE TROVE OF ARMOR PARTS AND EQUIPMENT...
...WHICH IS NOW YOURS.
DRONES ARE ALREADY EN ROUTE TO COLLECT THEM. WELL DONE, BRAM VELSING. YOU PROVE MY WISDOM IN ALLOWING YOU TO RETURN TO MY SERVICE.
STARK'S DESIGNS ARE ALWAYS IMPRESSIVE, COMING AS THEY DO FROM A HOPELESS SYBARITE.
PERHAPS I CAN SALVAGE SOMETHING TO INCORPORATE INTO MY NEXT-GENERATION DOOMBOTS...
MY GRACE. FORGIVE THE INTERRUPTION...
APPROACH ME, CHILD.
OUR SPIES REPORT THE CAPTURED OPERATOR OF THE IRON MAN HAS ARRIVED IN THE ZMAJ CAMP...
AND? HE IS BUT AN ERRAND BOY. LET THE SAVAGES SHOOT HIM.
THIS ISN'T JUST AN IRON MAN OPERATOR.
STARK CAME IN PERSON.
HE WHAT?

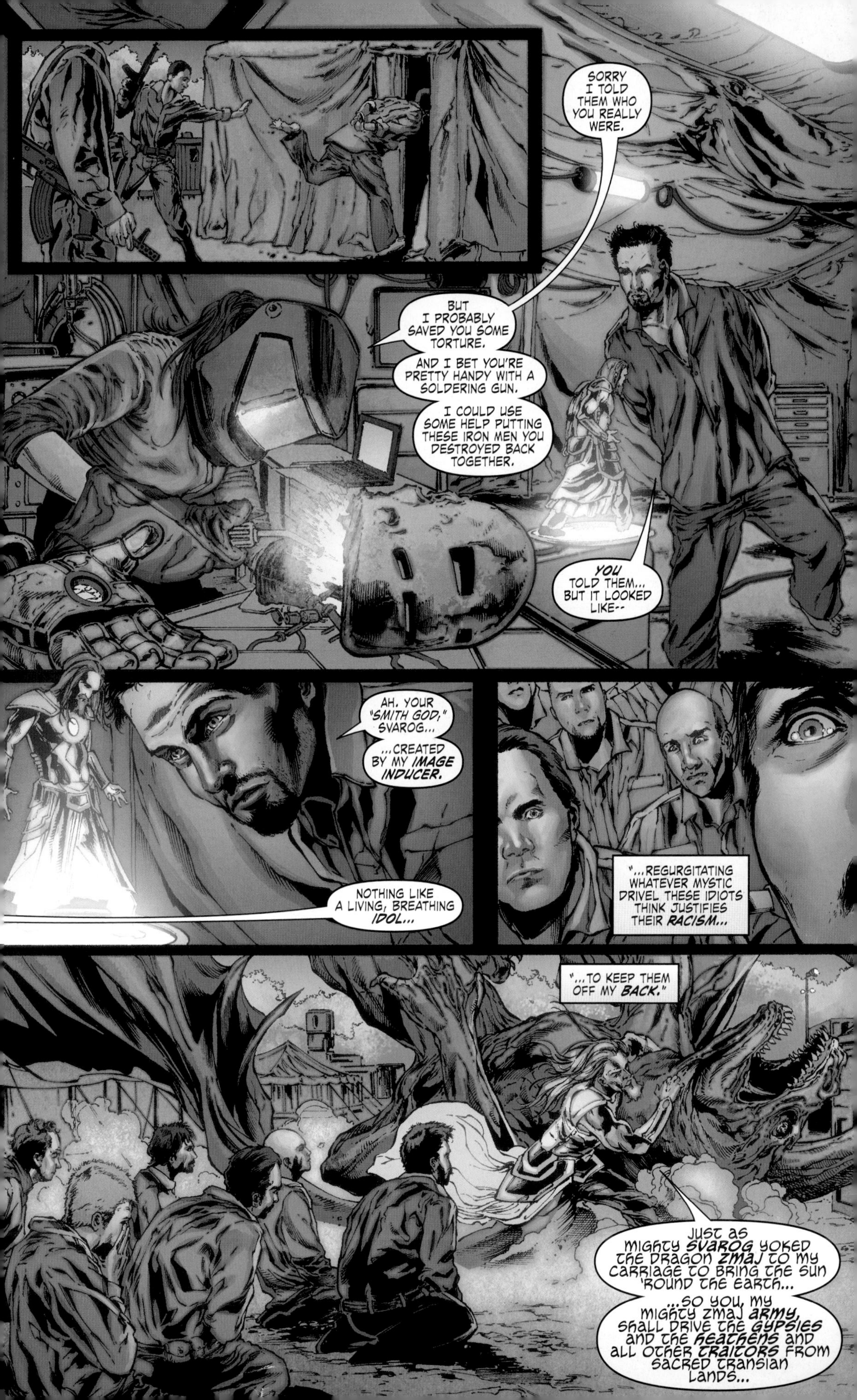
SORRY I TOLD THEM WHO YOU REALLY WERE.
BUT I PROBABLY SAVED YOU SOME TORTURE.
AND I BET YOU'RE PRETTY HANDY WITH A SOLDERING GUN.
I COULD USE SOME HELP PUTTING THESE IRON MEN YOU DESTROYED BACK TOGETHER.
YOU TOLD THEM... BUT IT LOOKED LIKE--
AH. YOUR "SMITH GOD," SVAROG...
...CREATED BY MY IMAGE INDUCER.
NOTHING LIKE A LIVING, BREATHING IDOL...
"...REGURGITATING WHATEVER MYSTIC DRIVEL THESE IDIOTS THINK JUSTIFIES THEIR RACISM...
"...TO KEEP THEM OFF MY BACK."
JUST AS MIGHTY SVAROG YOKED THE DRAGON ZMAJ TO MY CARRIAGE TO BRING THE SUN 'ROUND THE EARTH...
...SO YOU, MY MIGHTY ZMAJ ARMY, SHALL DRIVE THE GYPSIES AND THE HEATHENS AND ALL OTHER TRAITORS FROM SACRED TRANSIAN LANDS...

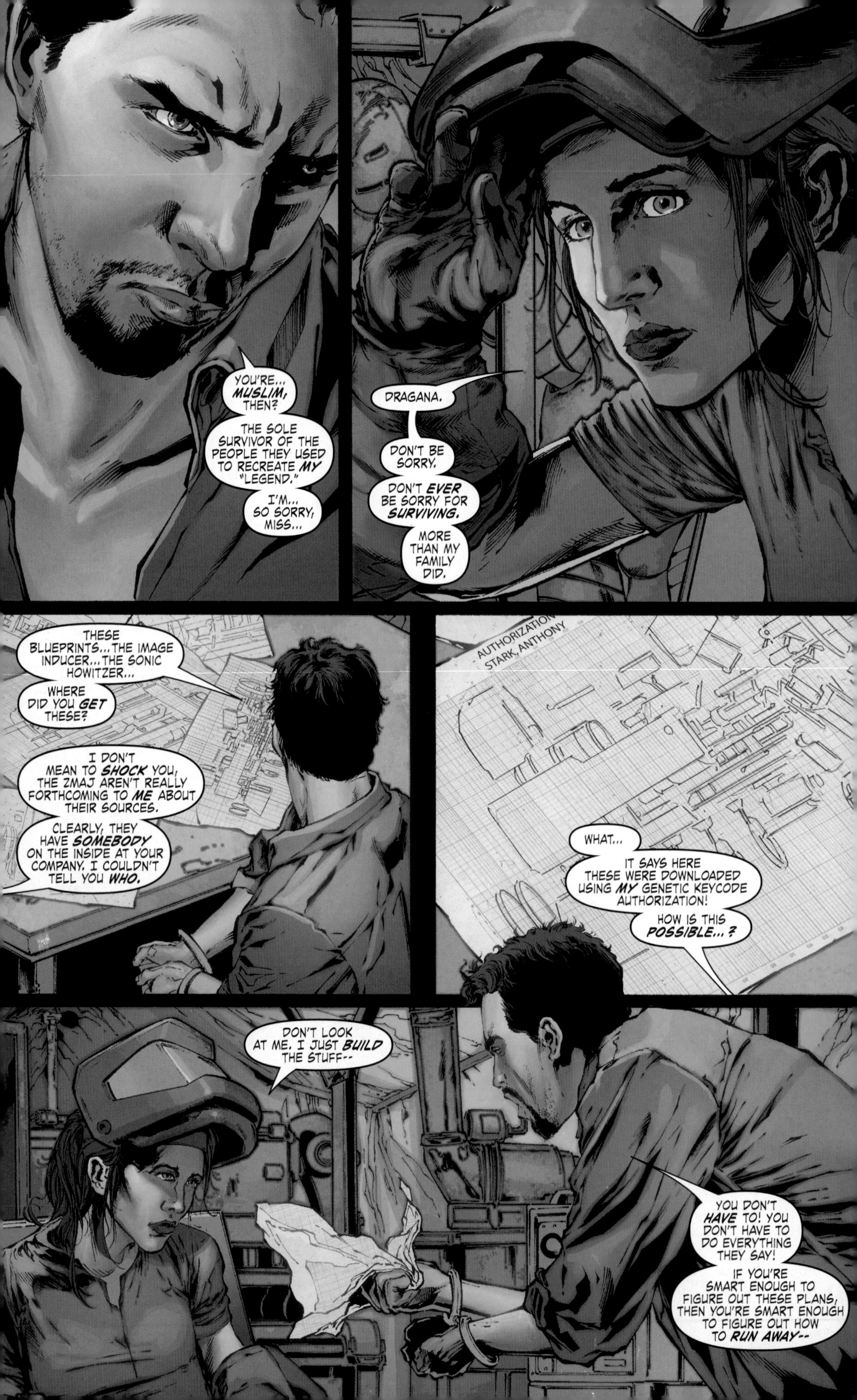
YOU'RE... MUSLIM, THEN?
THE SOLE SURVIVOR OF THE PEOPLE THEY USED TO RECREATE MY "LEGEND."
I'M... SO SORRY, MISS...
DRAGANA.
DON'T BE SORRY.
DON'T EVER BE SORRY FOR SURVIVING.
MORE THAN MY FAMILY DID.
THESE BLUEPRINTS... THE IMAGE INDUCER... THE SONIC HOWITZER...
WHERE DID YOU GET THESE?
I DON'T MEAN TO SHOCK YOU, THE ZMAJ AREN'T REALLY FORTHCOMING TO ME ABOUT THEIR SOURCES.
CLEARLY, THEY HAVE SOMEBODY ON THE INSIDE AT YOUR COMPANY. I COULDN'T TELL YOU WHO.
AUTHORIZATION
STARK, ANTHONY
WHAT...
IT SAYS HERE THESE WERE DOWNLOADED USING MY GENETIC KEYCODE AUTHORIZATION!
HOW IS THIS POSSIBLE...?
DON'T LOOK AT ME. I JUST BUILD THE STUFF--
YOU DON'T HAVE TO! YOU DON'T HAVE TO DO EVERYTHING THEY SAY!
IF YOU'RE SMART ENOUGH TO FIGURE OUT THESE PLANS, THEN YOU'RE SMART ENOUGH TO FIGURE OUT HOW TO RUN AWAY--

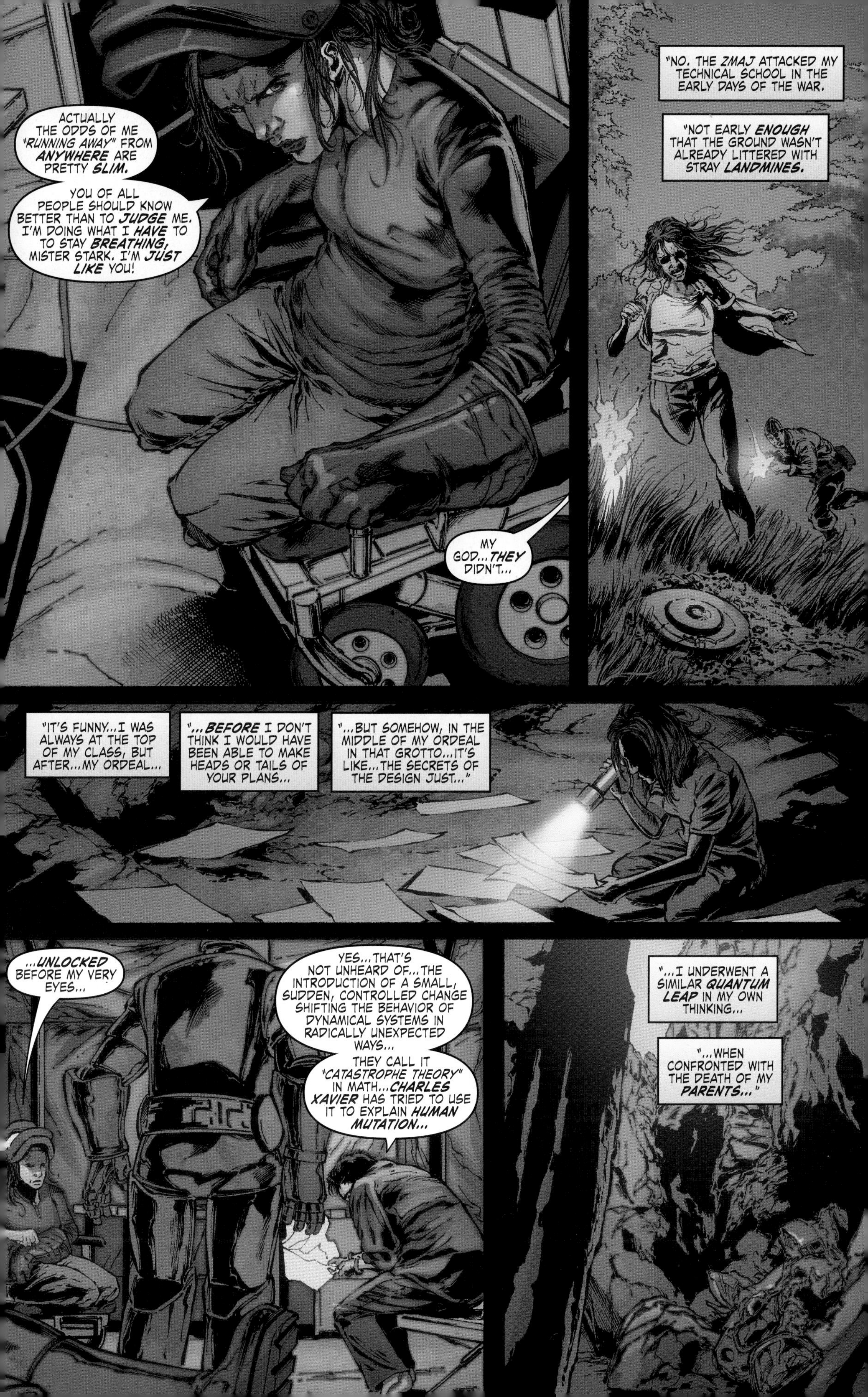
ACTUALLY THE ODDS OF ME "RUNNING AWAY" FROM ANYWHERE ARE PRETTY SLIM.
YOU OF ALL PEOPLE SHOULD KNOW BETTER THAN TO JUDGE ME. I'M DOING WHAT I HAVE TO TO STAY BREATHING, MISTER STARK. I'M JUST LIKE YOU!
MY GOD...THEY DIDN'T...
"NO. THE ZMAJ ATTACKED MY TECHNICAL SCHOOL IN THE EARLY DAYS OF THE WAR.
"NOT EARLY ENOUGH THAT THE GROUND WASN'T ALREADY LITTERED WITH STRAY LANDMINES.
"IT'S FUNNY...I WAS ALWAYS AT THE TOP OF MY CLASS, BUT AFTER...MY ORDEAL...
"...BEFORE I DON'T THINK I WOULD HAVE BEEN ABLE TO MAKE HEADS OR TAILS OF YOUR PLANS...
"...BUT SOMEHOW, IN THE MIDDLE OF MY ORDEAL IN THAT GROTTO...IT'S LIKE...THE SECRETS OF THE DESIGN JUST..."
...UNLOCKED BEFORE MY VERY EYES...
YES...THAT'S NOT UNHEARD OF...THE INTRODUCTION OF A SMALL, SUDDEN, CONTROLLED CHANGE SHIFTING THE BEHAVIOR OF DYNAMICAL SYSTEMS IN RADICALLY UNEXPECTED WAYS...
THEY CALL IT "CATASTROPHE THEORY" IN MATH...CHARLES XAVIER HAS TRIED TO USE IT TO EXPLAIN HUMAN MUTATION...
"...I UNDERWENT A SIMILAR QUANTUM LEAP IN MY OWN THINKING...
"...WHEN CONFRONTED WITH THE DEATH OF MY PARENTS..."

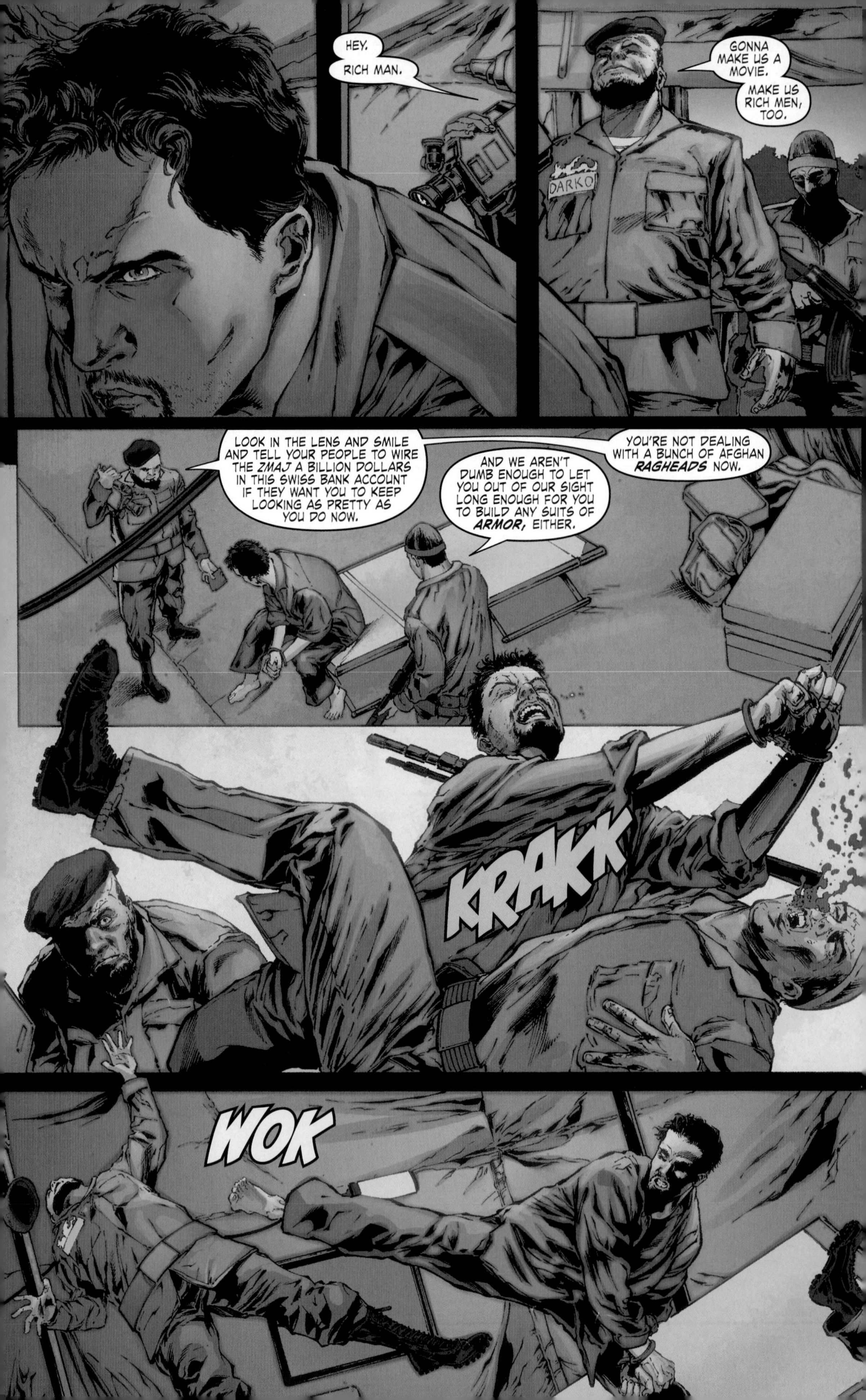
HEY.
RICH MAN.
GONNA MAKE US A MOVIE.
MAKE US RICH MEN, TOO.
DARKO
LOOK IN THE LENS AND SMILE AND TELL YOUR PEOPLE TO WIRE THE ZMAJ A BILLION DOLLARS IN THIS SWISS BANK ACCOUNT IF THEY WANT YOU TO KEEP LOOKING AS PRETTY AS YOU DO NOW.
YOU'RE NOT DEALING WITH A BUNCH OF AFGHAN RAGHEADS NOW.
AND WE AREN'T DUMB ENOUGH TO LET YOU OUT OF OUR SIGHT LONG ENOUGH FOR YOU TO BUILD ANY SUITS OF ARMOR, EITHER.
KRAKK
WOK

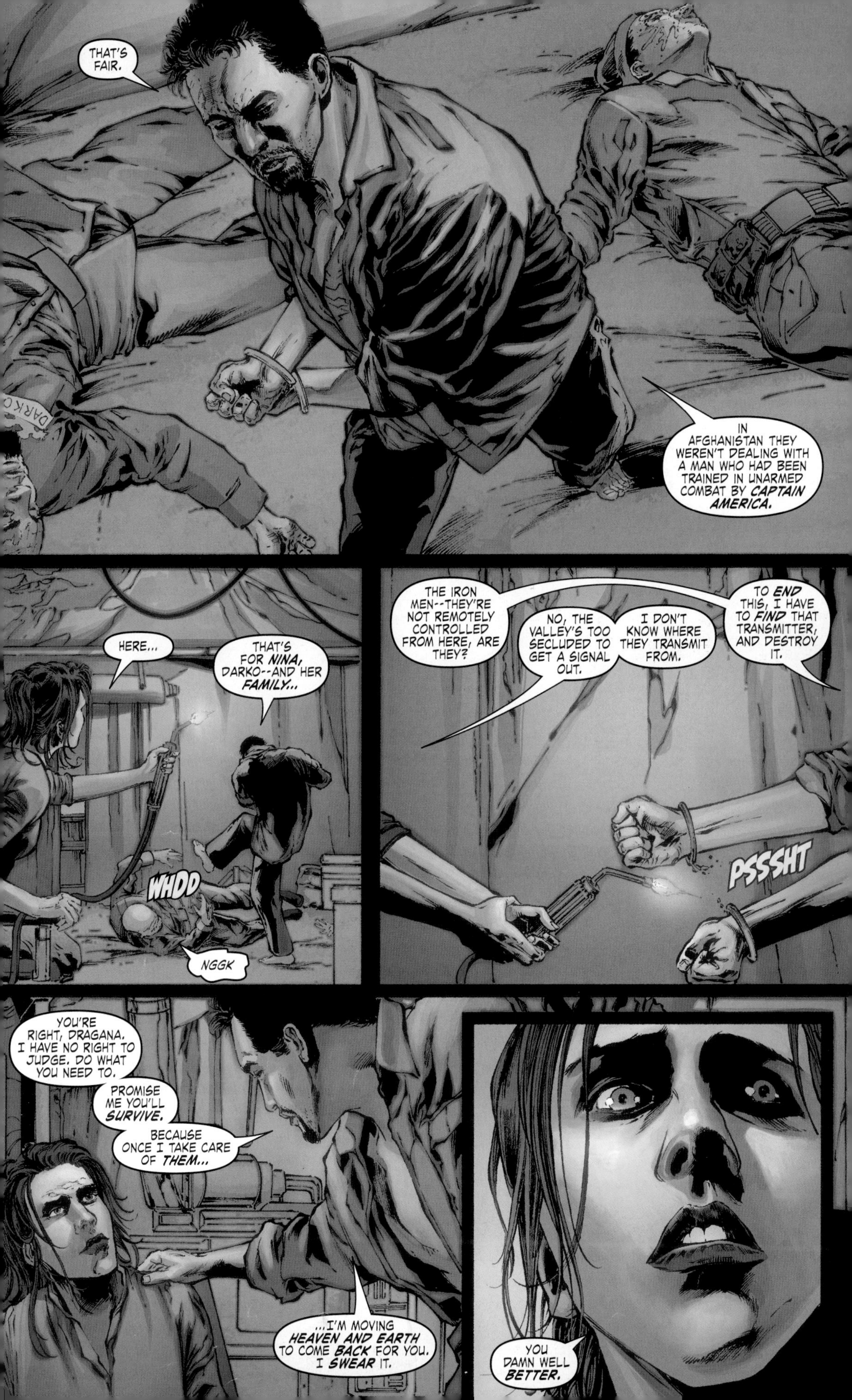
THAT'S FAIR.
DARKO
IN AFGHANISTAN THEY WEREN'T DEALING WITH A MAN WHO HAD BEEN TRAINED IN UNARMED COMBAT BY *CAPTAIN AMERICA*.
HERE...
THAT'S FOR *NINA*, DARKO--AND HER *FAMILY*...
WHDD
NGGK
THE IRON MEN--THEY'RE NOT REMOTELY CONTROLLED FROM HERE, ARE THEY?
NO, THE VALLEY'S TOO SECLUDED TO GET A SIGNAL OUT.
I DON'T KNOW WHERE THEY TRANSMIT FROM.
TO *END* THIS, I HAVE TO *FIND* THAT TRANSMITTER, AND DESTROY IT.
PSSSHT
YOU'RE RIGHT, DRAGANA. I HAVE NO RIGHT TO JUDGE. DO WHAT YOU NEED TO.
PROMISE ME YOU'LL *SURVIVE*.
BECAUSE ONCE I TAKE CARE OF *THEM*...
...I'M MOVING *HEAVEN AND EARTH* TO COME *BACK* FOR YOU. I *SWEAR* IT.
YOU DAMN WELL *BETTER*.

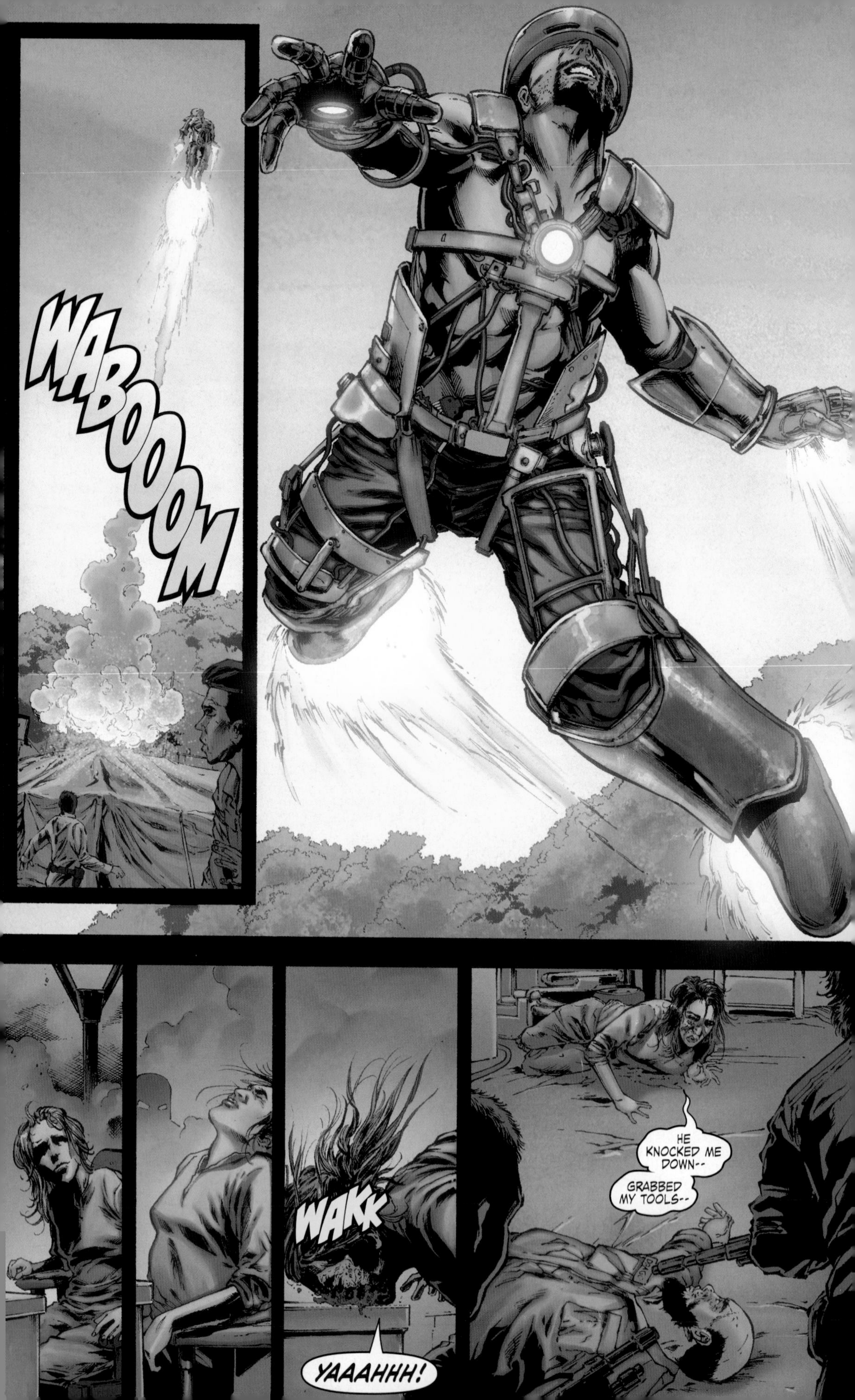
WABOOOM
WAKK
YAAAHHH!
HE KNOCKED ME DOWN--
GRABBED MY TOOLS--

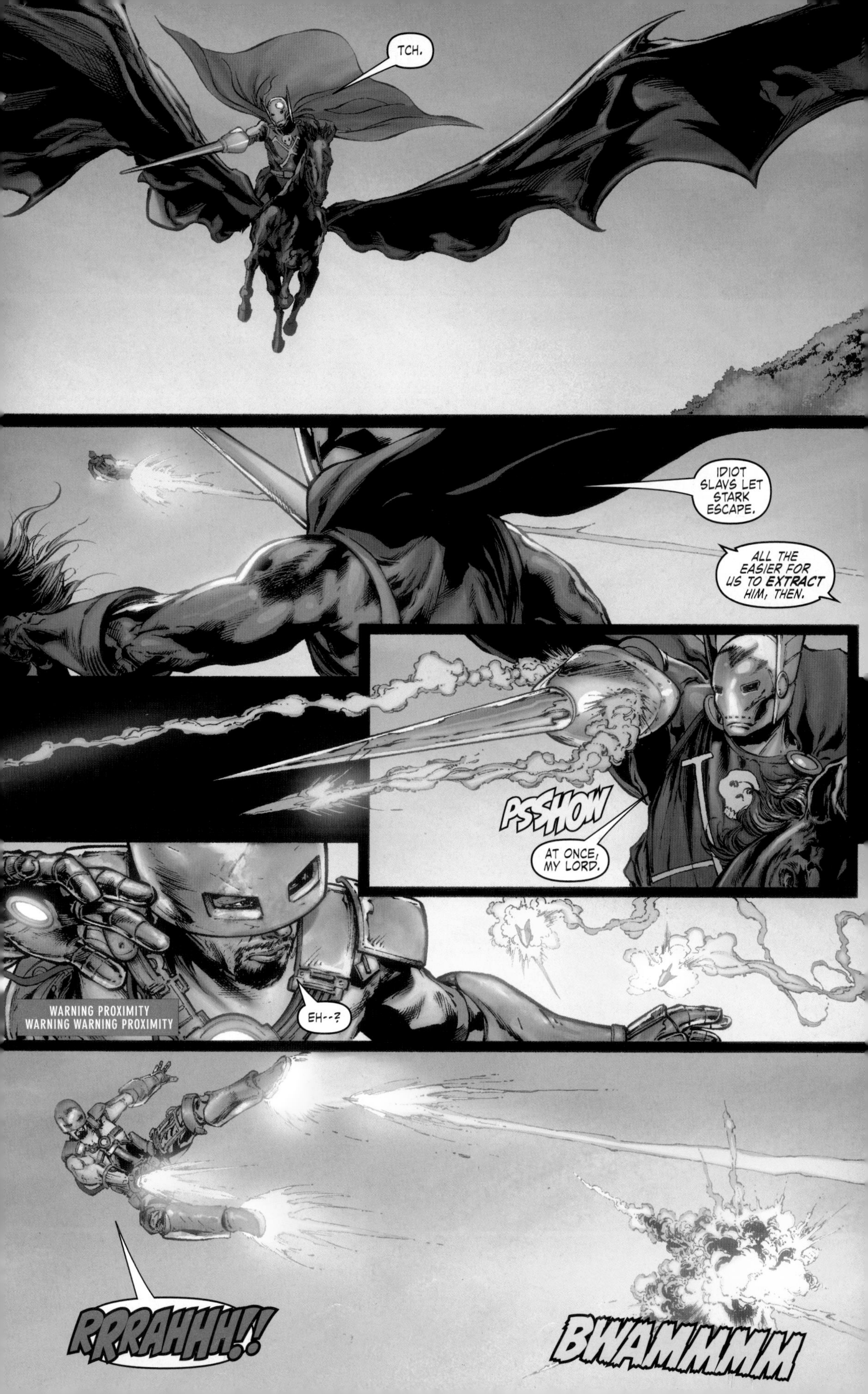
TCH.
IDIOT SLAVS LET STARK ESCAPE.
ALL THE EASIER FOR US TO EXTRACT HIM, THEN.
PSSHOW
AT ONCE, MY LORD.
WARNING PROXIMITY WARNING WARNING PROXIMITY
EH--?
RRRAHHH!!
BWAMMMMM

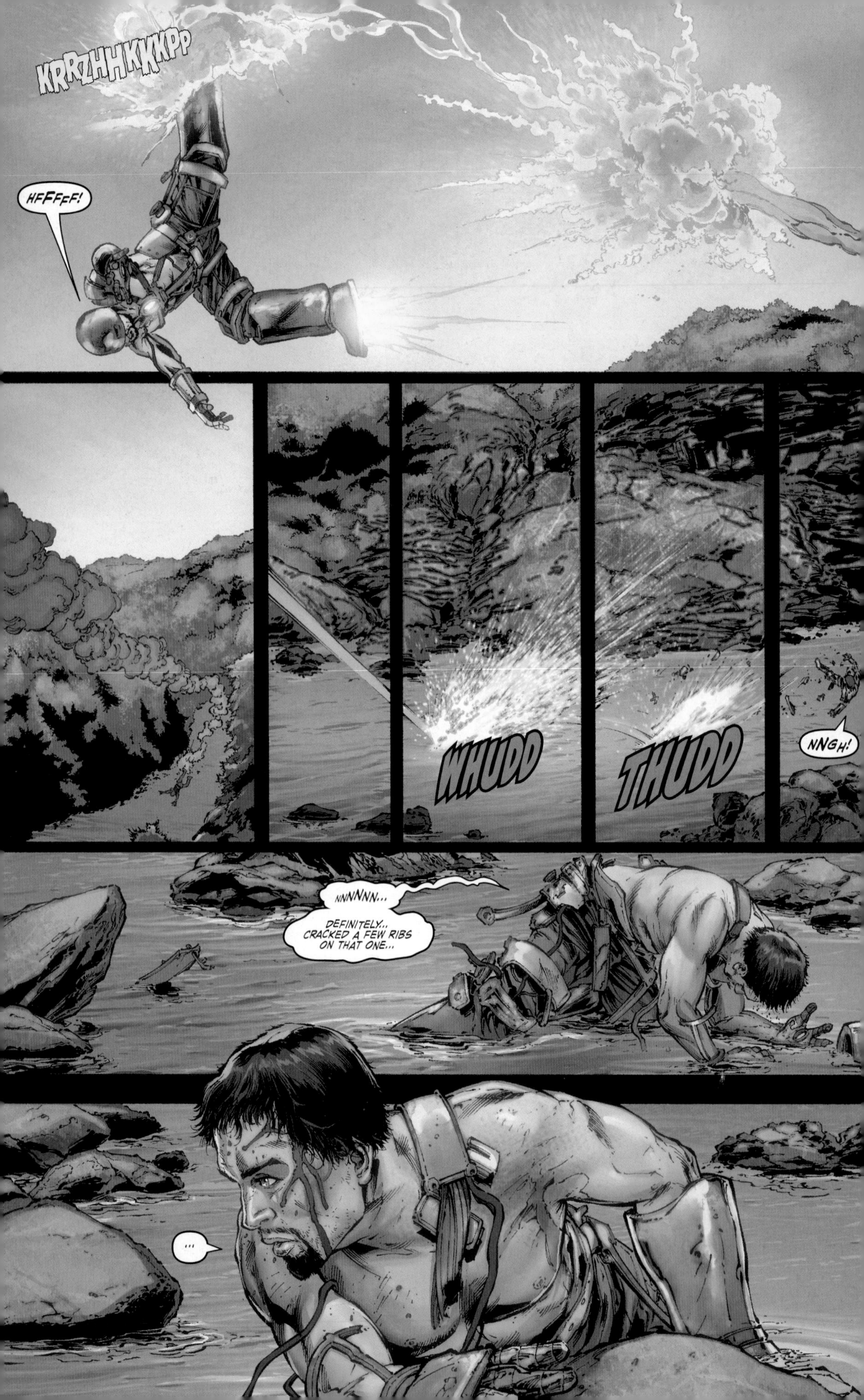
KRRZHHKKKPP
HFFFFF!
WHUDD
THUDD
NNGH!
NNNNNN...
DEFINITELY... CRACKED A FEW RIBS ON THAT ONE...
...

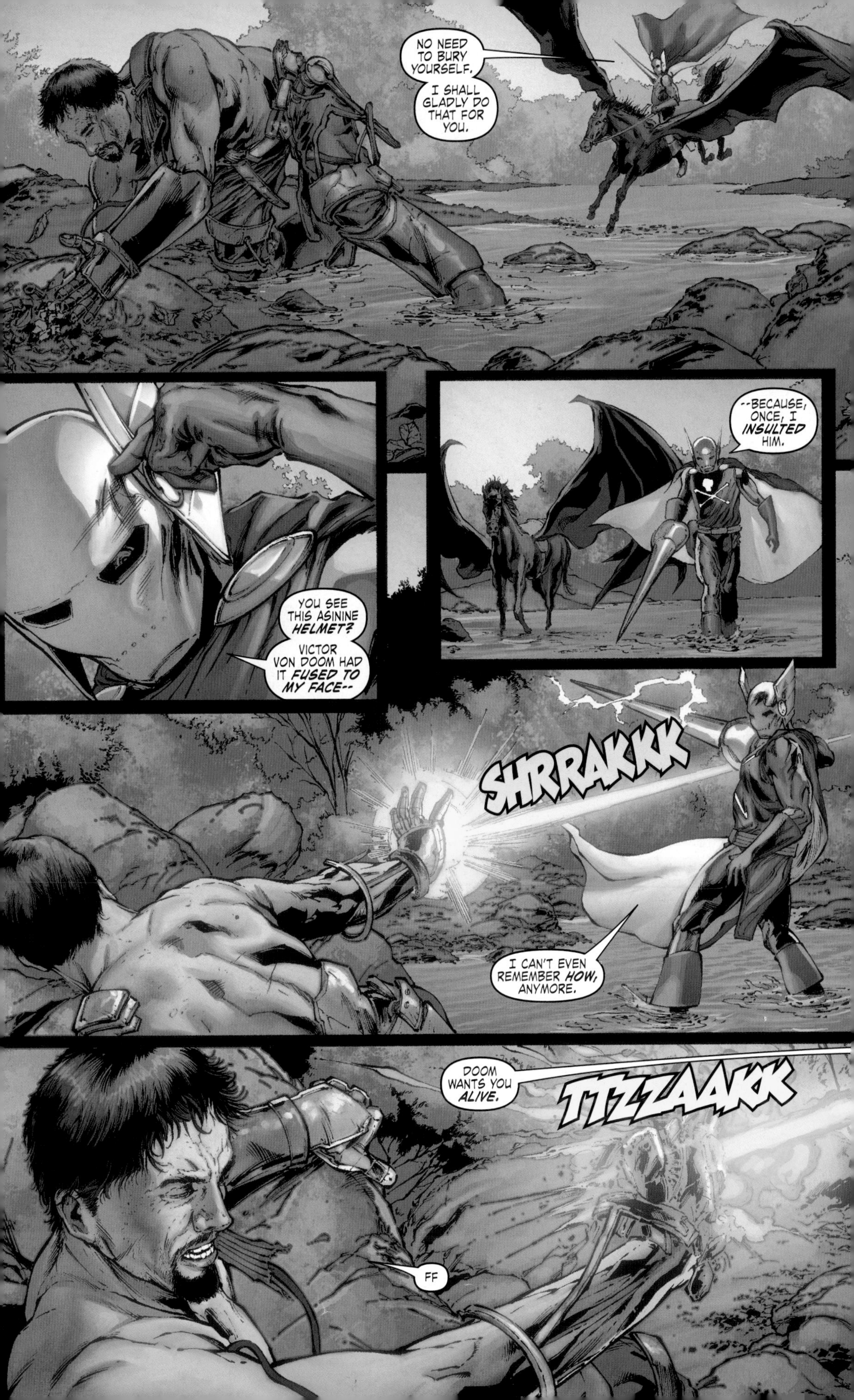
NO NEED TO BURY YOURSELF.
I SHALL GLADLY DO THAT FOR YOU.
YOU SEE THIS ASININE *HELMET?*
VICTOR VON DOOM HAD IT *FUSED TO MY FACE--*
--BECAUSE, ONCE, I *INSULTED* HIM.
SHRRAKKK
I CAN'T EVEN REMEMBER *HOW,* ANYMORE.
DOOM WANTS YOU *ALIVE.*
TTZZAAKK
FF

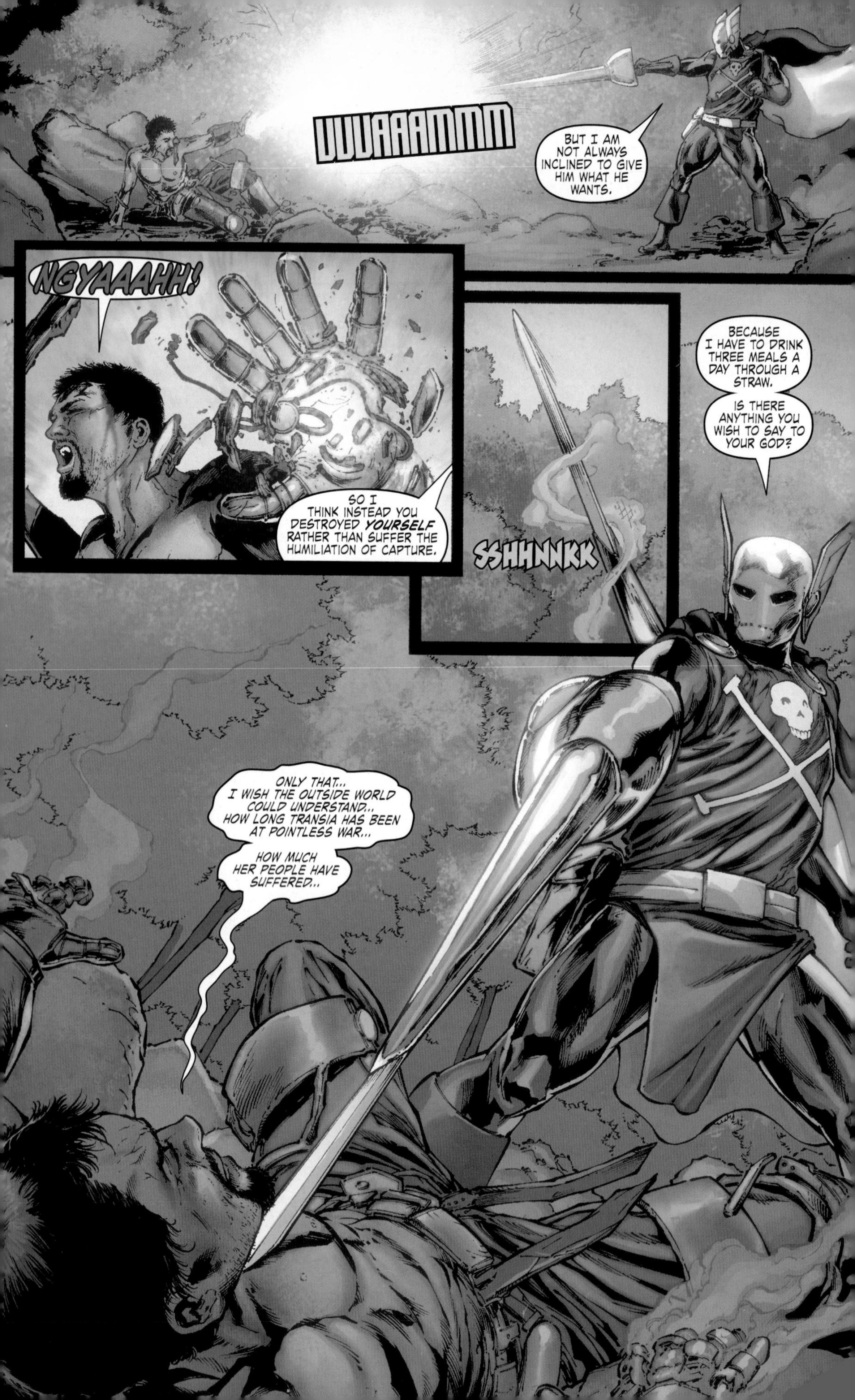
VVVRAAMMM
BUT I AM NOT ALWAYS INCLINED TO GIVE HIM WHAT HE WANTS.
NGYAAAHH!
SO I THINK INSTEAD YOU DESTROYED *YOURSELF* RATHER THAN SUFFER THE HUMILIATION OF CAPTURE.
SSHHNNKK
BECAUSE I HAVE TO DRINK THREE MEALS A DAY THROUGH A STRAW.
IS THERE ANYTHING YOU WISH TO SAY TO YOUR GOD?
ONLY THAT... I WISH THE OUTSIDE WORLD COULD UNDERSTAND... HOW LONG TRANSIA HAS BEEN AT POINTLESS WAR...
HOW MUCH HER PEOPLE HAVE SUFFERED...

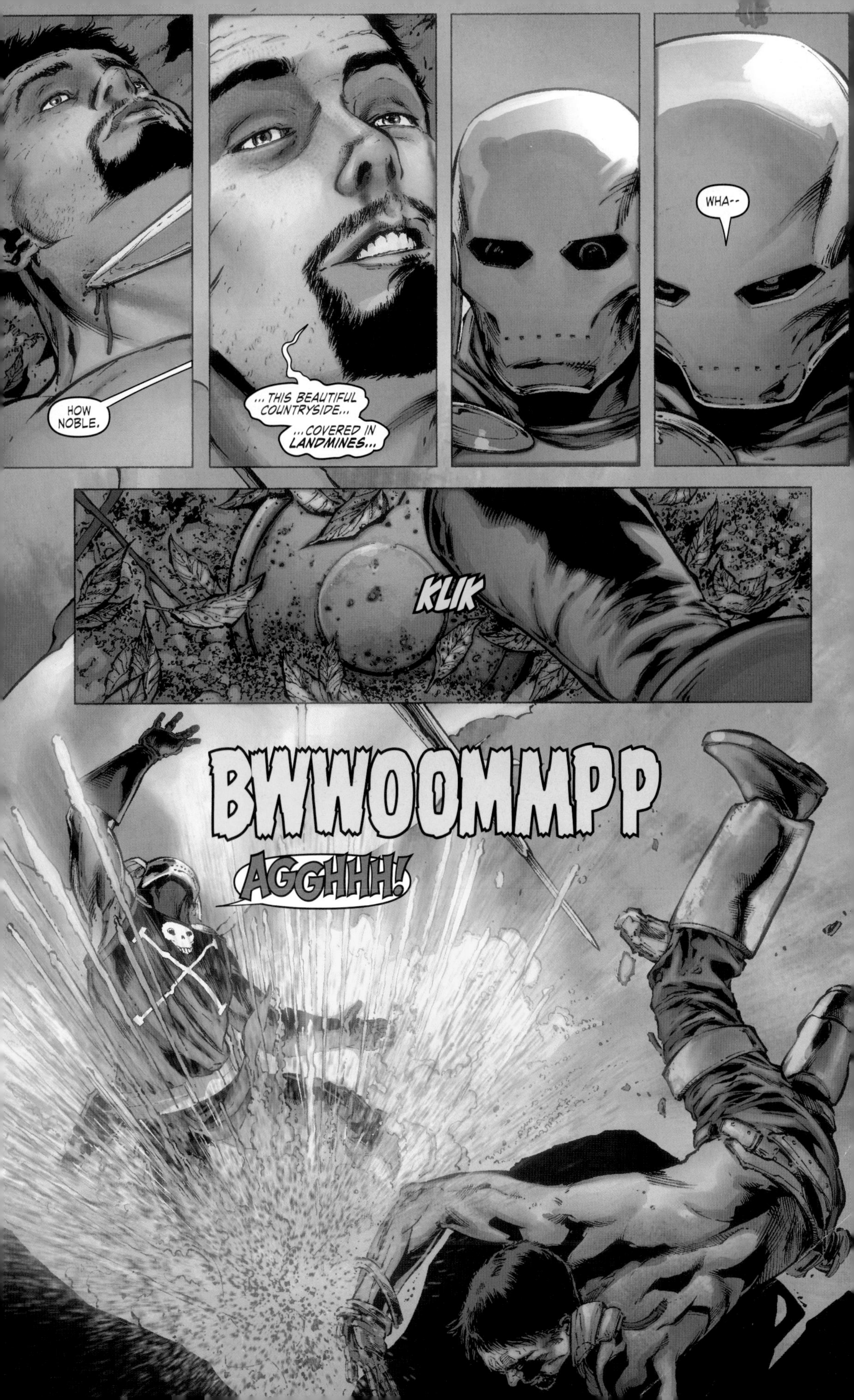
HOW NOBLE.
...THIS BEAUTIFUL COUNTRYSIDE...
...COVERED IN LANDMINES...
WHA--
KLIK
BWWOOMMPP
AGGHHH!

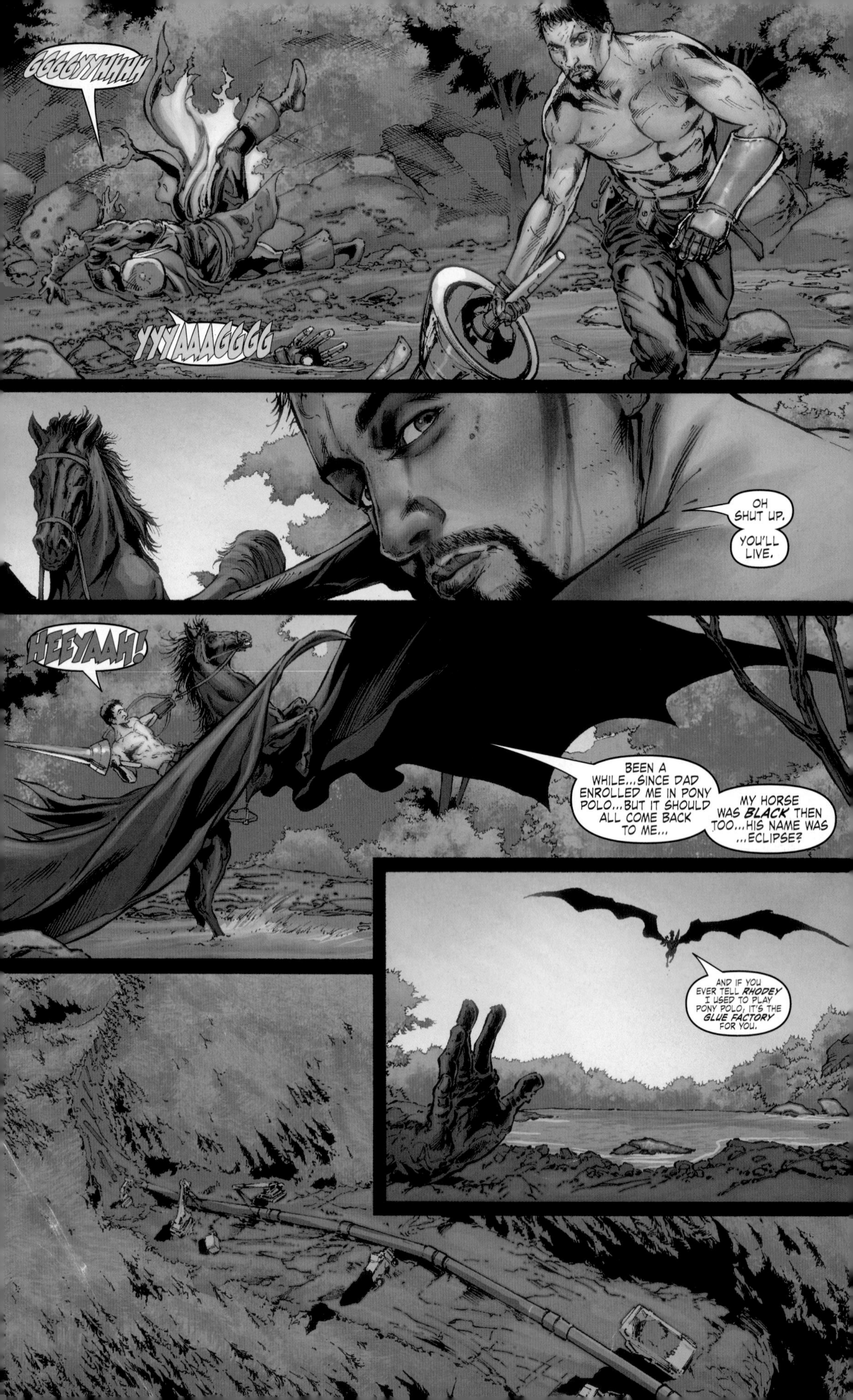
GGGGYYHHHH
YYYAAAGGGG
OH SHUT UP.
YOU'LL LIVE.
HEEYAAH!
BEEN A WHILE...SINCE DAD ENROLLED ME IN PONY POLO...BUT IT SHOULD ALL COME BACK TO ME...
MY HORSE WAS BLACK THEN TOO...HIS NAME WAS ...ECLIPSE?
AND IF YOU EVER TELL RHODEY I USED TO PLAY PONY POLO, IT'S THE GLUE FACTORY FOR YOU.

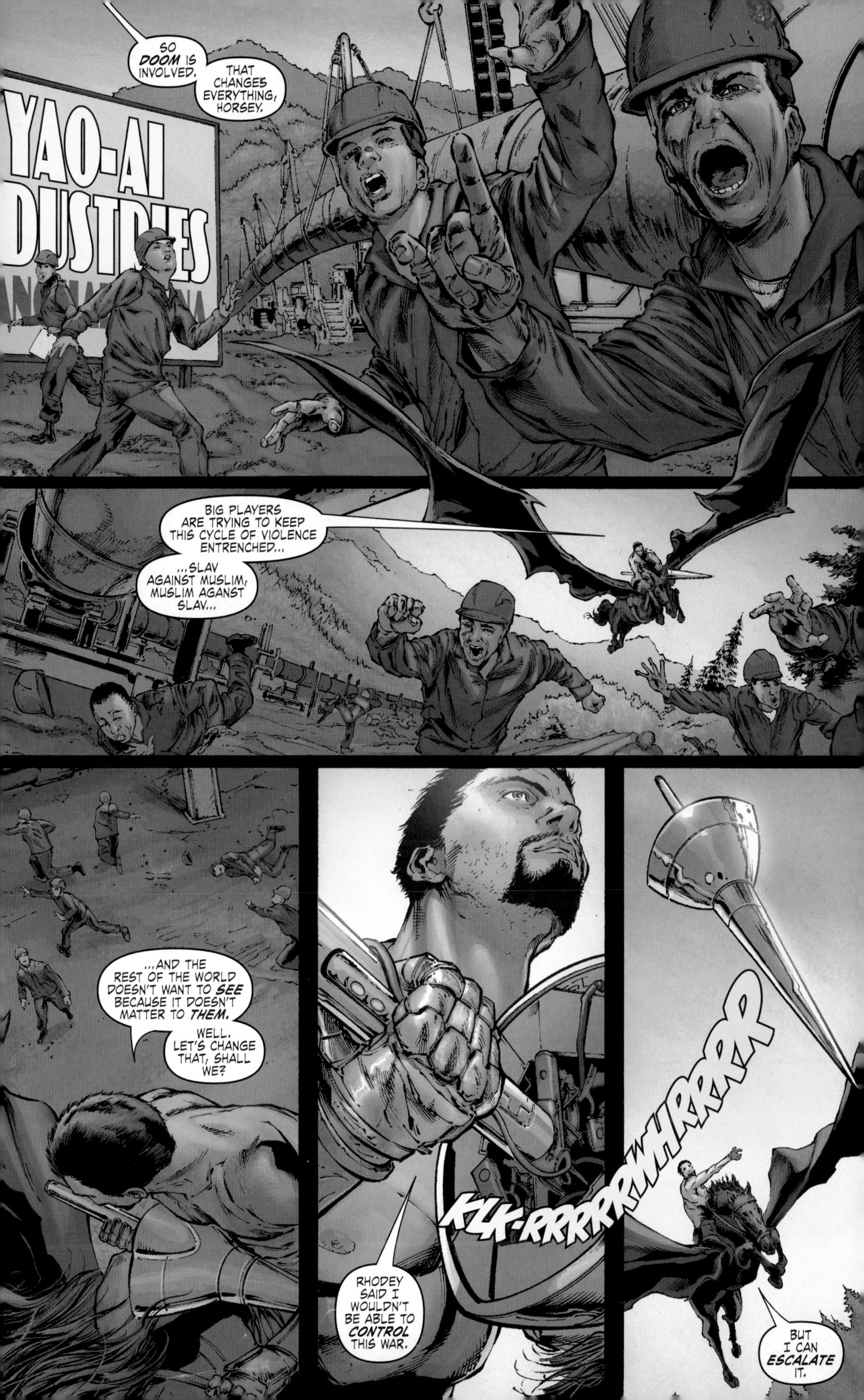
SO *DOOM* IS INVOLVED.
THAT CHANGES EVERYTHING, HORSEY.
YAO-AI
DUSTRIES
BIG PLAYERS ARE TRYING TO KEEP THIS CYCLE OF VIOLENCE ENTRENCHED...
...SLAV AGAINST MUSLIM, MUSLIM AGANST SLAV...
...AND THE REST OF THE WORLD DOESN'T WANT TO *SEE* BECAUSE IT DOESN'T MATTER TO *THEM.*
WELL. LET'S CHANGE THAT, SHALL WE?
RHODEY SAID I WOULDN'T BE ABLE TO *CONTROL* THIS WAR.
KLK-RRRRRWHRRRR
BUT I CAN *ESCALATE* IT.

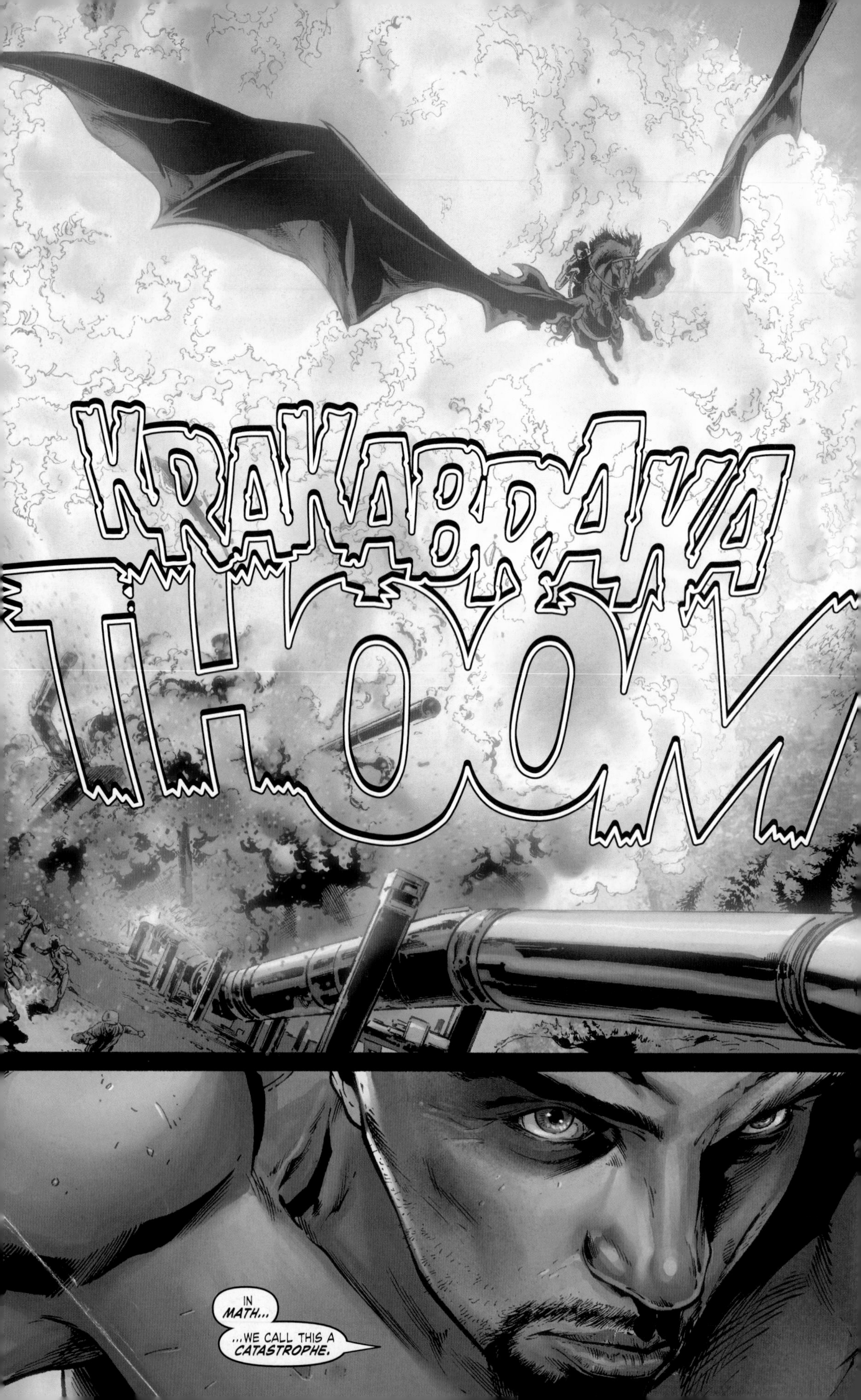
KRAKABBAKA
THOOM
IN MATH...
...WE CALL THIS A CATASTROPHE.

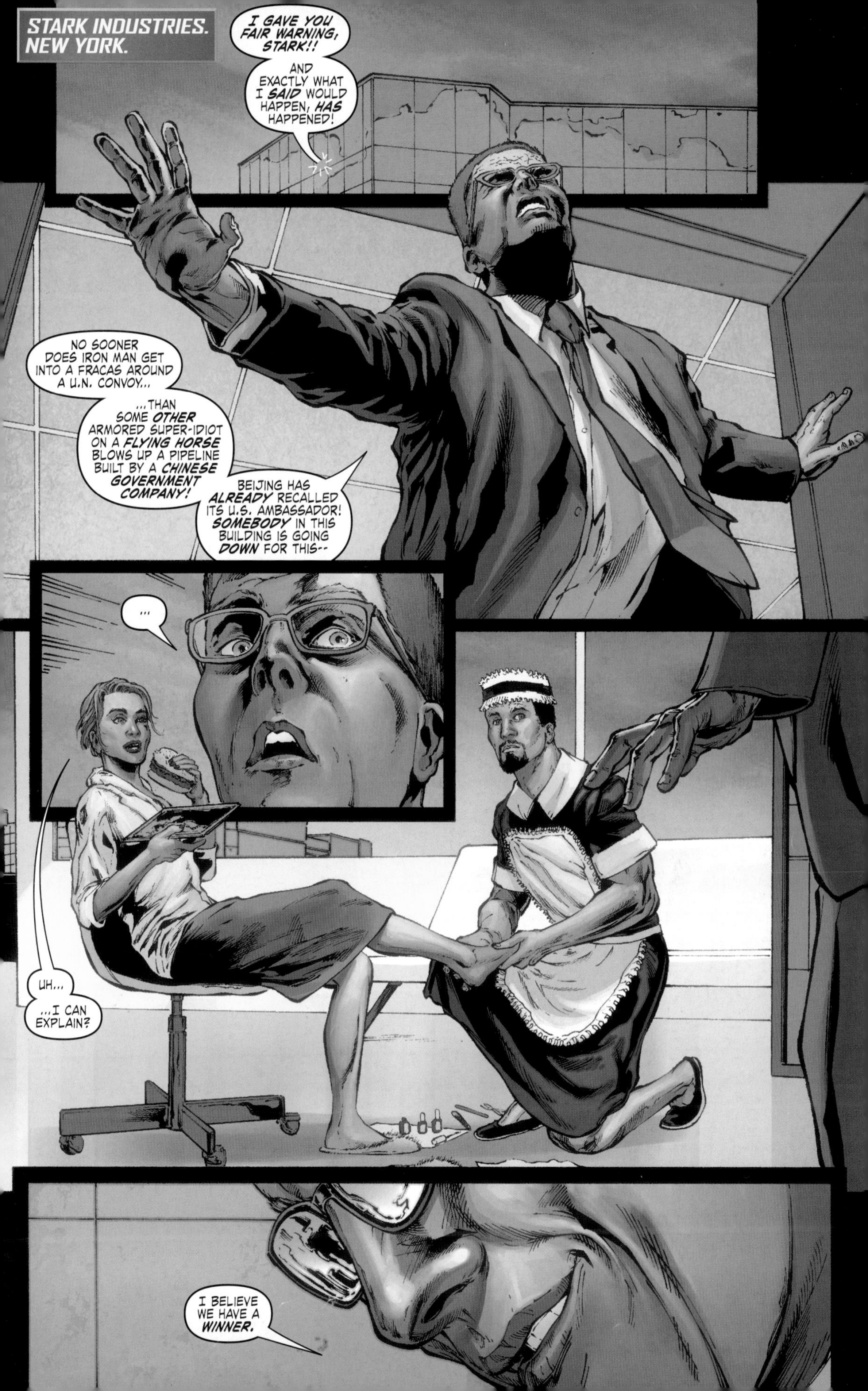
STARK INDUSTRIES. NEW YORK.
I GAVE YOU FAIR WARNING, STARK!!
AND EXACTLY WHAT I SAID WOULD HAPPEN, HAS HAPPENED!
NO SOONER DOES IRON MAN GET INTO A FRACAS AROUND A U.N. CONVOY...
...THAN SOME OTHER ARMORED SUPER-IDIOT ON A FLYING HORSE BLOWS UP A PIPELINE BUILT BY A CHINESE GOVERNMENT COMPANY!
BEIJING HAS ALREADY RECALLED ITS U.S. AMBASSADOR! SOMEBODY IN THIS BUILDING IS GOING DOWN FOR THIS--
...
UH...
...I CAN EXPLAIN?
I BELIEVE WE HAVE A WINNER.

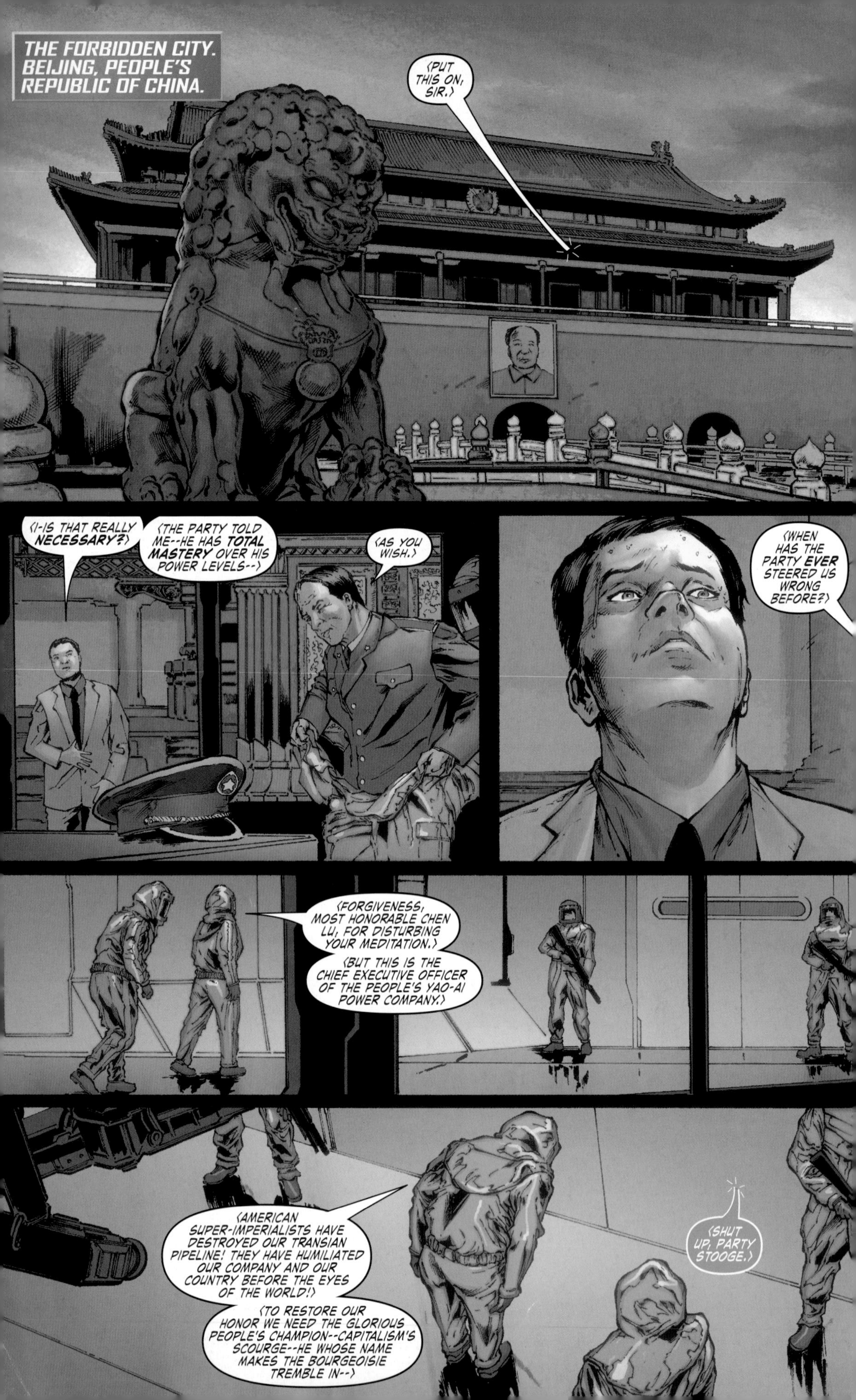
THE FORBIDDEN CITY. BEIJING, PEOPLE'S REPUBLIC OF CHINA.
⟨PUT THIS ON, SIR.⟩
⟨I-IS THAT REALLY NECESSARY?⟩
⟨THE PARTY TOLD ME--HE HAS TOTAL MASTERY OVER HIS POWER LEVELS--⟩
⟨AS YOU WISH.⟩
⟨WHEN HAS THE PARTY EVER STEERED US WRONG BEFORE?⟩
⟨FORGIVENESS, MOST HONORABLE CHEN LU, FOR DISTURBING YOUR MEDITATION.⟩
⟨BUT THIS IS THE CHIEF EXECUTIVE OFFICER OF THE PEOPLE'S YAO-AI POWER COMPANY.⟩
⟨AMERICAN SUPER-IMPERIALISTS HAVE DESTROYED OUR TRANSIAN PIPELINE! THEY HAVE HUMILIATED OUR COMPANY AND OUR COUNTRY BEFORE THE EYES OF THE WORLD!⟩
⟨TO RESTORE OUR HONOR WE NEED THE GLORIOUS PEOPLE'S CHAMPION--CAPITALISM'S SCOURGE--HE WHOSE NAME MAKES THE BOURGEOISIE TREMBLE IN--⟩
⟨SHUT UP, PARTY STOOGE.⟩

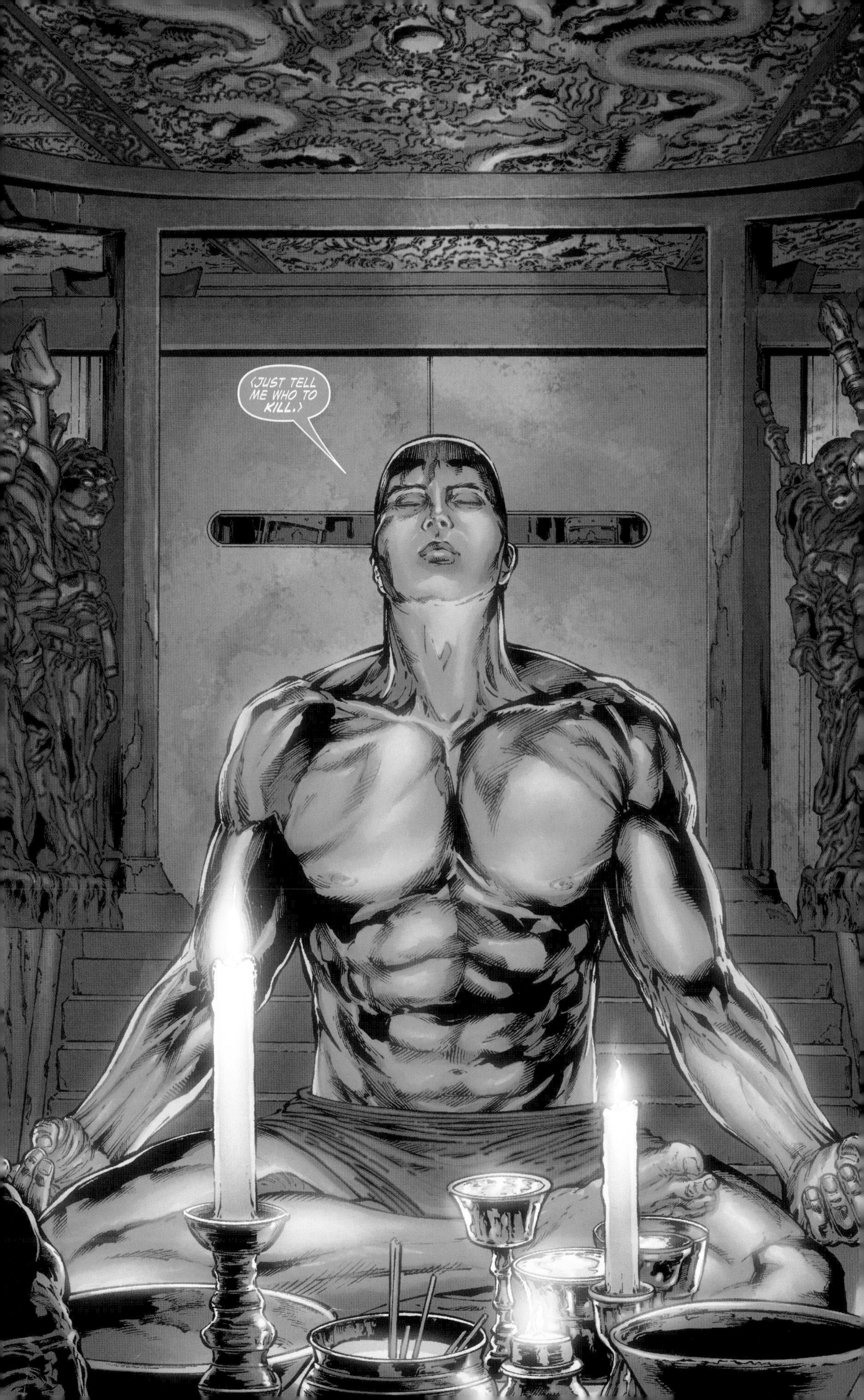
‹JUST TELL ME WHO TO KILL.›

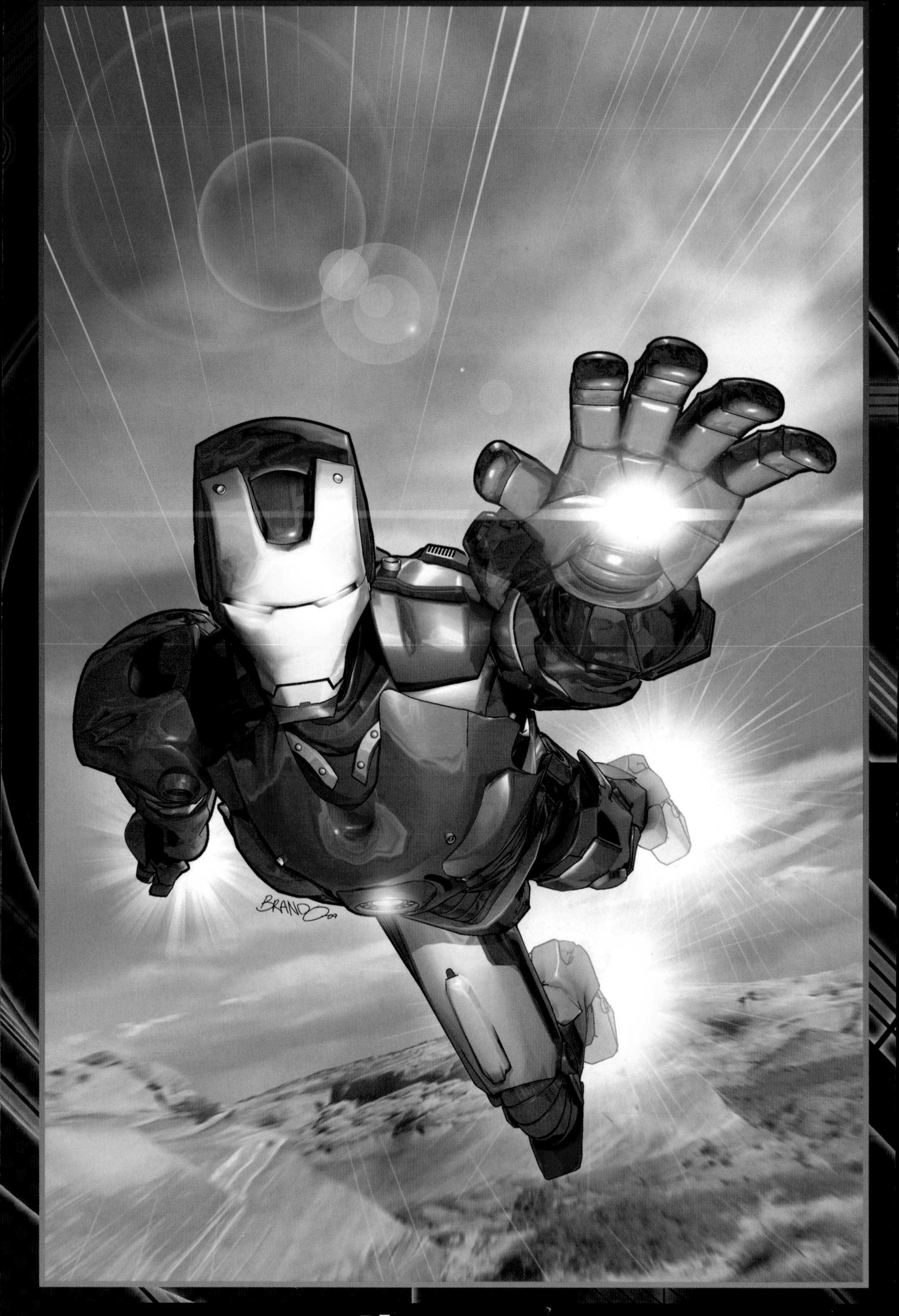

IRON MAN LEGACY 4

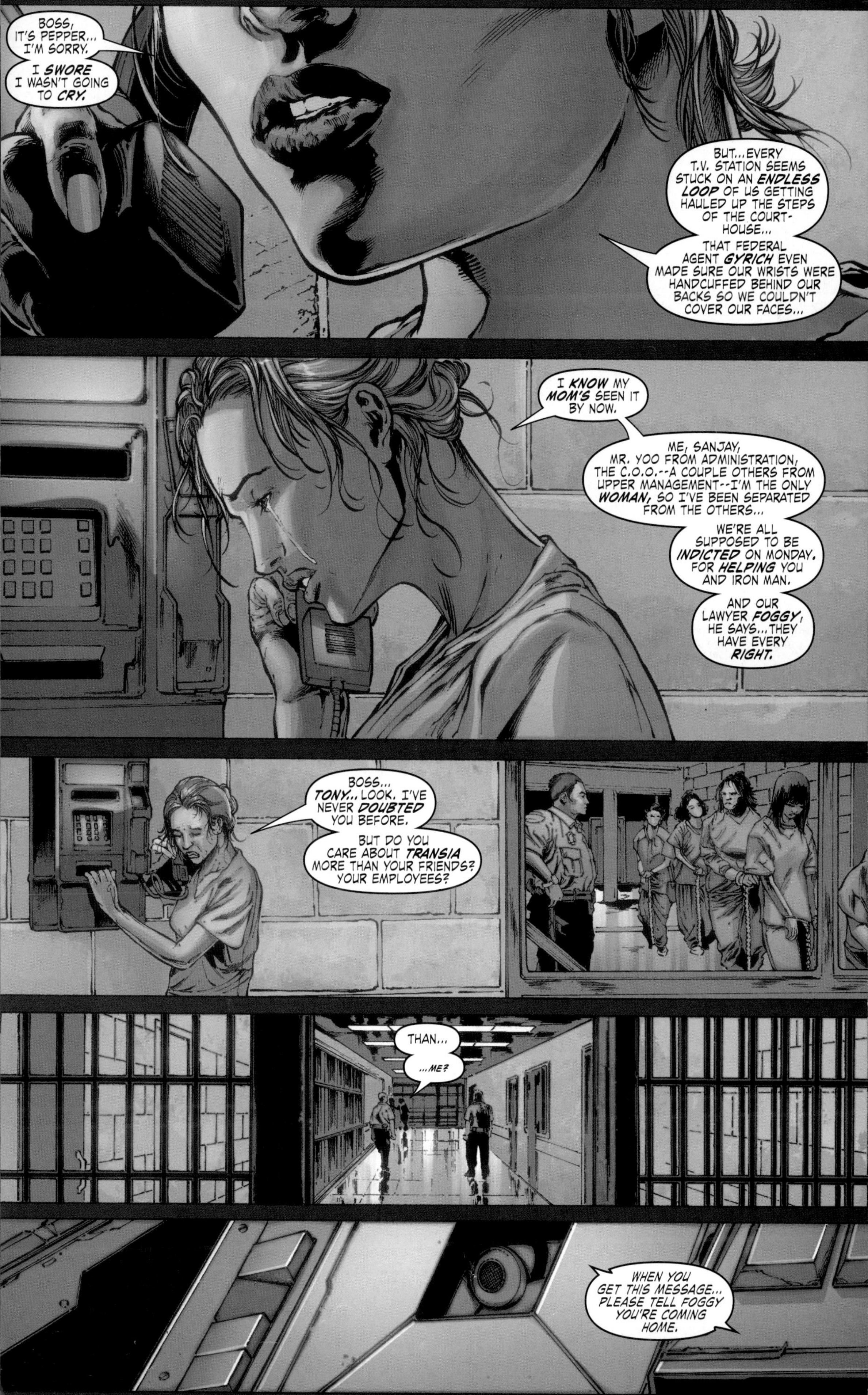
BOSS, IT'S PEPPER... I'M SORRY.
I SWORE I WASN'T GOING TO CRY.
BUT...EVERY T.V. STATION SEEMS STUCK ON AN ENDLESS LOOP OF US GETTING HAULED UP THE STEPS OF THE COURT-HOUSE...
THAT FEDERAL AGENT GYRICH EVEN MADE SURE OUR WRISTS WERE HANDCUFFED BEHIND OUR BACKS SO WE COULDN'T COVER OUR FACES...
I KNOW MY MOM'S SEEN IT BY NOW.
ME, SANJAY, MR. YOO FROM ADMINISTRATION, THE C.O.O.--A COUPLE OTHERS FROM UPPER MANAGEMENT--I'M THE ONLY WOMAN, SO I'VE BEEN SEPARATED FROM THE OTHERS...
WE'RE ALL SUPPOSED TO BE INDICTED ON MONDAY. FOR HELPING YOU AND IRON MAN.
AND OUR LAWYER FOGGY, HE SAYS...THEY HAVE EVERY RIGHT.
BOSS... TONY... LOOK. I'VE NEVER DOUBTED YOU BEFORE.
BUT DO YOU CARE ABOUT TRANSIA MORE THAN YOUR FRIENDS? YOUR EMPLOYEES?
THAN...
...ME?
WHEN YOU GET THIS MESSAGE... PLEASE TELL FOGGY YOU'RE COMING HOME.

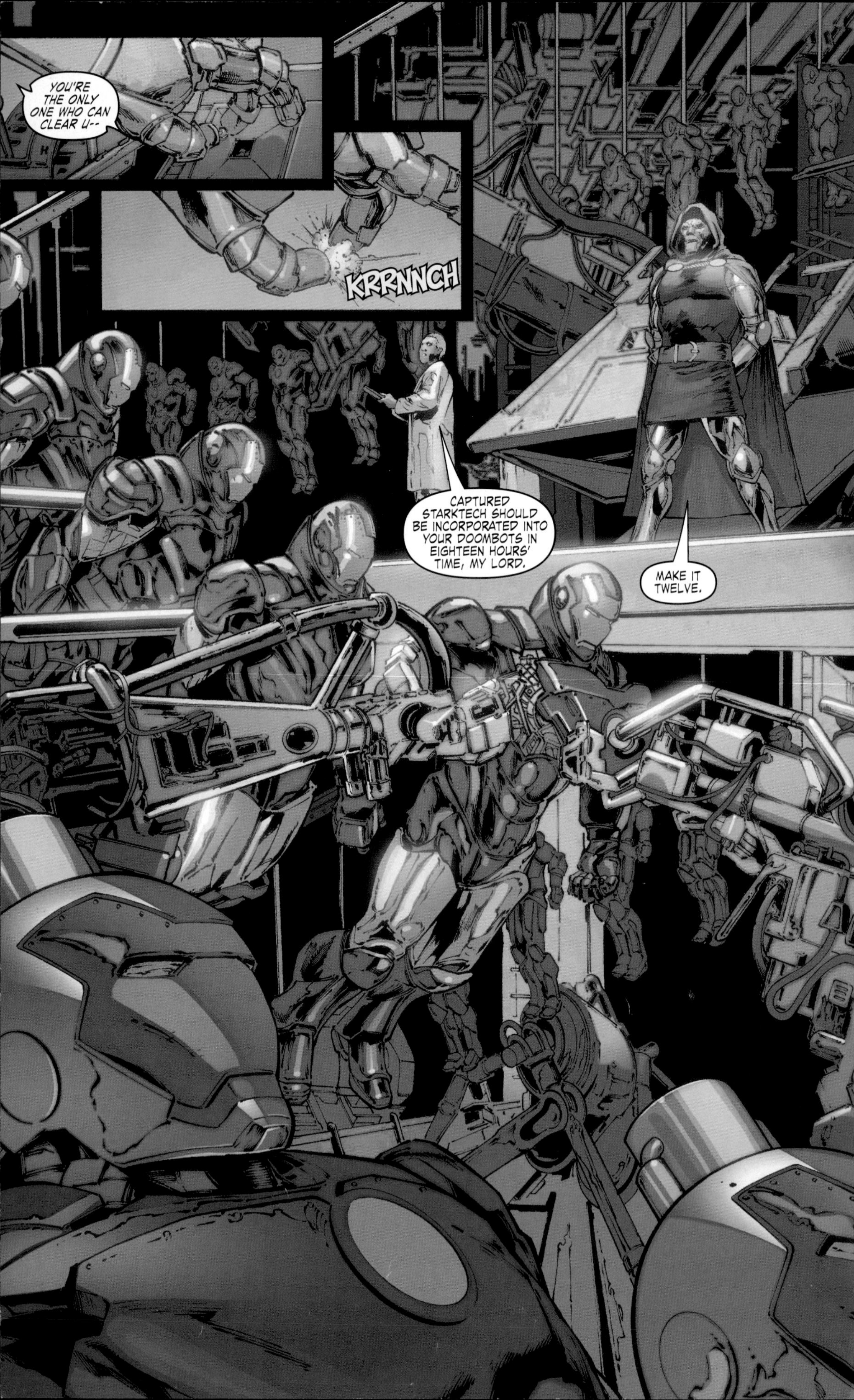
YOU'RE THE ONLY ONE WHO CAN CLEAR U--
KRRNNCH
CAPTURED STARKTECH SHOULD BE INCORPORATED INTO YOUR DOOMBOTS IN EIGHTEEN HOURS' TIME, MY LORD.
MAKE IT TWELVE.

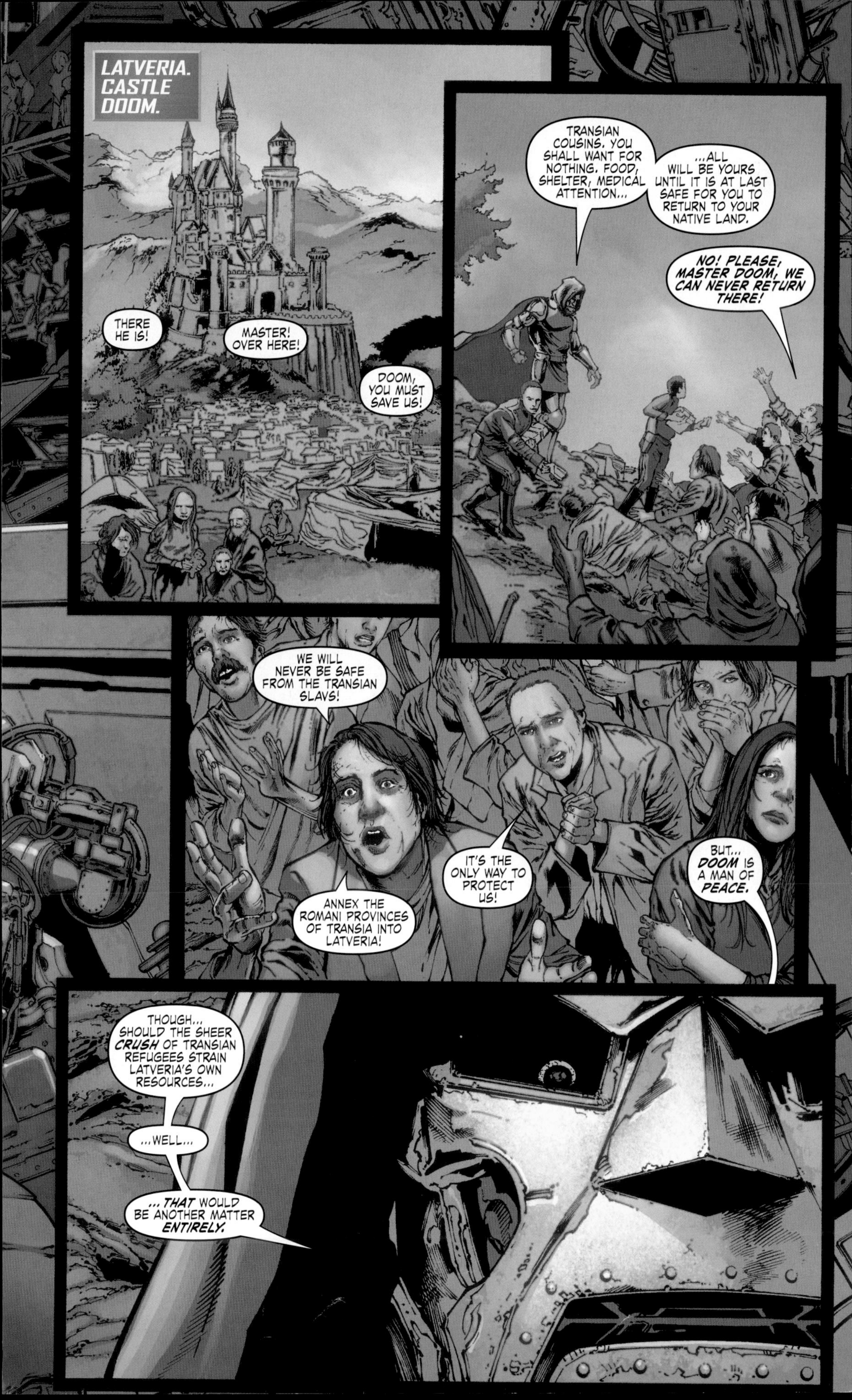
LATVERIA. CASTLE DOOM.
THERE HE IS!
MASTER! OVER HERE!
DOOM, YOU MUST SAVE US!
TRANSIAN COUSINS. YOU SHALL WANT FOR NOTHING. FOOD, SHELTER, MEDICAL ATTENTION...
...ALL WILL BE YOURS UNTIL IT IS AT LAST SAFE FOR YOU TO RETURN TO YOUR NATIVE LAND.
NO! PLEASE, MASTER DOOM, WE CAN NEVER RETURN THERE!
WE WILL NEVER BE SAFE FROM THE TRANSIAN SLAVS!
ANNEX THE ROMANI PROVINCES OF TRANSIA INTO LATVERIA!
IT'S THE ONLY WAY TO PROTECT US!
BUT... DOOM IS A MAN OF PEACE.
THOUGH... SHOULD THE SHEER CRUSH OF TRANSIAN REFUGEES STRAIN LATVERIA'S OWN RESOURCES...
...WELL...
...THAT WOULD BE ANOTHER MATTER ENTIRELY.

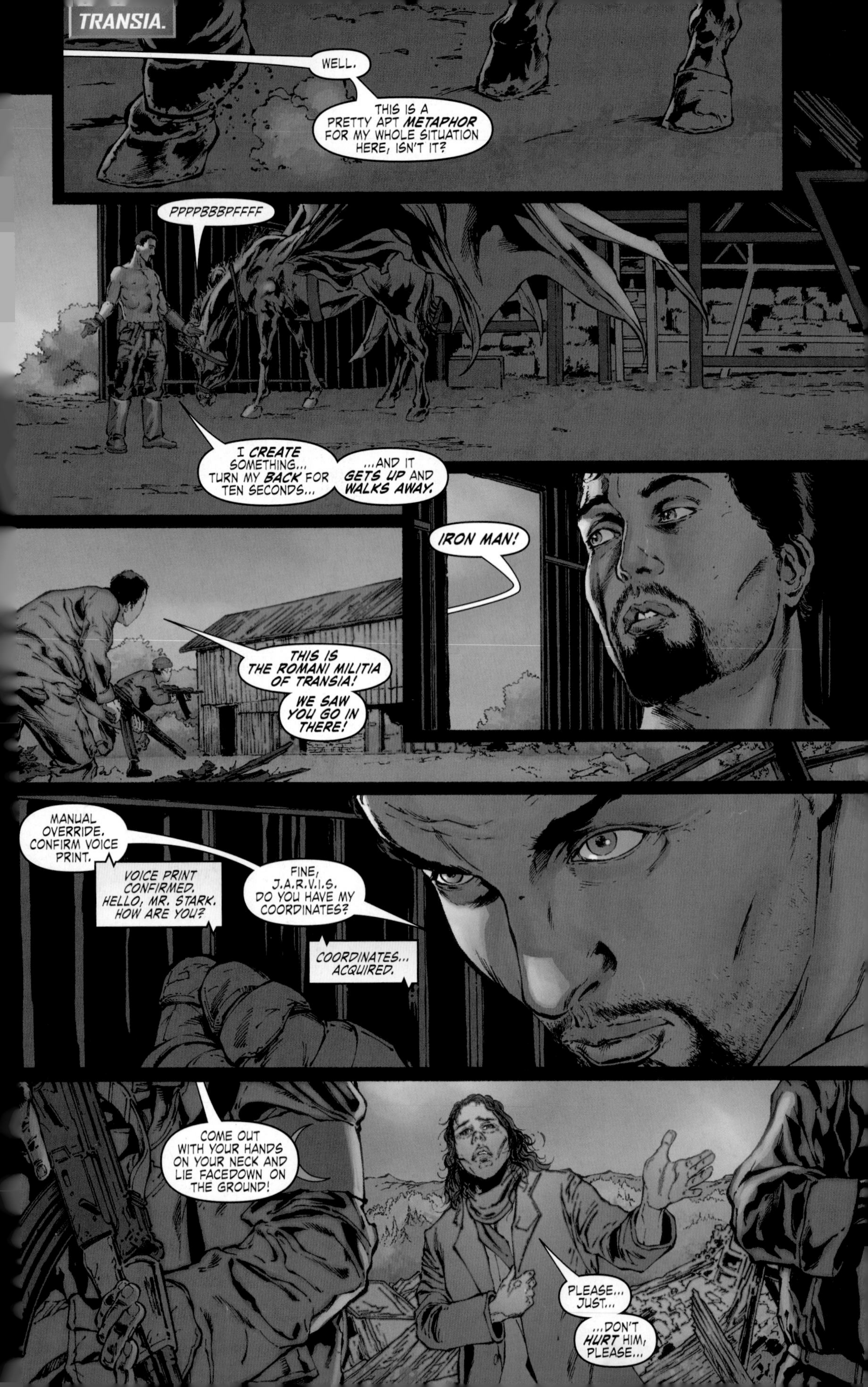
TRANSIA.
WELL.
THIS IS A PRETTY APT METAPHOR FOR MY WHOLE SITUATION HERE, ISN'T IT?
PPPPBBBPFFFF
I CREATE SOMETHING... TURN MY BACK FOR TEN SECONDS...
...AND IT GETS UP AND WALKS AWAY.
IRON MAN!
THIS IS THE ROMANI MILITIA OF TRANSIA!
WE SAW YOU GO IN THERE!
MANUAL OVERRIDE. CONFIRM VOICE PRINT.
VOICE PRINT CONFIRMED. HELLO, MR. STARK. HOW ARE YOU?
FINE, J.A.R.V.I.S. DO YOU HAVE MY COORDINATES?
COORDINATES... ACQUIRED.
COME OUT WITH YOUR HANDS ON YOUR NECK AND LIE FACEDOWN ON THE GROUND!
PLEASE... JUST...
...DON'T HURT HIM, PLEASE...

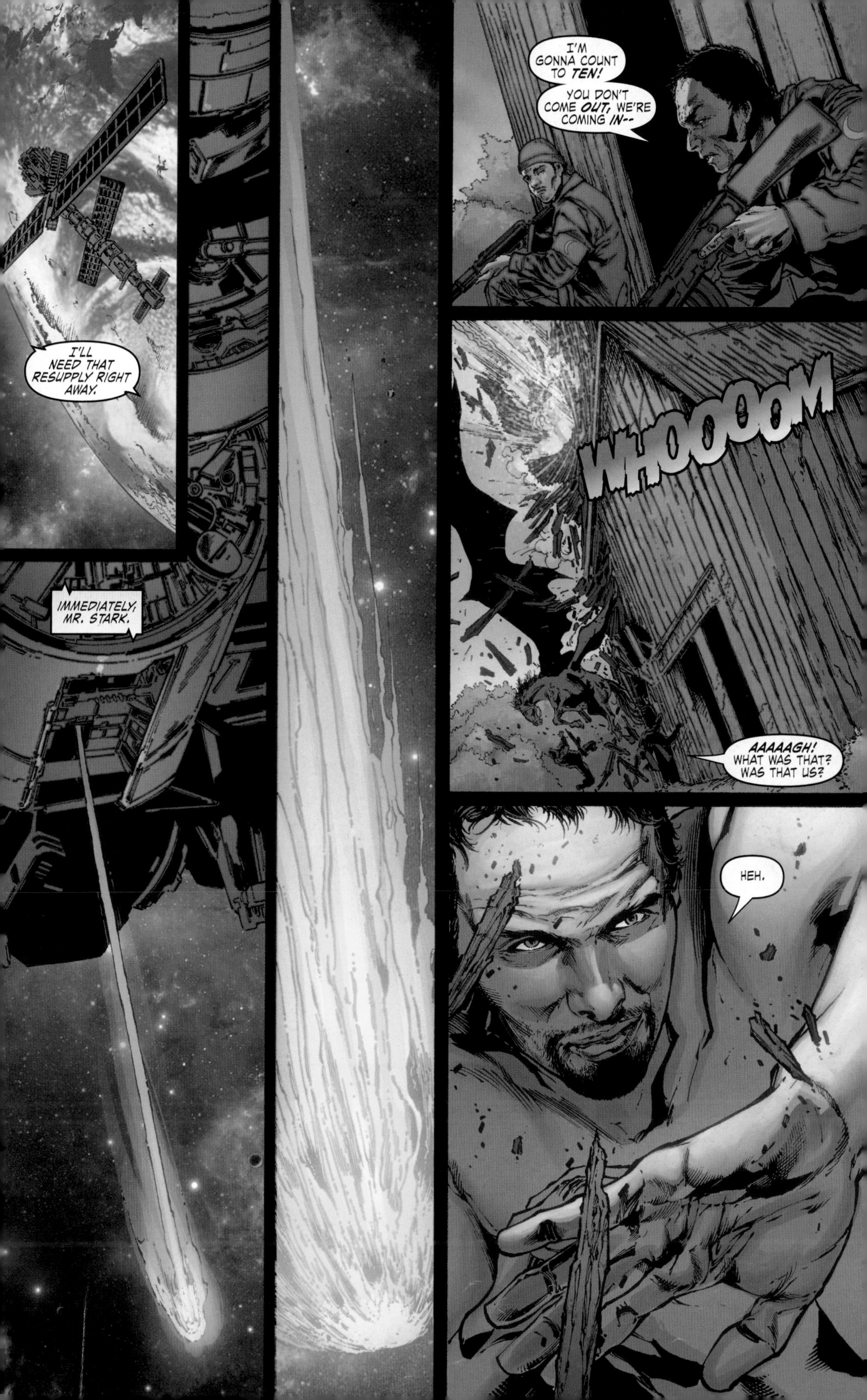
I'LL NEED THAT RESUPPLY RIGHT AWAY.
IMMEDIATELY, MR. STARK.
I'M GONNA COUNT TO TEN!
YOU DON'T COME OUT, WE'RE COMING IN--
WHOOOOM
AAAAAGH! WHAT WAS THAT? WAS THAT US?
HEH.

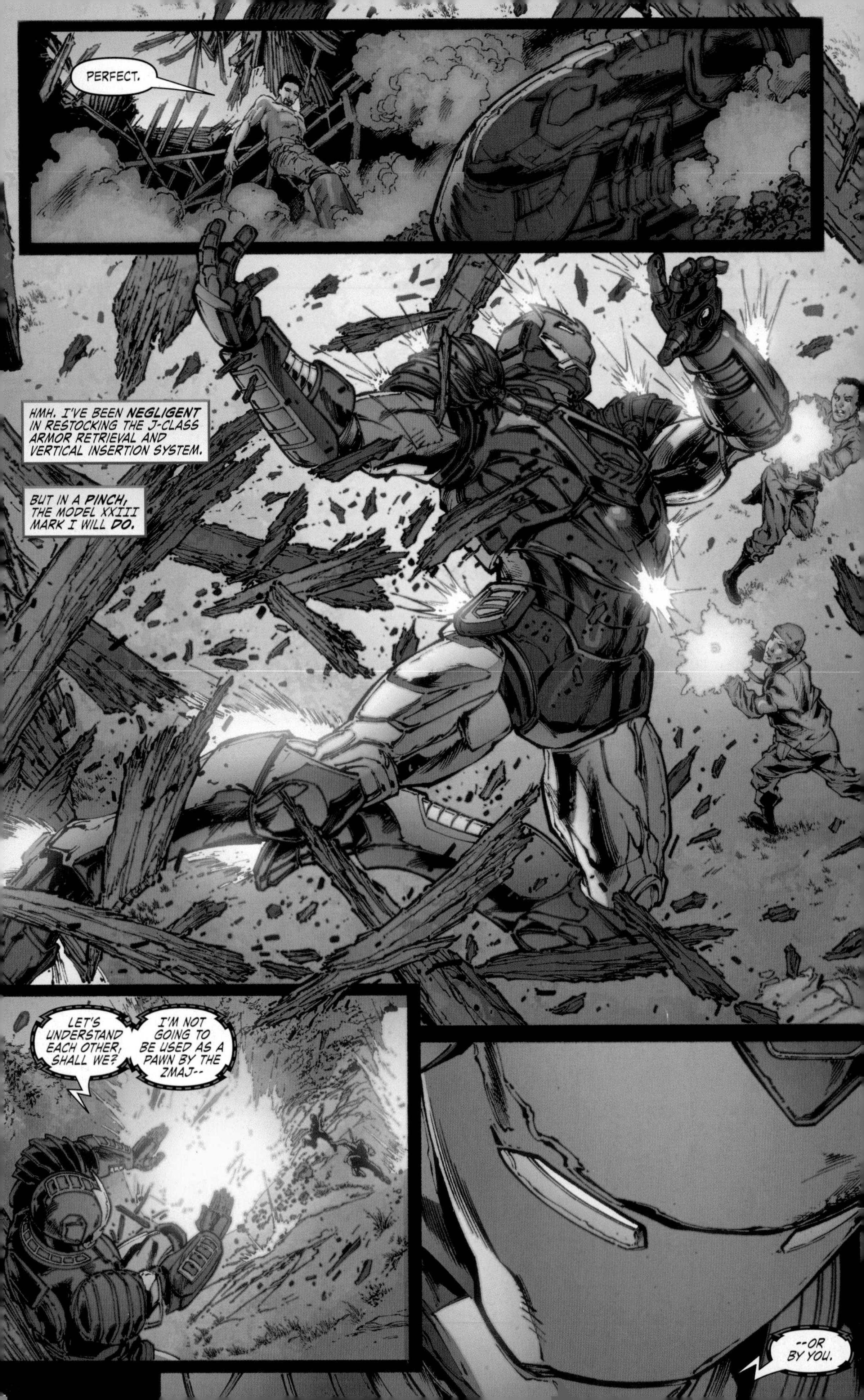
PERFECT.
HMH. I'VE BEEN NEGLIGENT IN RESTOCKING THE J-CLASS ARMOR RETRIEVAL AND VERTICAL INSERTION SYSTEM.
BUT IN A PINCH, THE MODEL XXIII MARK I WILL DO.
LET'S UNDERSTAND EACH OTHER, SHALL WE?
I'M NOT GOING TO BE USED AS A PAWN BY THE ZMAJ--
--OR BY YOU.

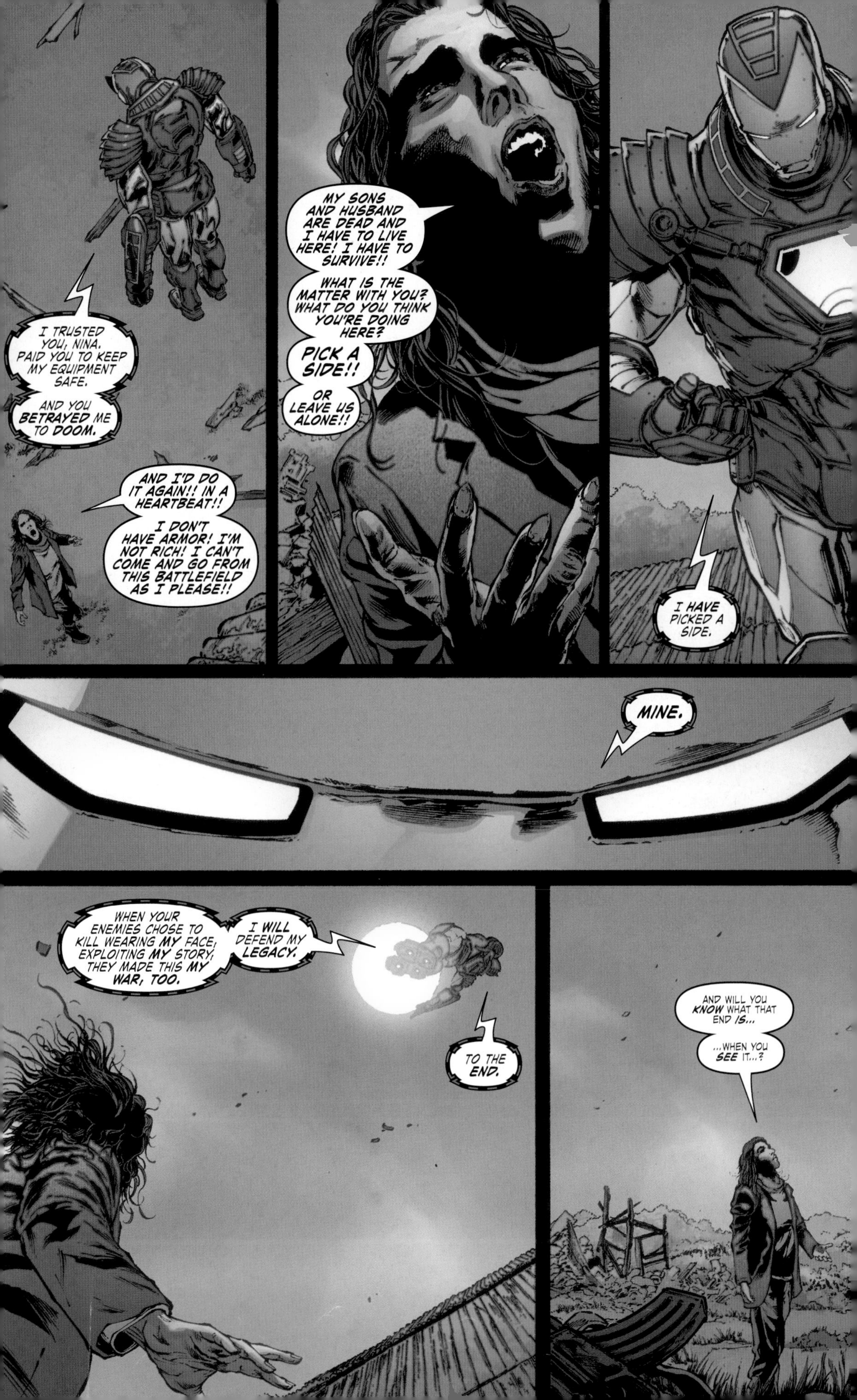
I TRUSTED YOU, NINA. PAID YOU TO KEEP MY EQUIPMENT SAFE.
AND YOU BETRAYED ME TO DOOM.
AND I'D DO IT AGAIN!! IN A HEARTBEAT!!
I DON'T HAVE ARMOR! I'M NOT RICH! I CAN'T COME AND GO FROM THIS BATTLEFIELD AS I PLEASE!!
MY SONS AND HUSBAND ARE DEAD AND I HAVE TO LIVE HERE! I HAVE TO SURVIVE!!
WHAT IS THE MATTER WITH YOU? WHAT DO YOU THINK YOU'RE DOING HERE?
PICK A SIDE!!
OR LEAVE US ALONE!!
I HAVE PICKED A SIDE.
MINE.
WHEN YOUR ENEMIES CHOSE TO KILL WEARING MY FACE, EXPLOITING MY STORY, THEY MADE THIS MY WAR, TOO.
I WILL DEFEND MY LEGACY.
TO THE END.
AND WILL YOU KNOW WHAT THAT END IS...
...WHEN YOU SEE IT...?

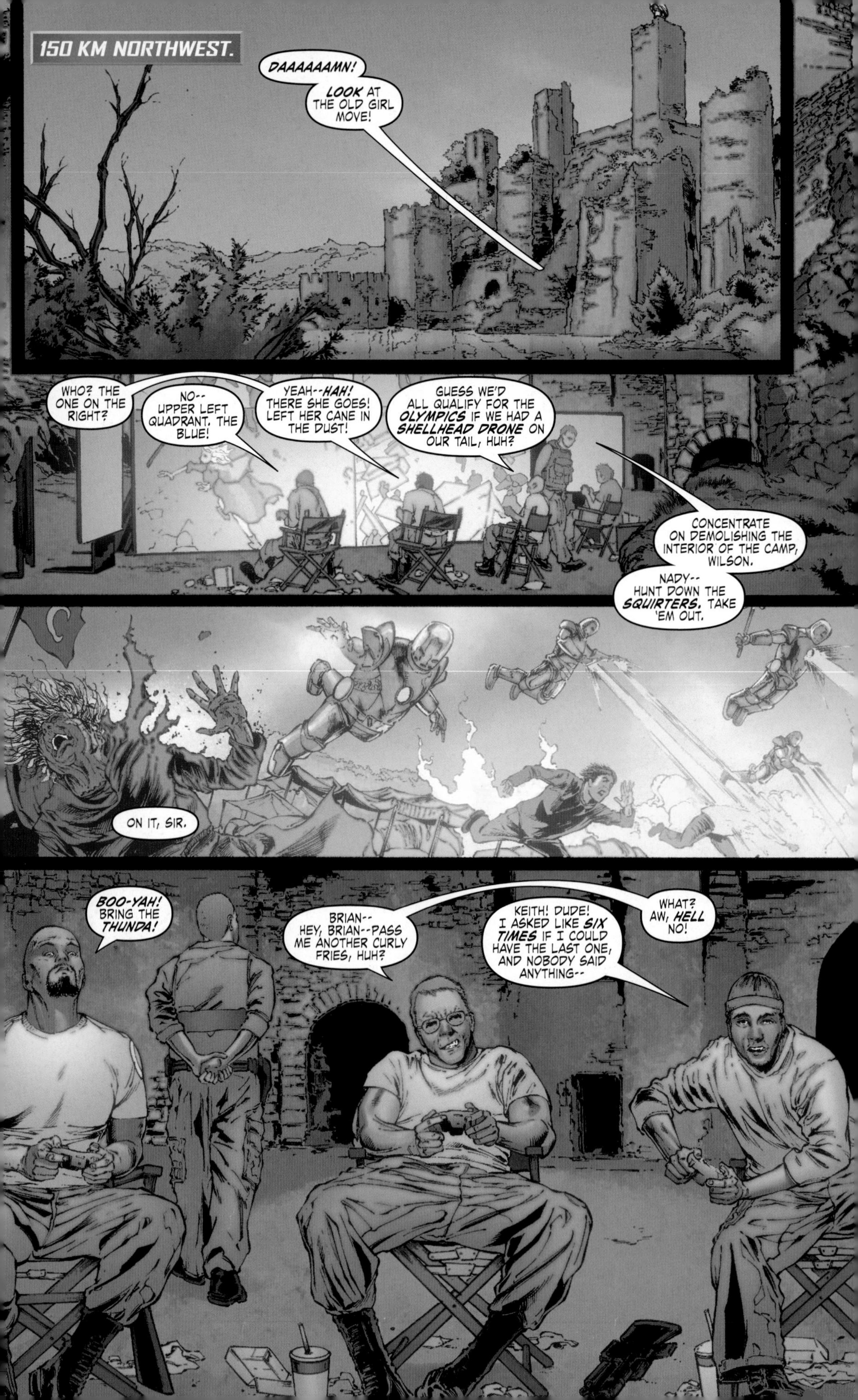
150 KM NORTHWEST.
DAAAAAAAMN!
LOOK AT THE OLD GIRL MOVE!
WHO? THE ONE ON THE RIGHT?
NO-- UPPER LEFT QUADRANT. THE BLUE!
YEAH--HAH! THERE SHE GOES! LEFT HER CANE IN THE DUST!
GUESS WE'D ALL QUALIFY FOR THE OLYMPICS IF WE HAD A SHELLHEAD DRONE ON OUR TAIL, HUH?
CONCENTRATE ON DEMOLISHING THE INTERIOR OF THE CAMP, WILSON.
NADY-- HUNT DOWN THE SQUIRTERS. TAKE 'EM OUT.
ON IT, SIR.
BOO-YAH! BRING THE THUNDA!
BRIAN-- HEY, BRIAN--PASS ME ANOTHER CURLY FRIES, HUH?
KEITH! DUDE! I ASKED LIKE SIX TIMES IF I COULD HAVE THE LAST ONE, AND NOBODY SAID ANYTHING--
WHAT? AW, HELL NO!

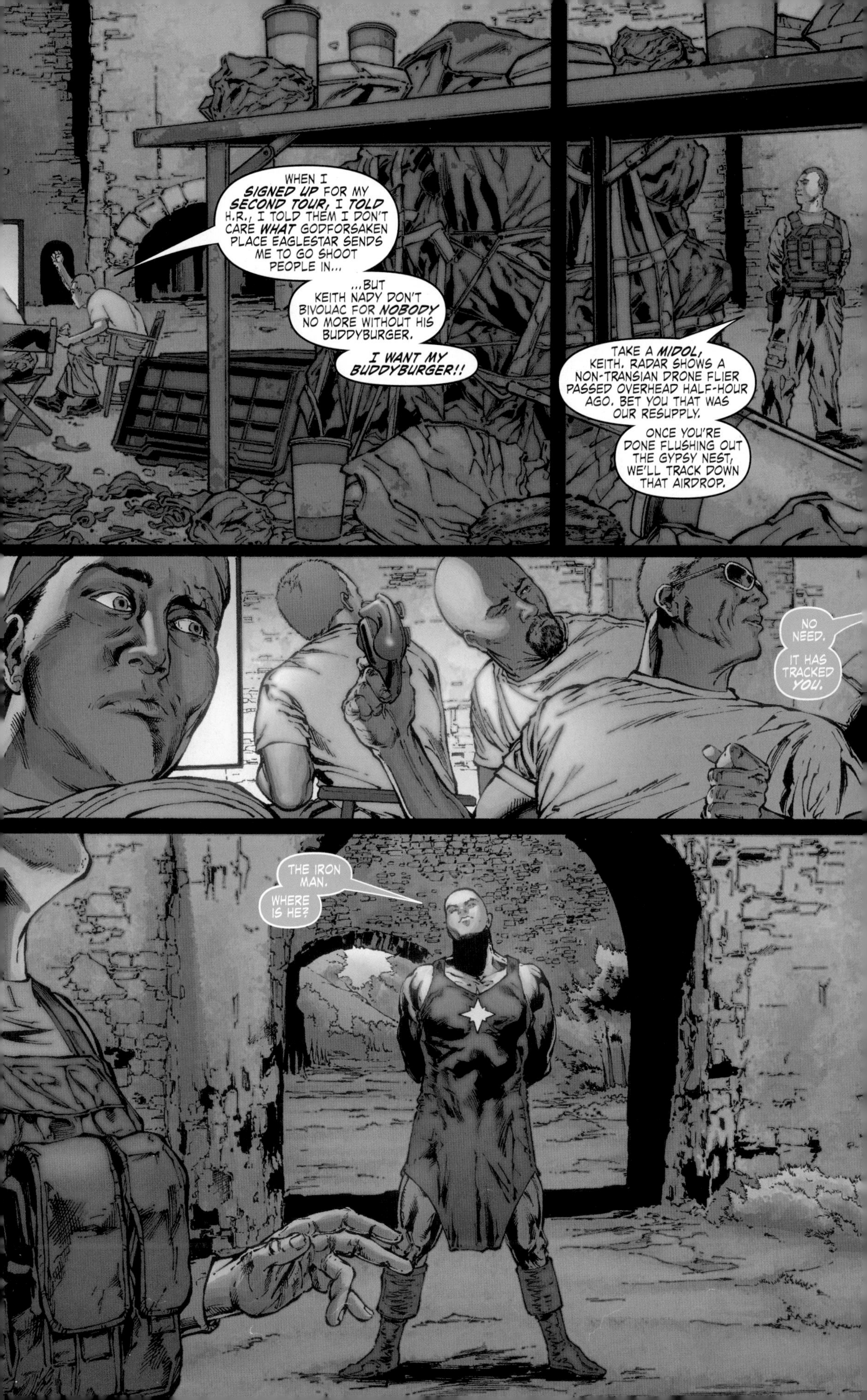
WHEN I SIGNED UP FOR MY SECOND TOUR, I TOLD H.R., I TOLD THEM I DON'T CARE WHAT GODFORSAKEN PLACE EAGLESTAR SENDS ME TO GO SHOOT PEOPLE IN...
...BUT KEITH NADY DON'T BIVOUAC FOR NOBODY NO MORE WITHOUT HIS BUDDYBURGER.
I WANT MY BUDDYBURGER!!
TAKE A MIDOL, KEITH. RADAR SHOWS A NON-TRANSIAN DRONE FLIER PASSED OVERHEAD HALF-HOUR AGO. BET YOU THAT WAS OUR RESUPPLY.
ONCE YOU'RE DONE FLUSHING OUT THE GYPSY NEST, WE'LL TRACK DOWN THAT AIRDROP.
NO NEED.
IT HAS TRACKED YOU.
THE IRON MAN.
WHERE IS HE?

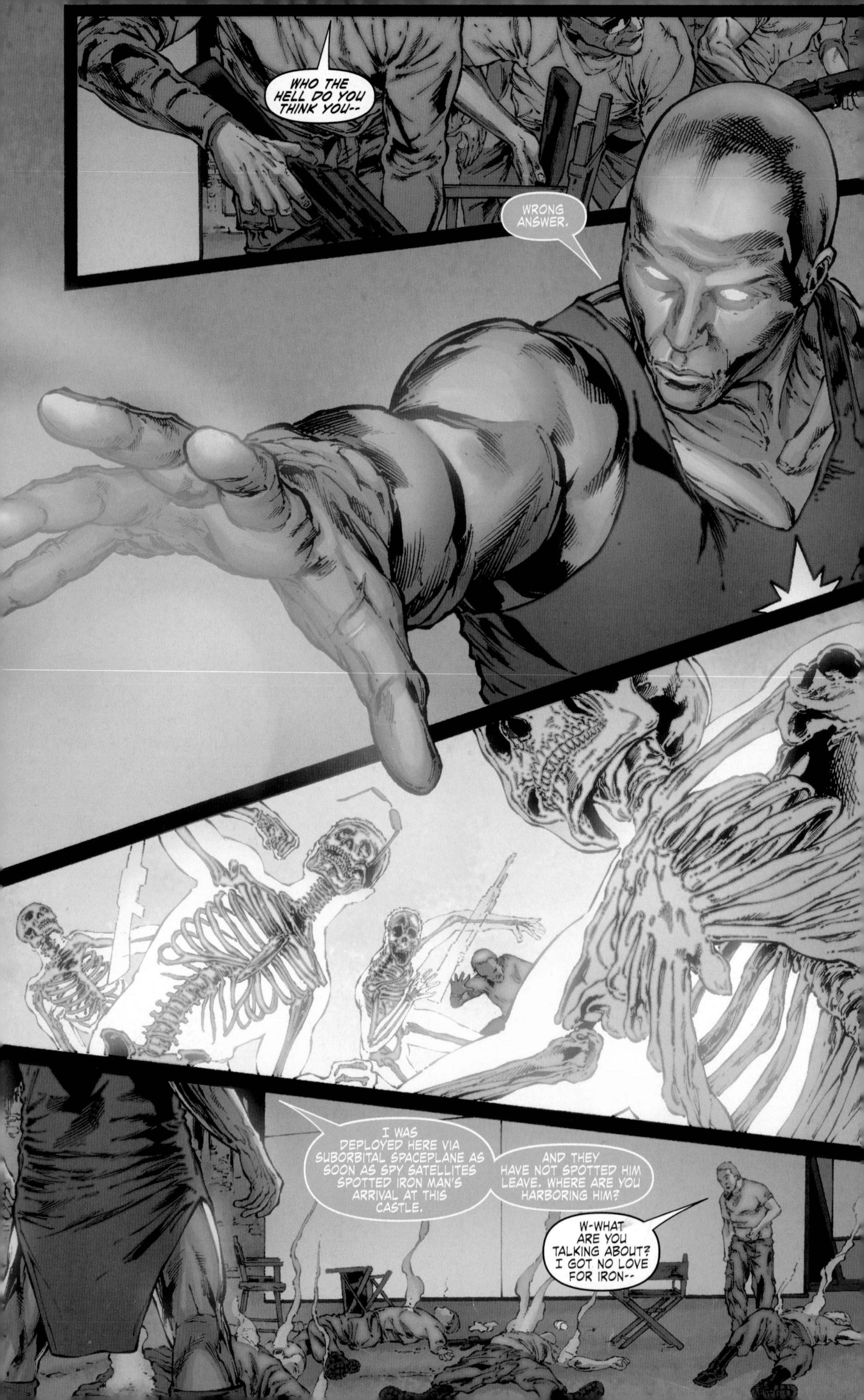
WHO THE HELL DO YOU THINK YOU--
WRONG ANSWER.
I WAS DEPLOYED HERE VIA SUBORBITAL SPACEPLANE AS SOON AS SPY SATELLITES SPOTTED IRON MAN'S ARRIVAL AT THIS CASTLE.
AND THEY HAVE NOT SPOTTED HIM LEAVE. WHERE ARE YOU HARBORING HIM?
W-WHAT ARE YOU TALKING ABOUT? I GOT NO LOVE FOR IRON--

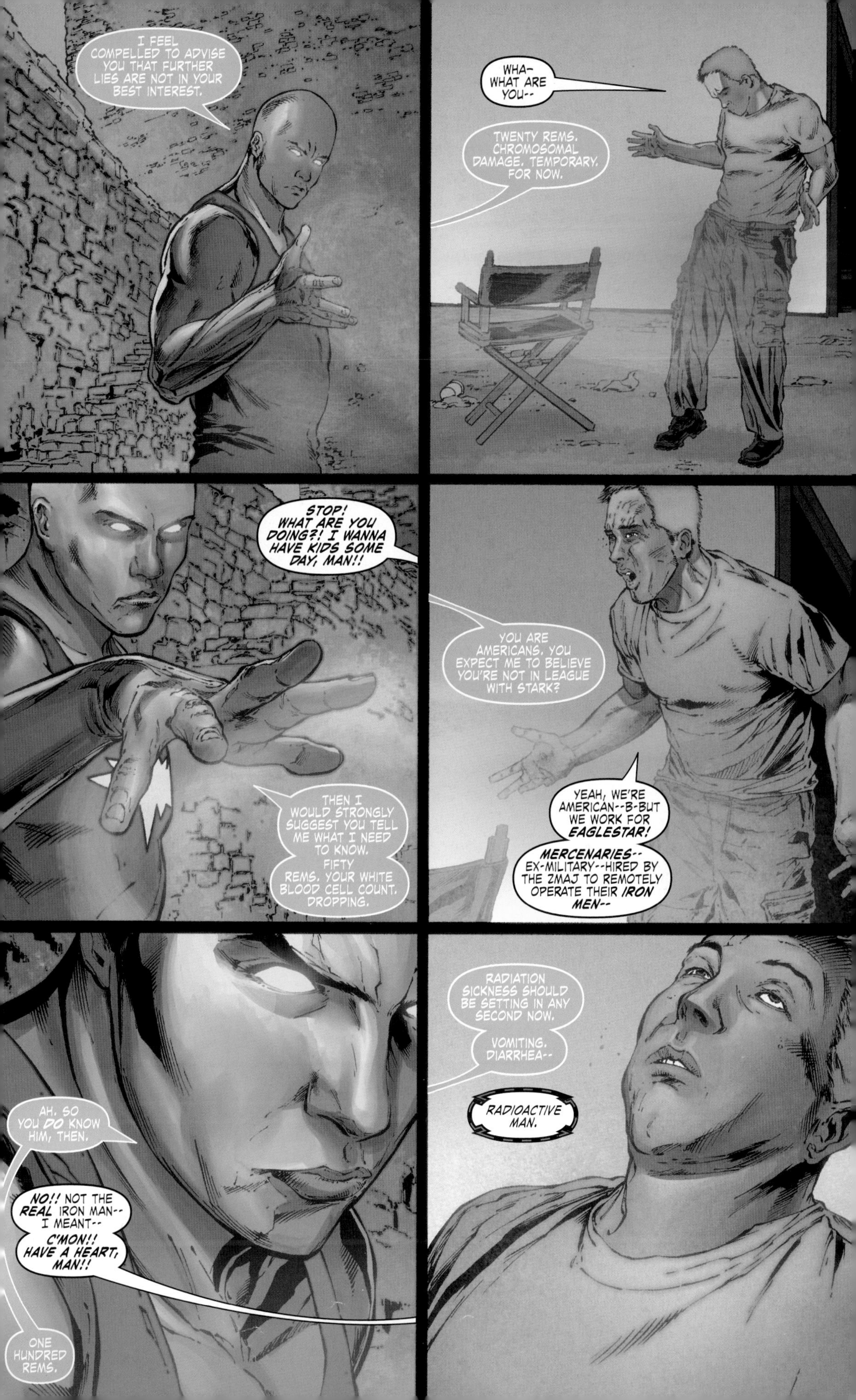
I FEEL COMPELLED TO ADVISE YOU THAT FURTHER LIES ARE NOT IN YOUR BEST INTEREST.
WHA- WHAT ARE YOU--
TWENTY REMS. CHROMOSOMAL DAMAGE. TEMPORARY. FOR NOW.
STOP! WHAT ARE YOU DOING?! I WANNA HAVE KIDS SOME DAY, MAN!!
THEN I WOULD STRONGLY SUGGEST YOU TELL ME WHAT I NEED TO KNOW.
FIFTY REMS. YOUR WHITE BLOOD CELL COUNT. DROPPING.
YOU ARE AMERICANS. YOU EXPECT ME TO BELIEVE YOU'RE NOT IN LEAGUE WITH STARK?
YEAH, WE'RE AMERICAN--B-BUT WE WORK FOR EAGLESTAR!
MERCENARIES--EX-MILITARY--HIRED BY THE ZMAJ TO REMOTELY OPERATE THEIR IRON MEN--
AH. SO YOU DO KNOW HIM, THEN.
NO!! NOT THE REAL IRON MAN--I MEANT--
C'MON!! HAVE A HEART, MAN!!
ONE HUNDRED REMS.
RADIATION SICKNESS SHOULD BE SETTING IN ANY SECOND NOW.
VOMITING. DIARRHEA--
RADIOACTIVE MAN.

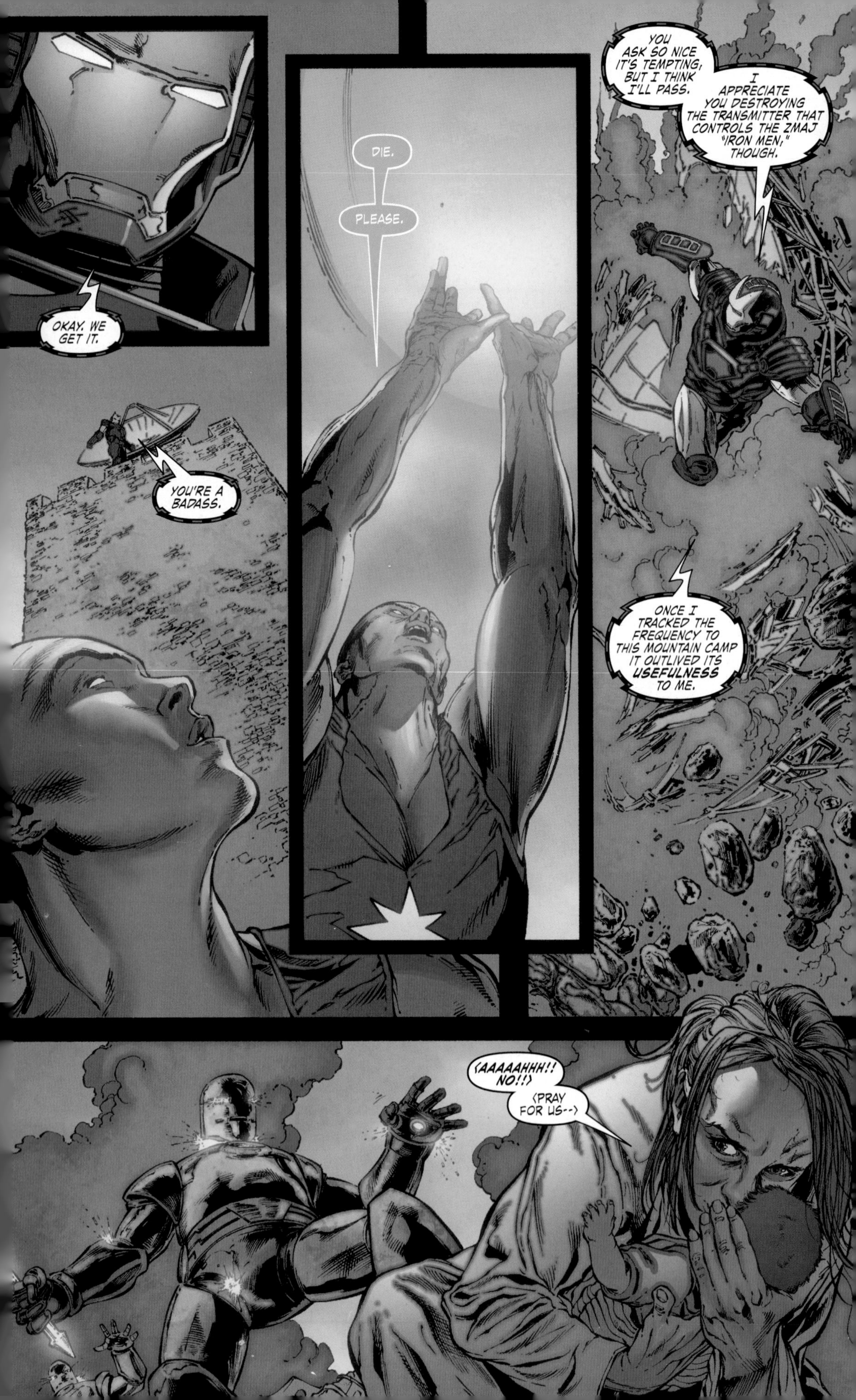
OKAY. WE GET IT.
YOU'RE A BADASS.
DIE.
PLEASE.
YOU ASK SO NICE IT'S TEMPTING, BUT I THINK I'LL PASS.
I APPRECIATE YOU DESTROYING THE TRANSMITTER THAT CONTROLS THE ZMAJ "IRON MEN," THOUGH.
ONCE I TRACKED THE FREQUENCY TO THIS MOUNTAIN CAMP IT OUTLIVED ITS USEFULNESS TO ME.
‹AAAAAHHH!! NO!!›
‹PRAY FOR US--›

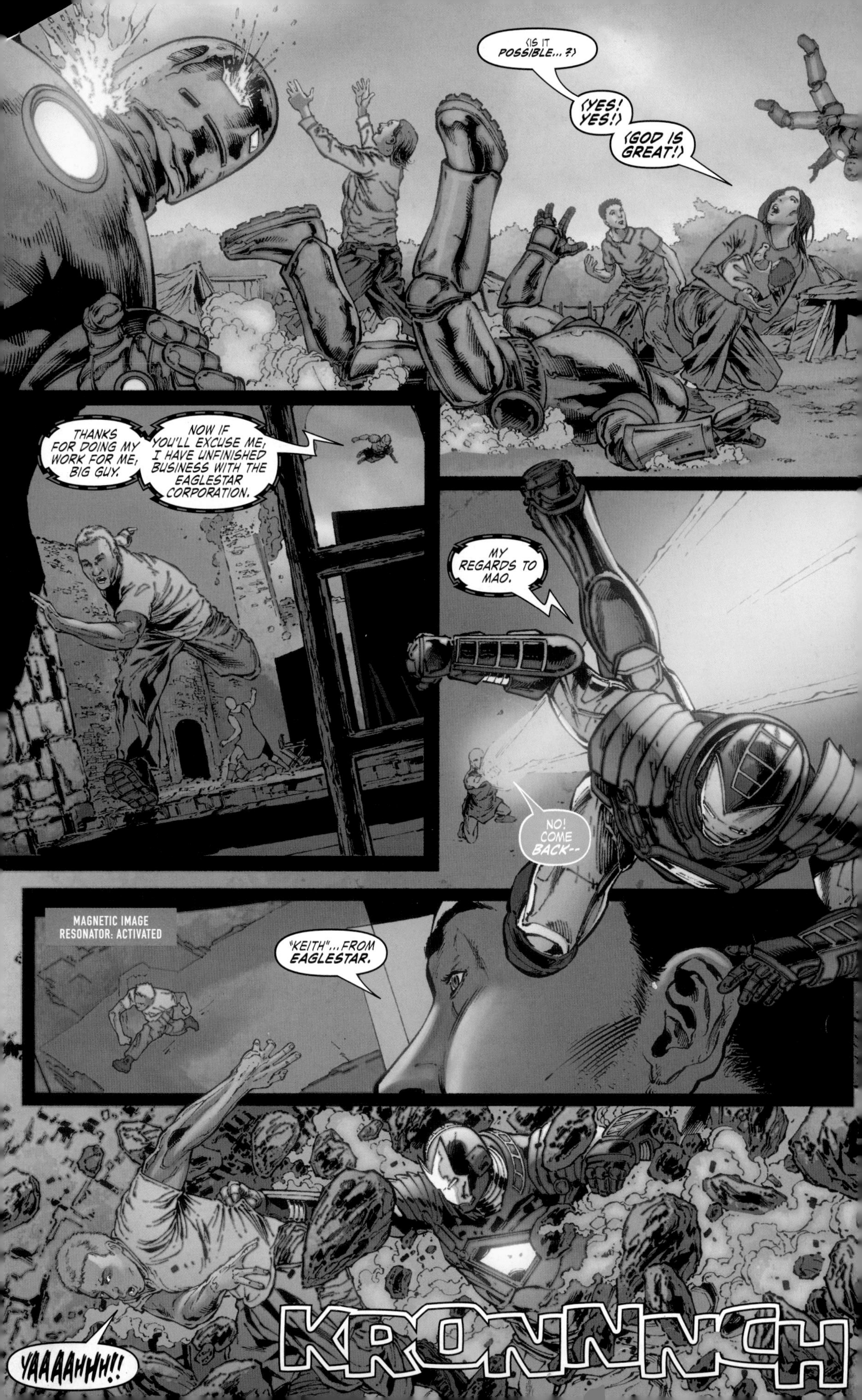
‹IS IT POSSIBLE...?›
‹YES! YES!›
‹GOD IS GREAT!›
THANKS FOR DOING MY WORK FOR ME, BIG GUY.
NOW IF YOU'LL EXCUSE ME, I HAVE UNFINISHED BUSINESS WITH THE EAGLESTAR CORPORATION.
MY REGARDS TO MAO.
NO! COME BACK--
MAGNETIC IMAGE RESONATOR: ACTIVATED
"KEITH"...FROM EAGLESTAR.
YAAAAHHH!!
KRONNNCH

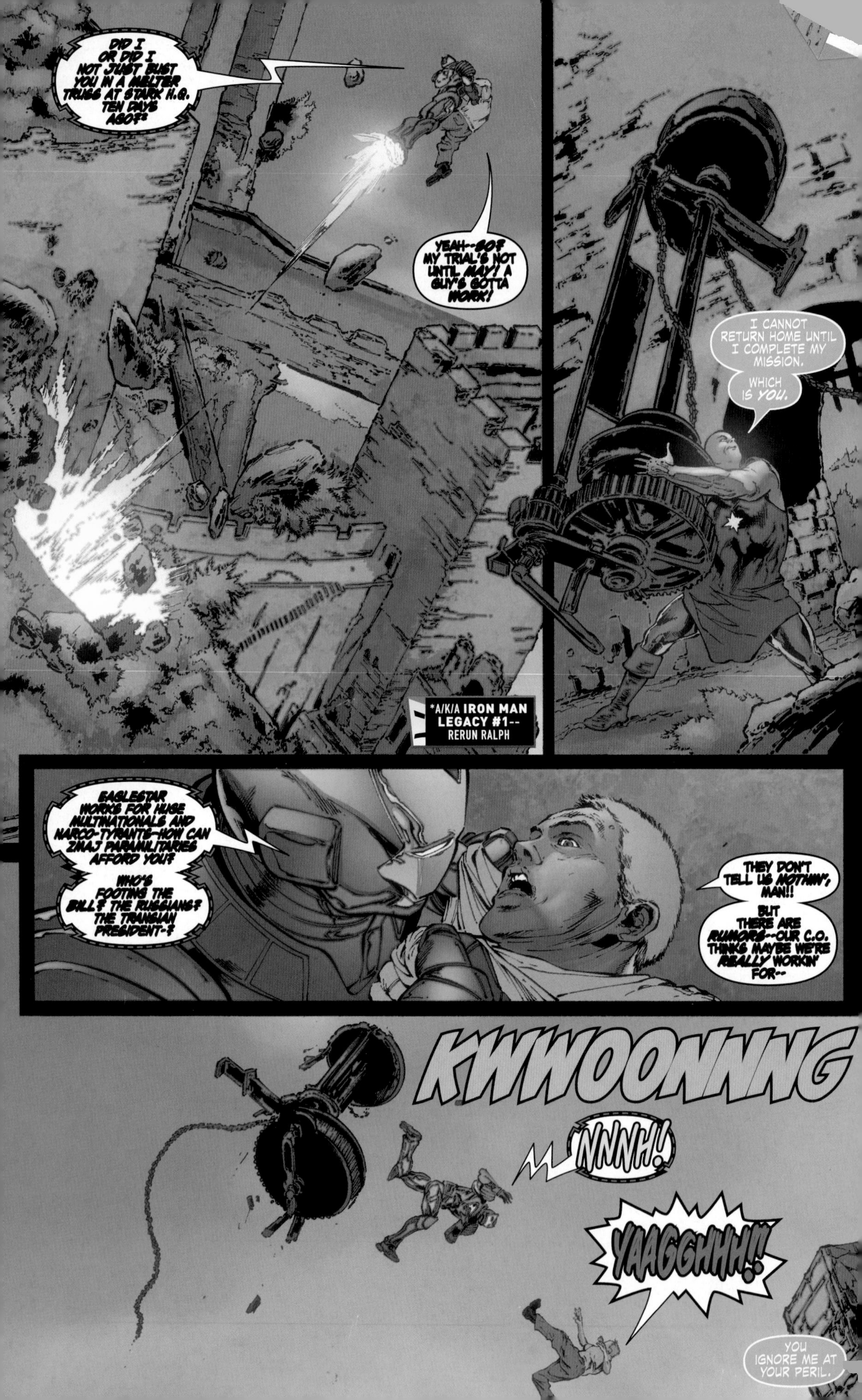
DID I OR DID I NOT JUST BUST YOU IN A MELTER TRUSS AT STARK H.Q. TEN DAYS AGO?*
YEAH--SO? MY TRIAL'S NOT UNTIL MAY! A GUY'S GOTTA WORK!
*A/K/A IRON MAN LEGACY #1-- RERUN RALPH
I CANNOT RETURN HOME UNTIL I COMPLETE MY MISSION.
WHICH IS YOU.
EAGLESTAR WORKS FOR HUGE MULTINATIONALS AND NARCO-TYRANTS--HOW CAN ZHAJ PARAMILITARIES AFFORD YOU?
WHO'S FOOTING THE BILL? THE RUSSIANS? THE TRANSIAN PRESIDENT-?
THEY DON'T TELL US NOTHIN', MAN!!
BUT THERE ARE RUMORS--OUR C.O. THINKS MAYBE WE'RE REALLY WORKIN' FOR--
KWWOONNNG
NNNH!
YAAGGHHH!!
YOU IGNORE ME AT YOUR PERIL.

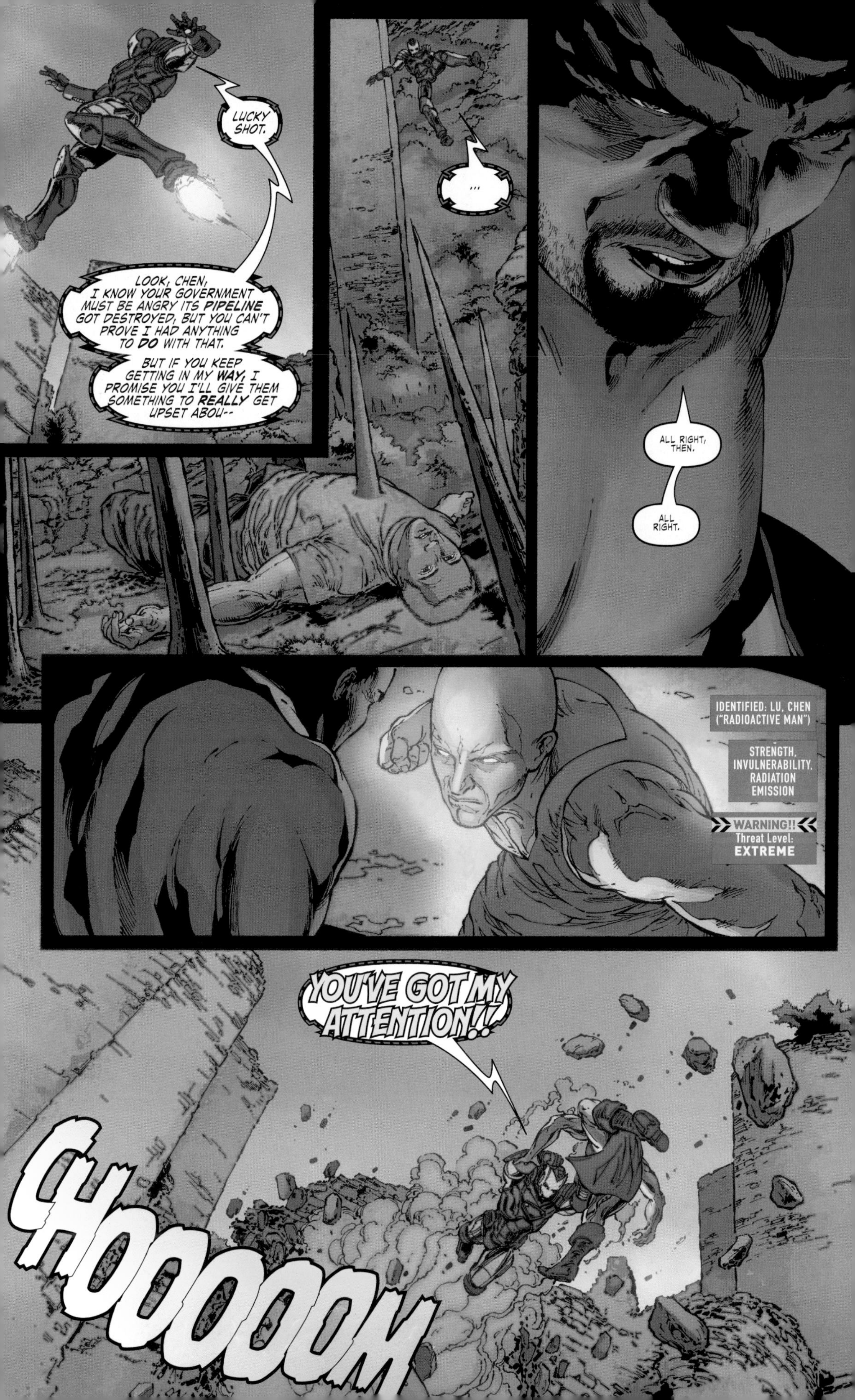

LUCKY SHOT.
LOOK, CHEN, I KNOW YOUR GOVERNMENT MUST BE ANGRY ITS PIPELINE GOT DESTROYED, BUT YOU CAN'T PROVE I HAD ANYTHING TO DO WITH THAT.
BUT IF YOU KEEP GETTING IN MY WAY, I PROMISE YOU I'LL GIVE THEM SOMETHING TO REALLY GET UPSET ABOU--
...
ALL RIGHT, THEN.
ALL RIGHT.
IDENTIFIED: LU, CHEN ("RADIOACTIVE MAN")
STRENGTH, INVULNERABILITY, RADIATION EMISSION
WARNING!! Threat Level: EXTREME
YOU'VE GOT MY ATTENTION!!
CHOOOOOOM

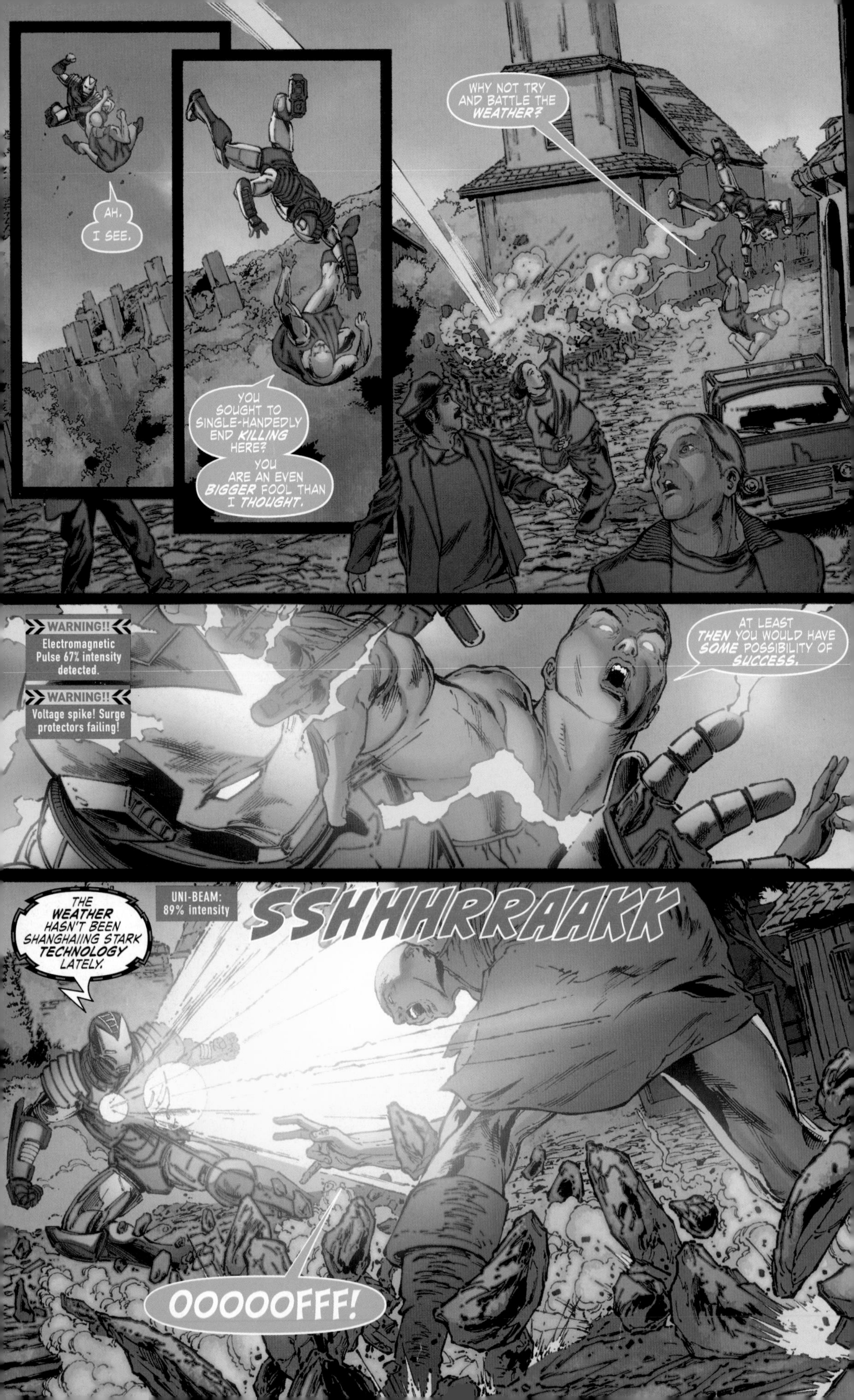
AH. I SEE.
YOU SOUGHT TO SINGLE-HANDEDLY END KILLING HERE?
YOU ARE AN EVEN BIGGER FOOL THAN I THOUGHT.
WHY NOT TRY AND BATTLE THE WEATHER?
WARNING!! Electromagnetic Pulse 67% intensity detected.
WARNING!! Voltage spike! Surge protectors failing!
AT LEAST THEN YOU WOULD HAVE SOME POSSIBILITY OF SUCCESS.
THE WEATHER HASN'T BEEN SHANGHAIING STARK TECHNOLOGY LATELY.
UNI-BEAM: 89% intensity
SSHHHRRAAKK
OOOOOFFF!

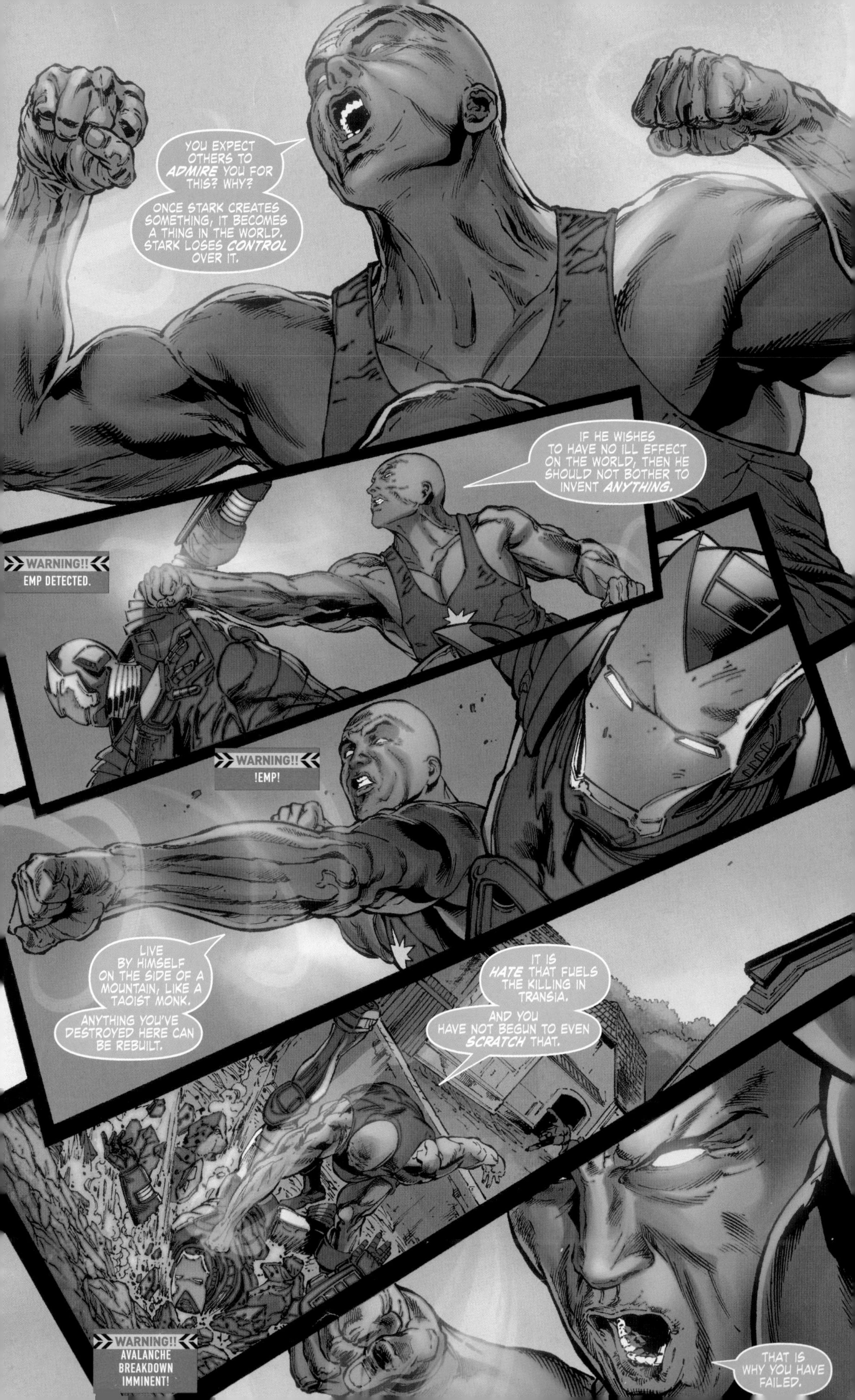

YOU EXPECT OTHERS TO *ADMIRE* YOU FOR THIS? WHY?
ONCE STARK CREATES SOMETHING, IT BECOMES A THING IN THE WORLD. STARK LOSES *CONTROL* OVER IT.
IF HE WISHES TO HAVE NO ILL EFFECT ON THE WORLD, THEN HE SHOULD NOT BOTHER TO INVENT *ANYTHING.*
WARNING!!
EMP DETECTED.
WARNING!!
!EMP!
LIVE BY HIMSELF ON THE SIDE OF A MOUNTAIN, LIKE A TAOIST MONK.
ANYTHING YOU'VE DESTROYED HERE CAN BE REBUILT.
IT IS *HATE* THAT FUELS THE KILLING IN TRANSIA.
AND YOU HAVE NOT BEGUN TO EVEN *SCRATCH* THAT.
WARNING!!
AVALANCHE BREAKDOWN IMMINENT!
THAT IS WHY YOU HAVE FAILED.

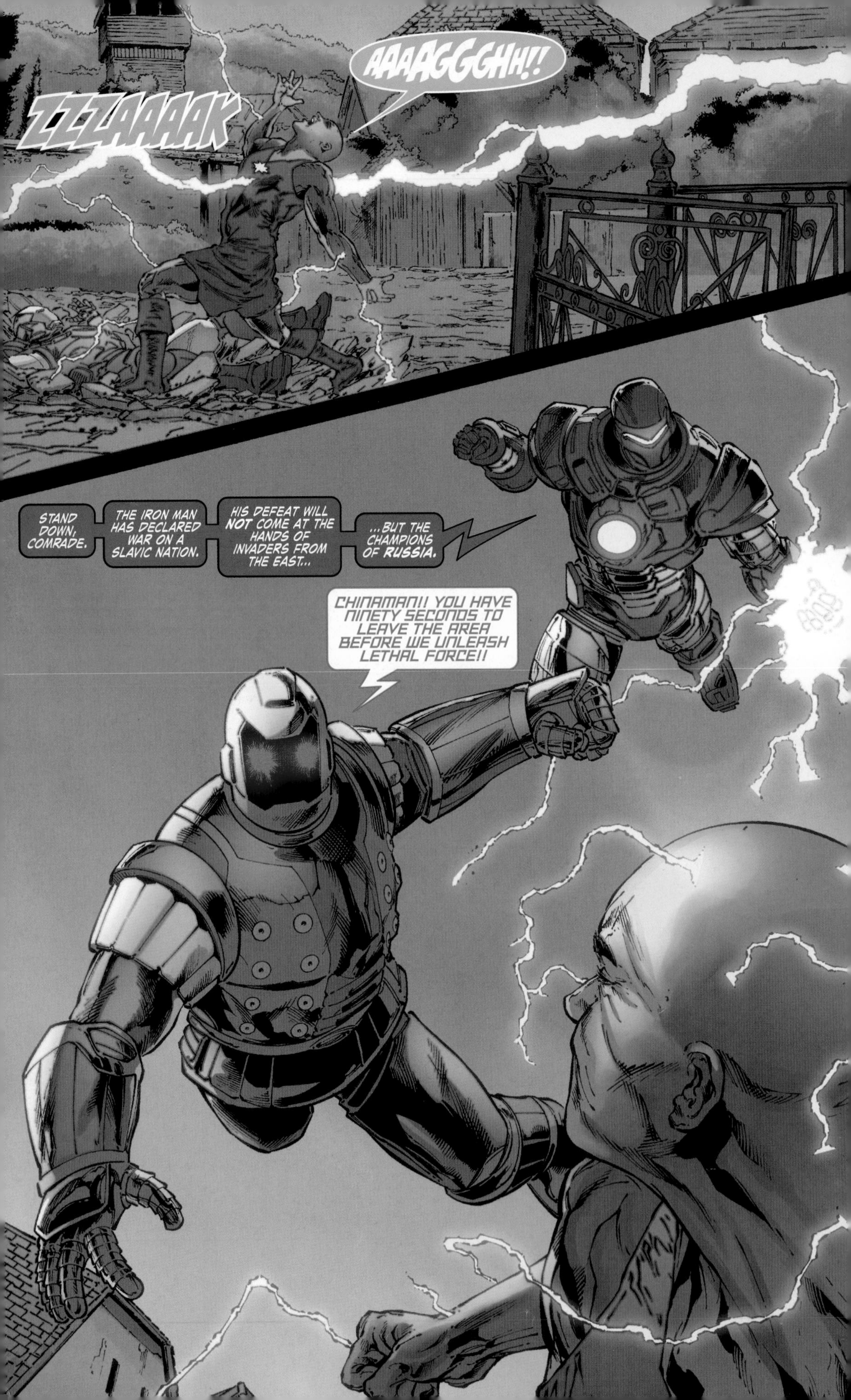

ZZZAAAAK
AAAAGGGHH!!
STAND DOWN, COMRADE.
THE IRON MAN HAS DECLARED WAR ON A SLAVIC NATION.
HIS DEFEAT WILL **NOT** COME AT THE HANDS OF INVADERS FROM THE EAST...
...BUT THE CHAMPIONS OF **RUSSIA**.
CHINAMAN!! YOU HAVE NINETY SECONDS TO LEAVE THE AREA BEFORE WE UNLEASH LETHAL FORCE!!

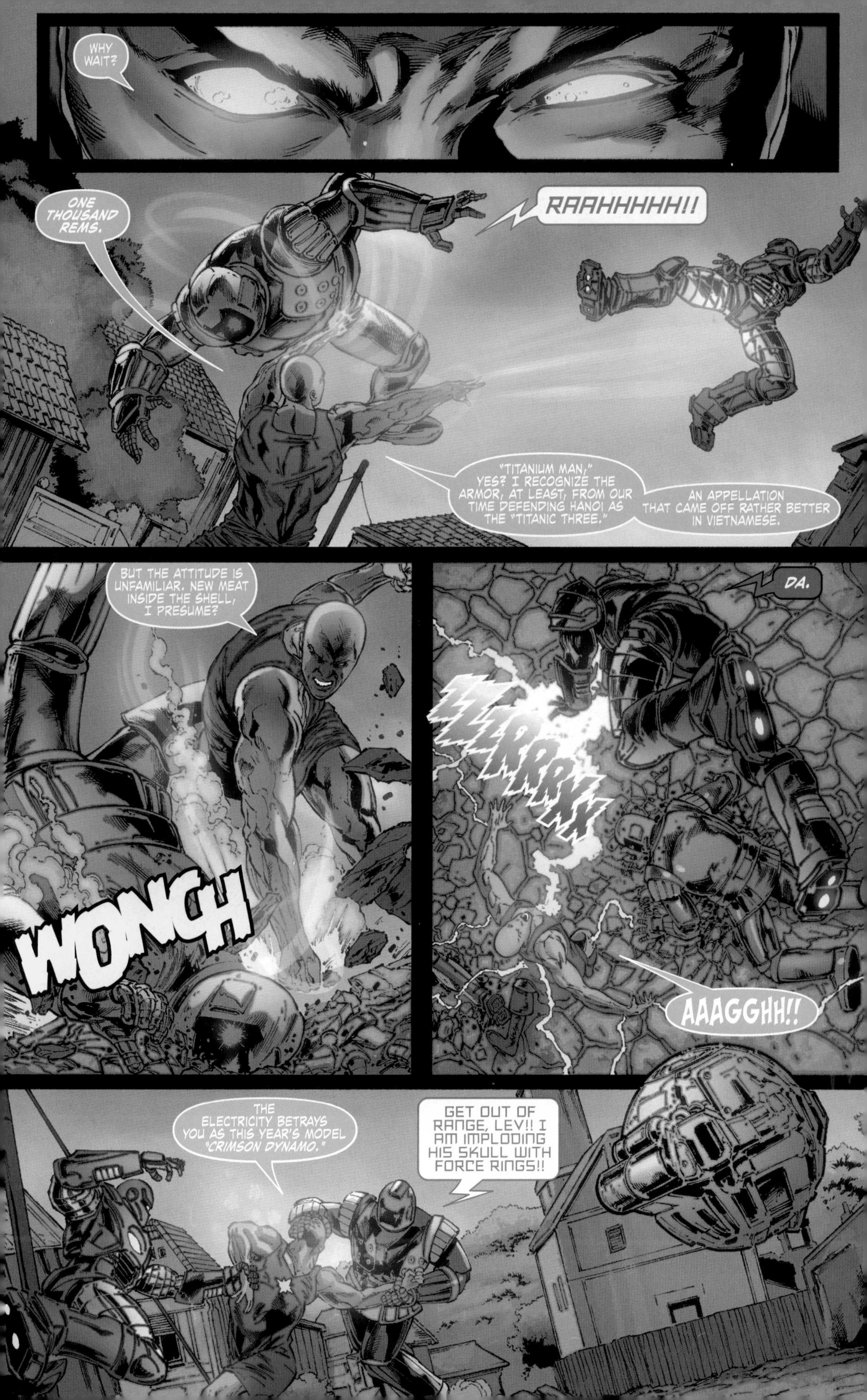

WHY WAIT?
ONE THOUSAND REMS.
RAAHHHHH!!
"TITANIUM MAN," YES? I RECOGNIZE THE ARMOR, AT LEAST, FROM OUR TIME DEFENDING HANOI AS THE "TITANIC THREE."
AN APPELLATION THAT CAME OFF RATHER BETTER IN VIETNAMESE.
BUT THE ATTITUDE IS UNFAMILIAR. NEW MEAT INSIDE THE SHELL, I PRESUME?
WONCH
DA.
ZZRRRX
AAAGGHH!!
THE ELECTRICITY BETRAYS YOU AS THIS YEAR'S MODEL "CRIMSON DYNAMO."
GET OUT OF RANGE, LEV!! I AM IMPLODING HIS SKULL WITH FORCE RINGS!!

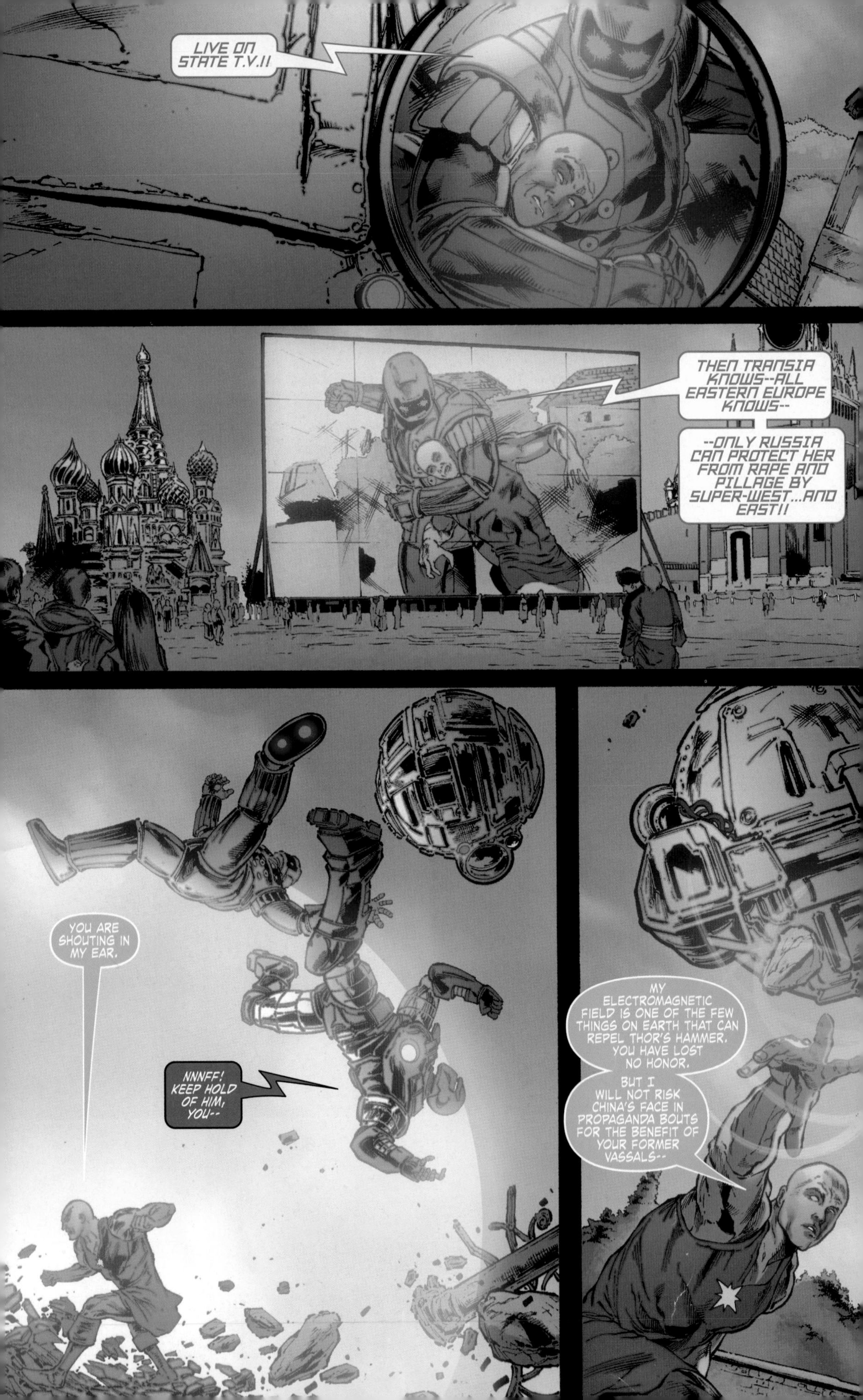
LIVE ON STATE T.V.!!
THEN TRANSIA KNOWS--ALL EASTERN EUROPE KNOWS--
--ONLY RUSSIA CAN PROTECT HER FROM RAPE AND PILLAGE BY SUPER-WEST...AND EAST!!
YOU ARE SHOUTING IN MY EAR.
NNNFF! KEEP HOLD OF HIM, YOU--
MY ELECTROMAGNETIC FIELD IS ONE OF THE FEW THINGS ON EARTH THAT CAN REPEL THOR'S HAMMER. YOU HAVE LOST NO HONOR.
BUT I WILL NOT RISK CHINA'S FACE IN PROPAGANDA BOUTS FOR THE BENEFIT OF YOUR FORMER VASSALS--

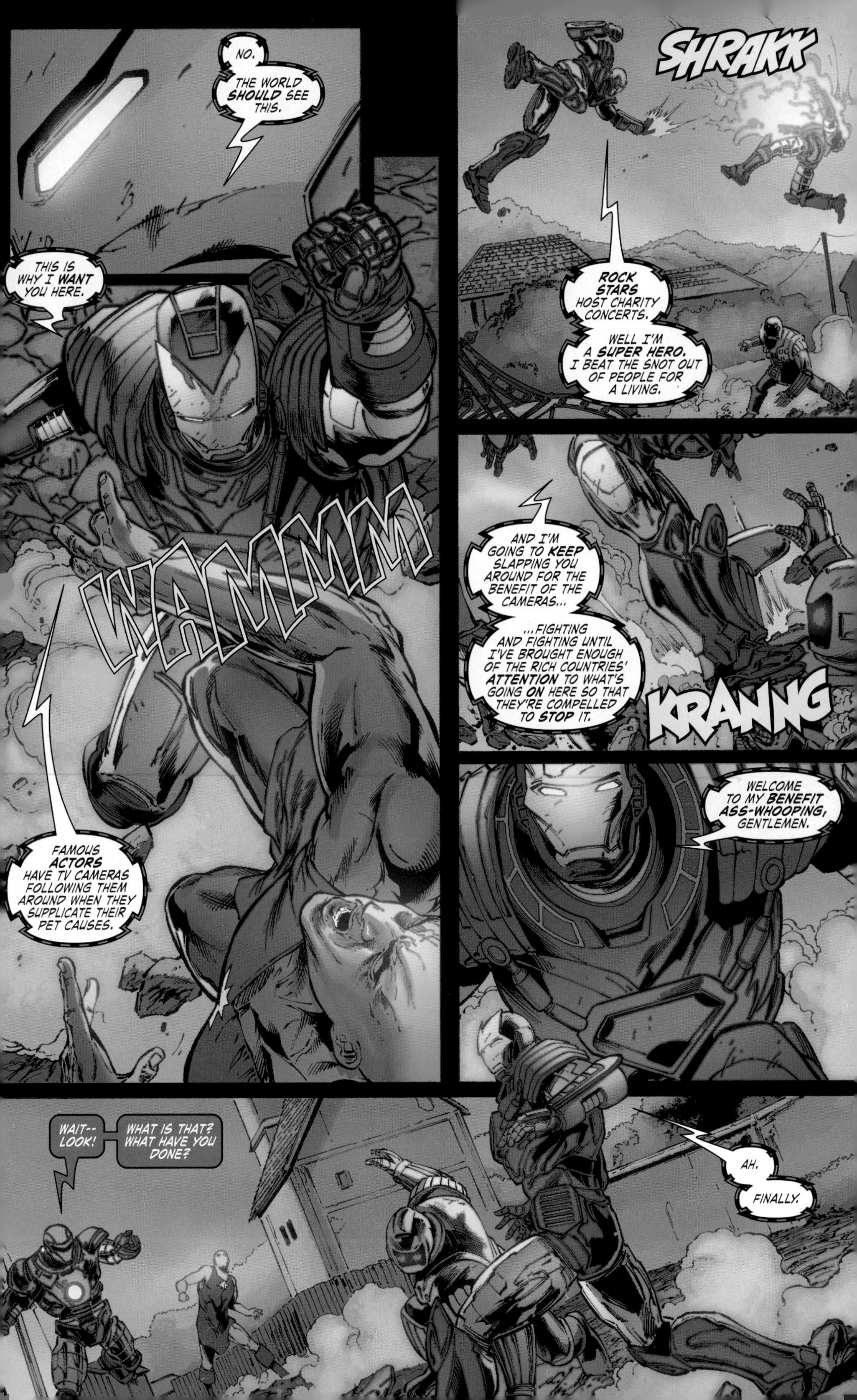

NO.
THE WORLD SHOULD SEE THIS.
THIS IS WHY I WANT YOU HERE.
WAMMM
FAMOUS ACTORS HAVE TV CAMERAS FOLLOWING THEM AROUND WHEN THEY SUPPLICATE THEIR PET CAUSES.
SHRAKK
ROCK STARS HOST CHARITY CONCERTS.
WELL I'M A SUPER HERO. I BEAT THE SNOT OUT OF PEOPLE FOR A LIVING.
AND I'M GOING TO KEEP SLAPPING YOU AROUND FOR THE BENEFIT OF THE CAMERAS...
...FIGHTING AND FIGHTING UNTIL I'VE BROUGHT ENOUGH OF THE RICH COUNTRIES' ATTENTION TO WHAT'S GOING ON HERE SO THAT THEY'RE COMPELLED TO STOP IT.
KRANNG
WELCOME TO MY BENEFIT ASS-WHOOPING, GENTLEMEN.
WAIT-- LOOK!
WHAT IS THAT? WHAT HAVE YOU DONE?
AH.
FINALLY.

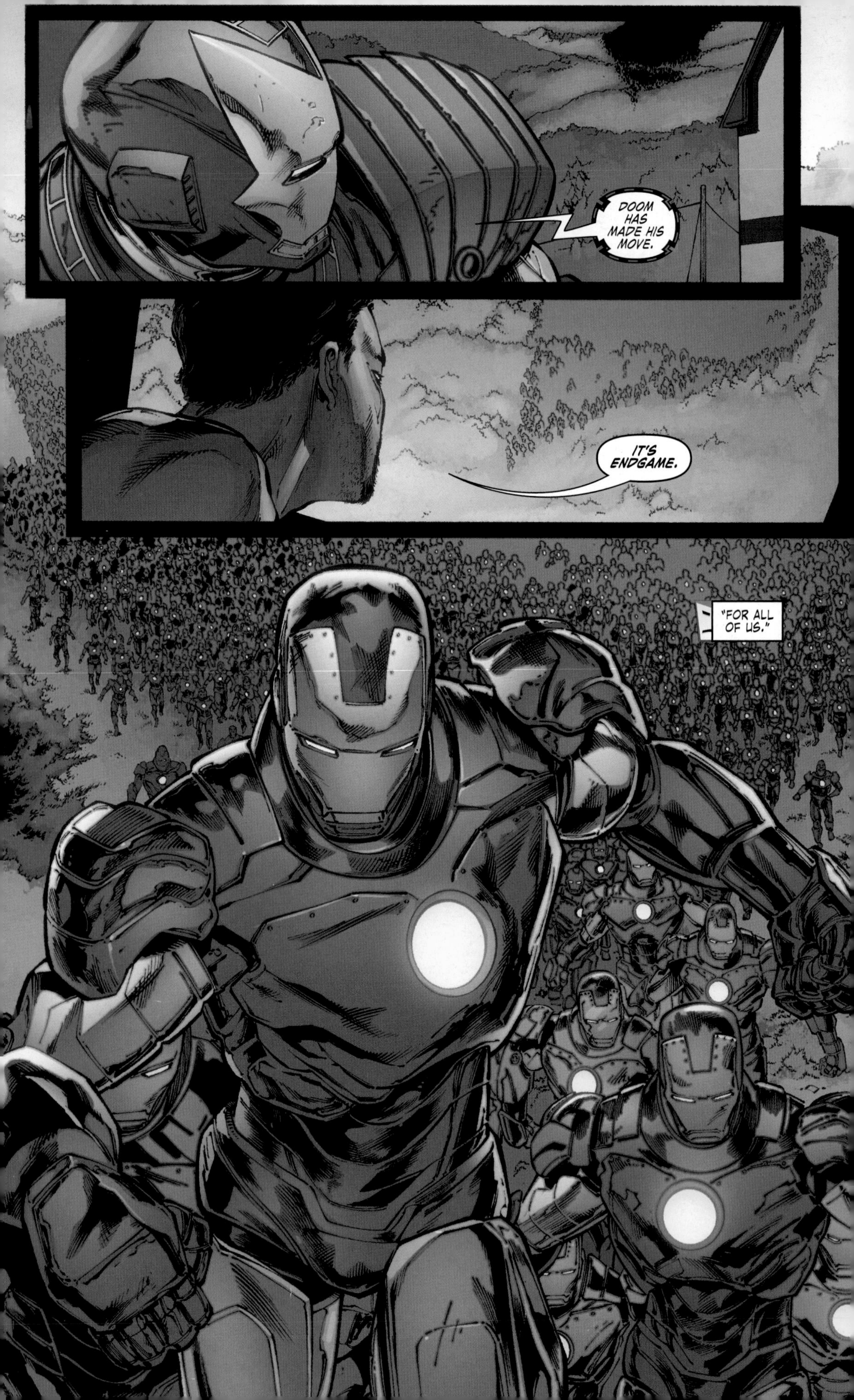
DOOM HAS MADE HIS MOVE.
IT'S ENDGAME.
"FOR ALL OF US."

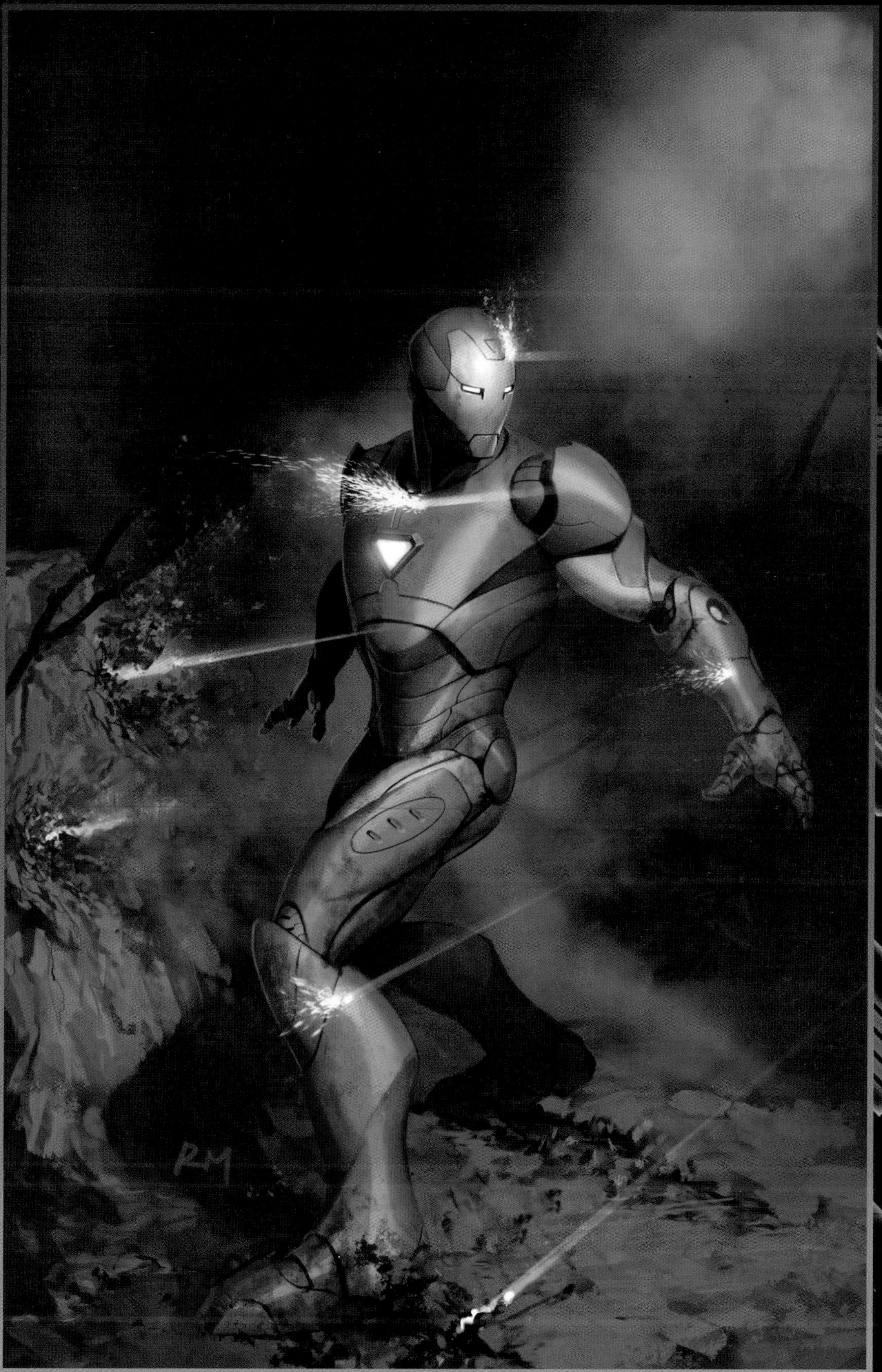

#1 VARIANT
BY RYAN MEINERDING

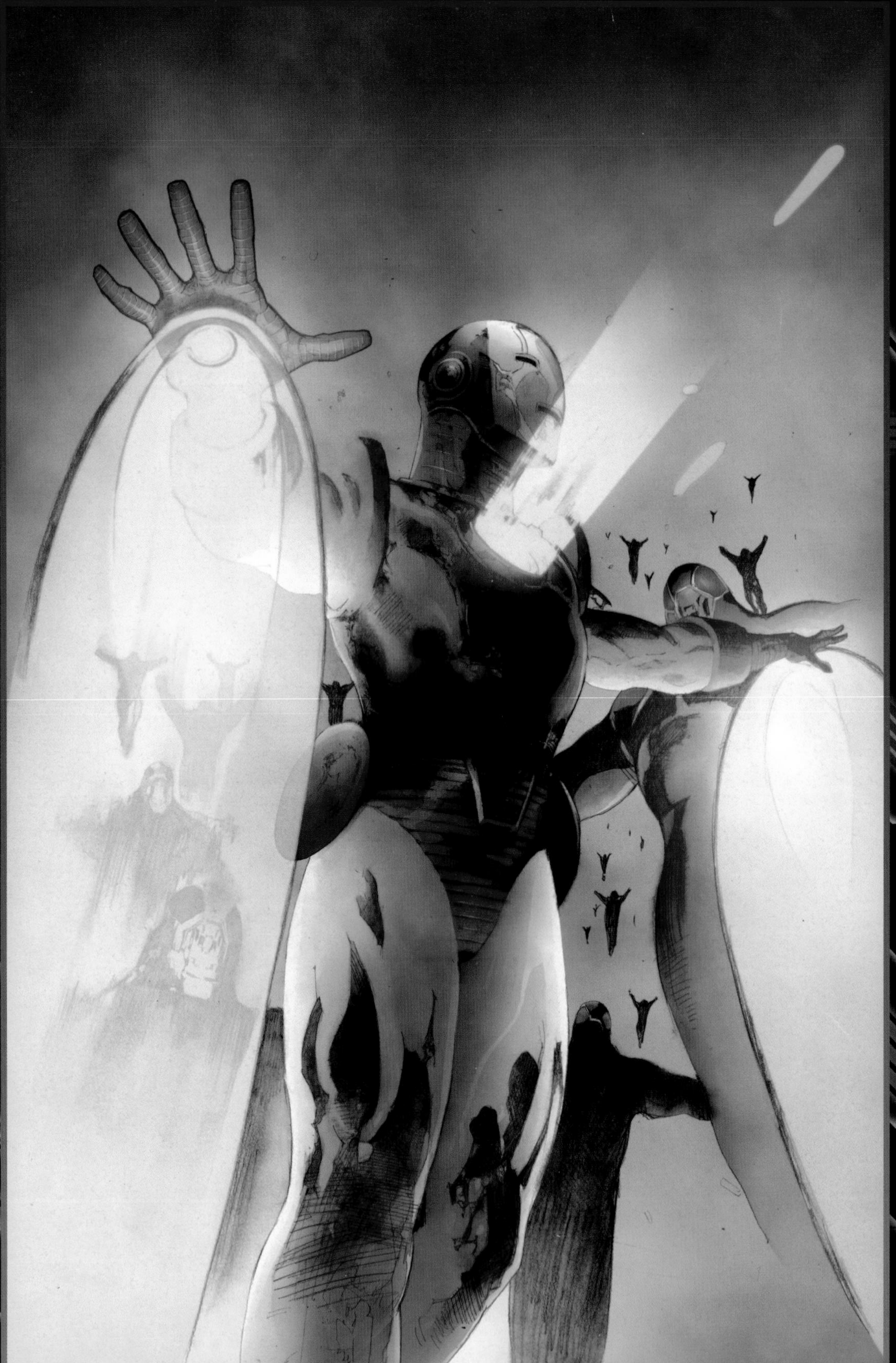

IRON MAN LEGACY 5

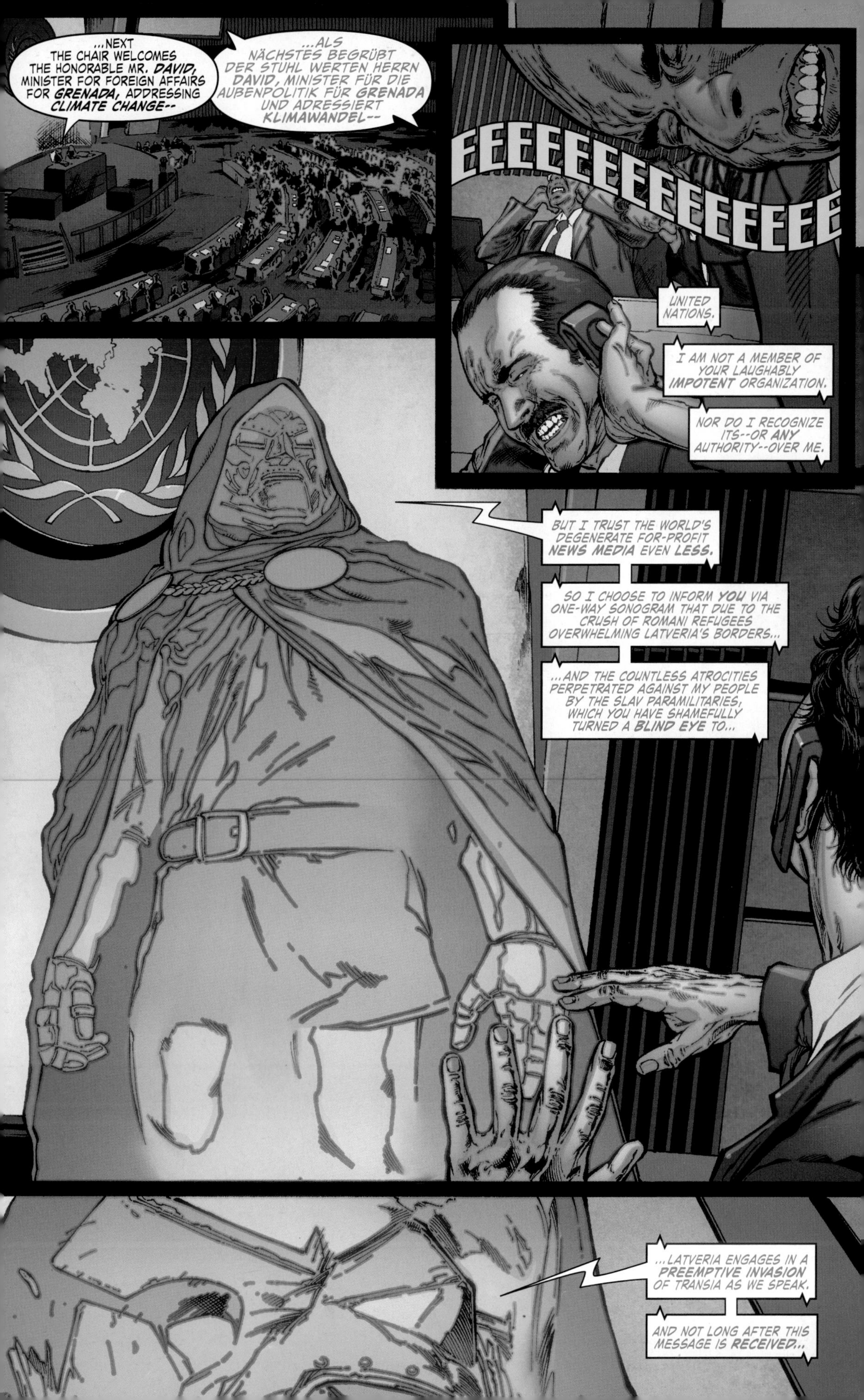
...NEXT THE CHAIR WELCOMES THE HONORABLE MR. DAVID, MINISTER FOR FOREIGN AFFAIRS FOR GRENADA, ADDRESSING CLIMATE CHANGE--
...ALS NÄCHSTES BEGRÜßT DER STUHL WERTEN HERRN DAVID, MINISTER FÜR DIE AUßENPOLITIK FÜR GRENADA UND ADRESSIERT KLIMAWANDEL--
EEEEEEEEEEEEEEEEEEE
UNITED NATIONS.
I AM NOT A MEMBER OF YOUR LAUGHABLY IMPOTENT ORGANIZATION.
NOR DO I RECOGNIZE ITS--OR ANY AUTHORITY--OVER ME.
BUT I TRUST THE WORLD'S DEGENERATE FOR-PROFIT NEWS MEDIA EVEN LESS.
SO I CHOOSE TO INFORM YOU VIA ONE-WAY SONOGRAM THAT DUE TO THE CRUSH OF ROMANI REFUGEES OVERWHELMING LATVERIA'S BORDERS...
...AND THE COUNTLESS ATROCITIES PERPETRATED AGAINST MY PEOPLE BY THE SLAV PARAMILITARIES, WHICH YOU HAVE SHAMEFULLY TURNED A BLIND EYE TO...
...LATVERIA ENGAGES IN A PREEMPTIVE INVASION OF TRANSIA AS WE SPEAK.
AND NOT LONG AFTER THIS MESSAGE IS RECEIVED...

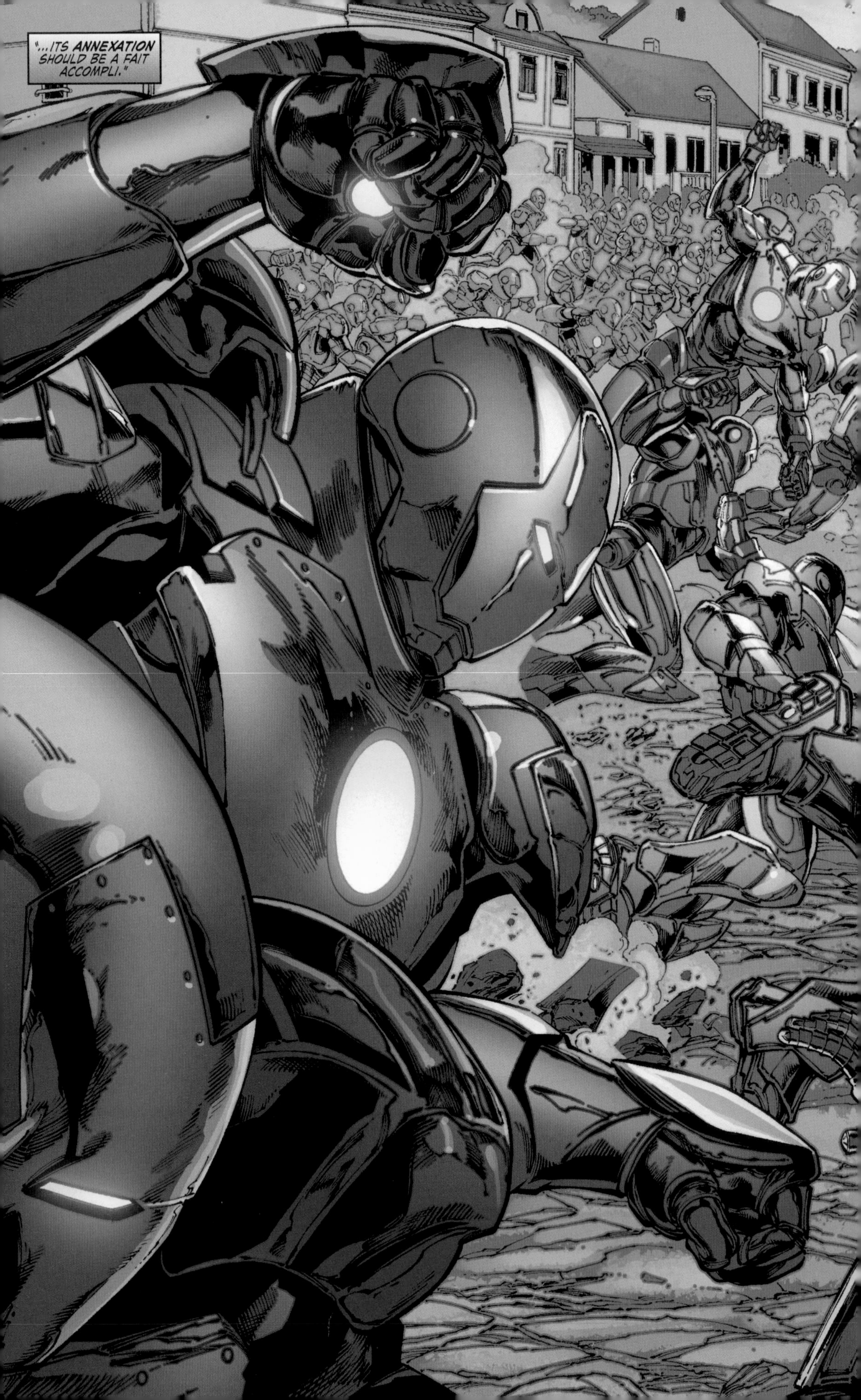
"...ITS ANNEXATION SHOULD BE A FAIT ACCOMPLI."

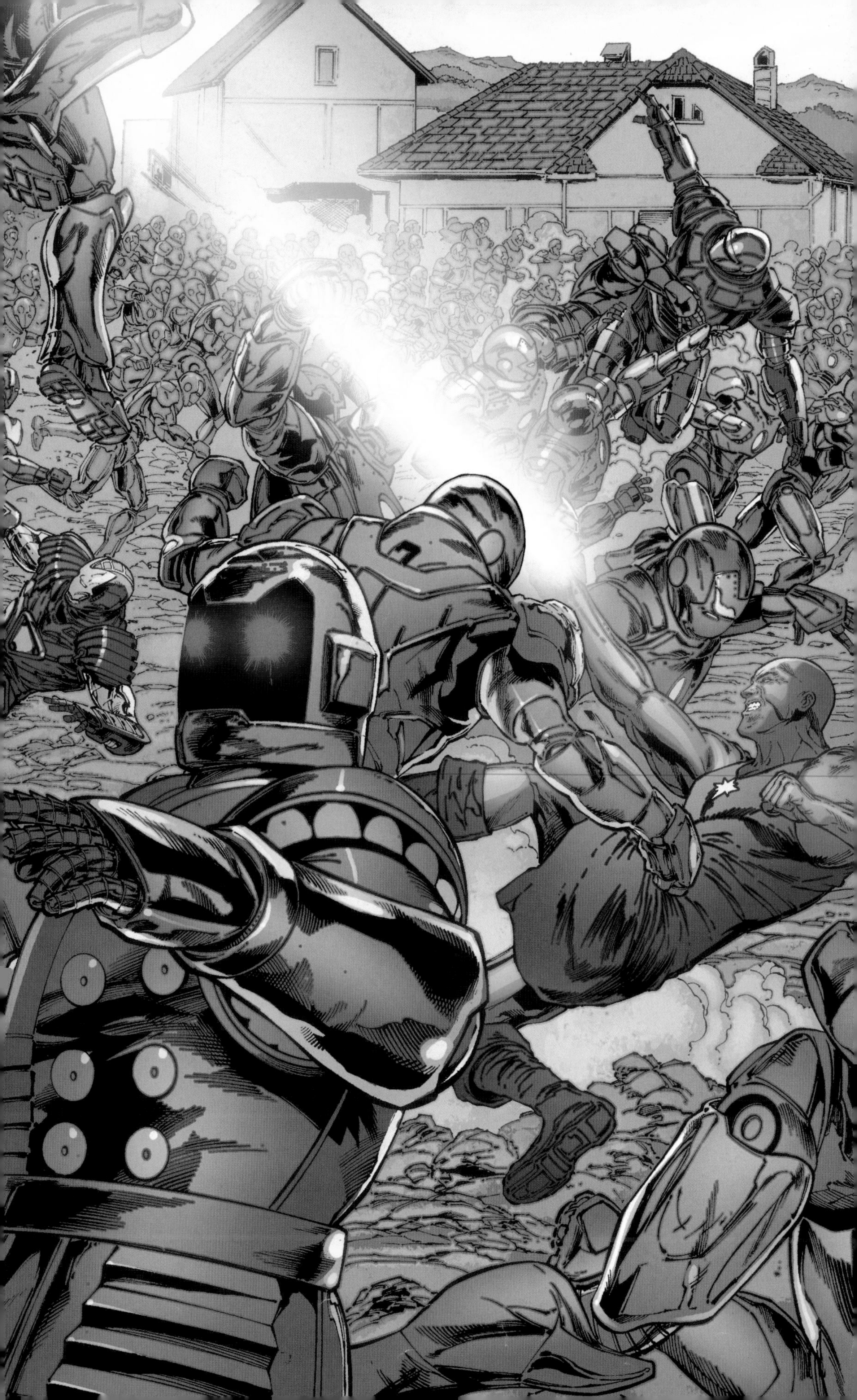

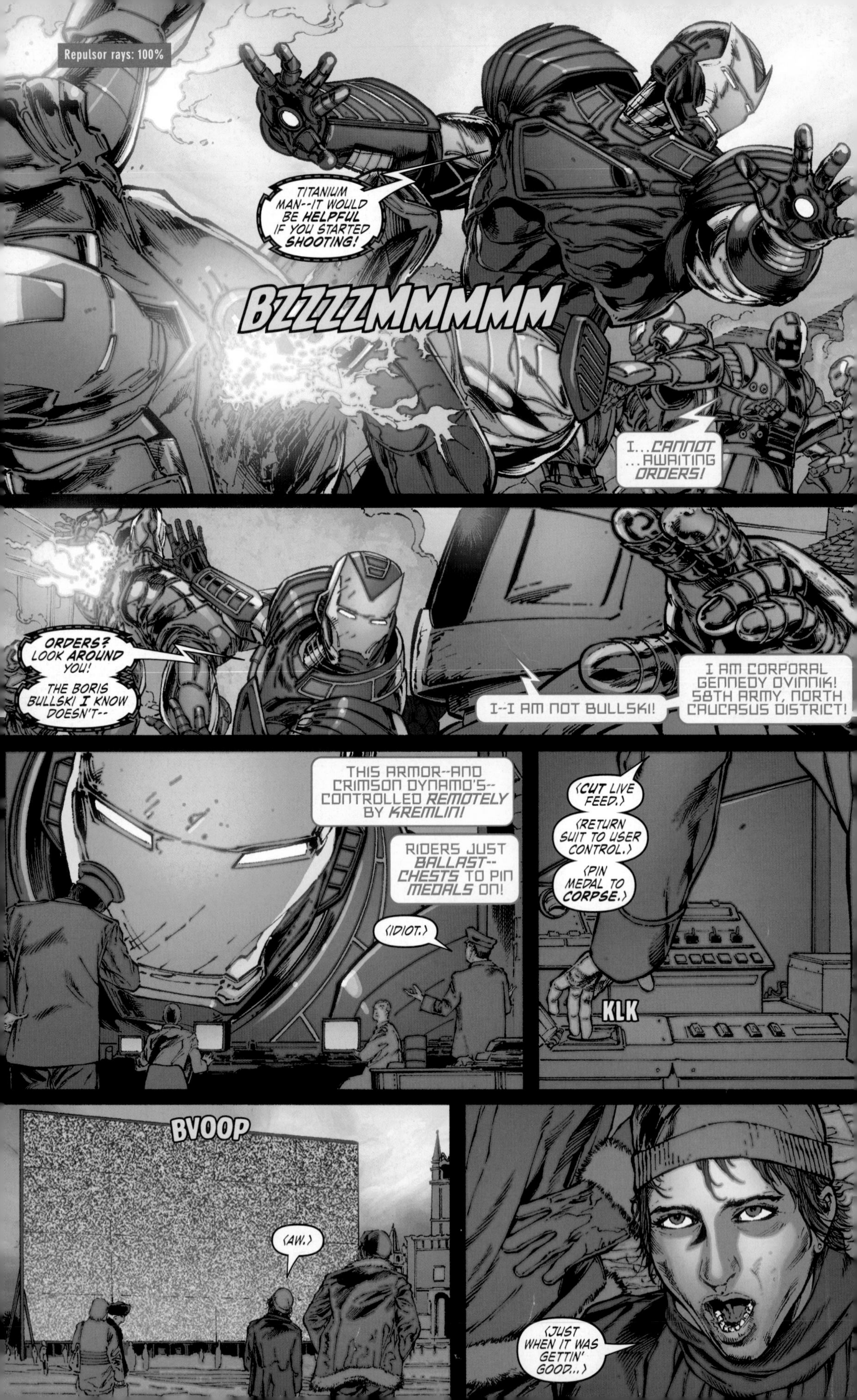

Repulsor rays: 100%
TITANIUM MAN--IT WOULD BE HELPFUL IF YOU STARTED SHOOTING!
BZZZZMMMMMM
I...CANNOT ...AWAITING ORDERS!
ORDERS? LOOK AROUND YOU!
THE BORIS BULLSKI I KNOW DOESN'T--
I--I AM NOT BULLSKI!
I AM CORPORAL GENNEDY OVINNIK! 58TH ARMY, NORTH CAUCASUS DISTRICT!
THIS ARMOR--AND CRIMSON DYNAMO'S--CONTROLLED REMOTELY BY KREMLIN!
RIDERS JUST BALLAST--CHESTS TO PIN MEDALS ON!
‹IDIOT.›
‹CUT LIVE FEED.›
‹RETURN SUIT TO USER CONTROL.›
‹PIN MEDAL TO CORPSE.›
KLK
BVOOP
‹AW.›
‹JUST WHEN IT WAS GETTIN' GOOD...›

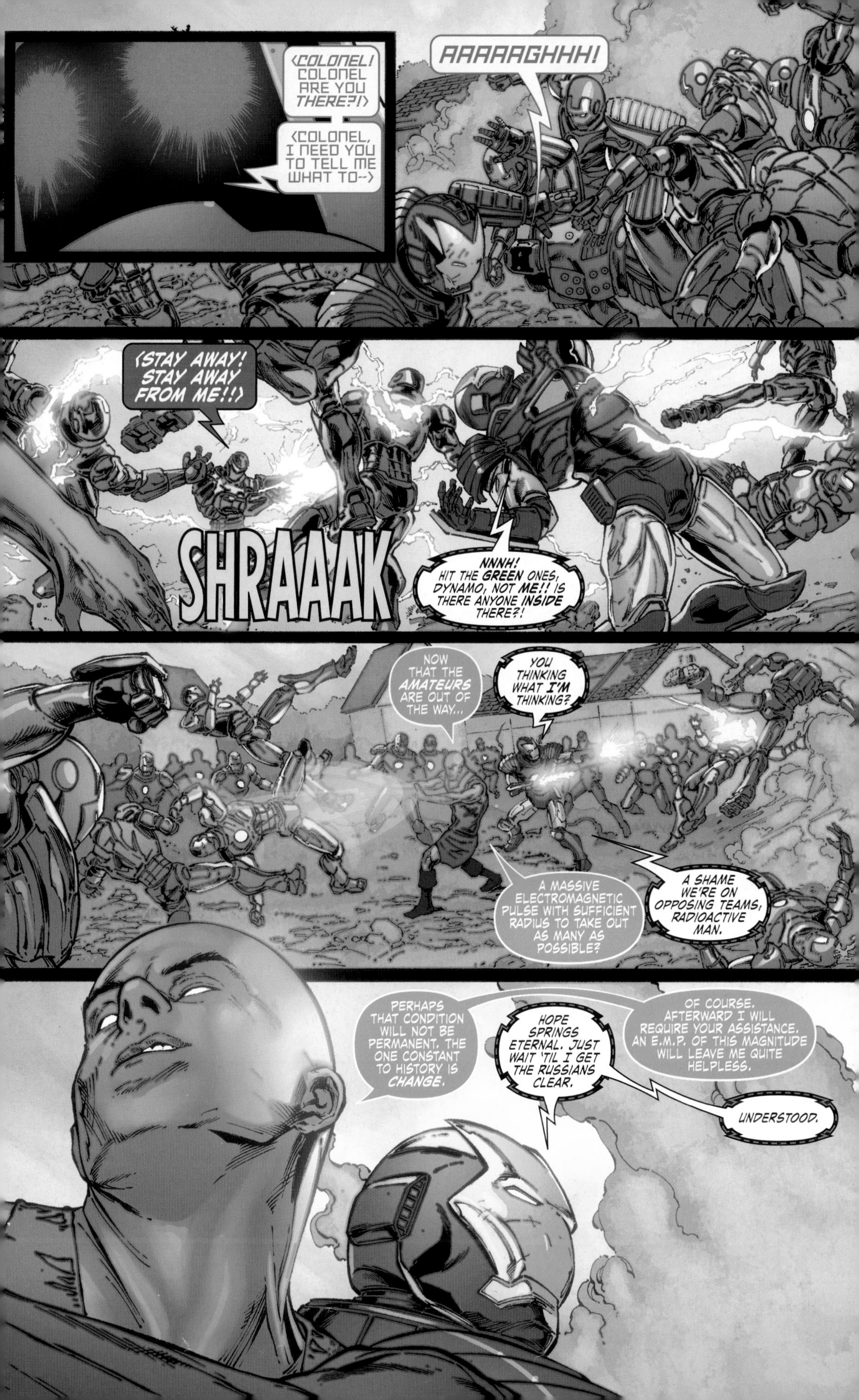

‹COLONEL! COLONEL ARE YOU THERE?!›
‹COLONEL, I NEED YOU TO TELL ME WHAT TO--›
AAAAAGHHH!
‹STAY AWAY! STAY AWAY FROM ME!!›
SHRAAAK
NNNH! HIT THE GREEN ONES, DYNAMO, NOT ME!! IS THERE ANYONE INSIDE THERE?!
NOW THAT THE AMATEURS ARE OUT OF THE WAY...
YOU THINKING WHAT I'M THINKING?
A MASSIVE ELECTROMAGNETIC PULSE WITH SUFFICIENT RADIUS TO TAKE OUT AS MANY AS POSSIBLE?
A SHAME WE'RE ON OPPOSING TEAMS, RADIOACTIVE MAN.
PERHAPS THAT CONDITION WILL NOT BE PERMANENT. THE ONE CONSTANT TO HISTORY IS CHANGE.
HOPE SPRINGS ETERNAL. JUST WAIT 'TIL I GET THE RUSSIANS CLEAR.
OF COURSE. AFTERWARD I WILL REQUIRE YOUR ASSISTANCE. AN E.M.P. OF THIS MAGNITUDE WILL LEAVE ME QUITE HELPLESS.
UNDERSTOOD.

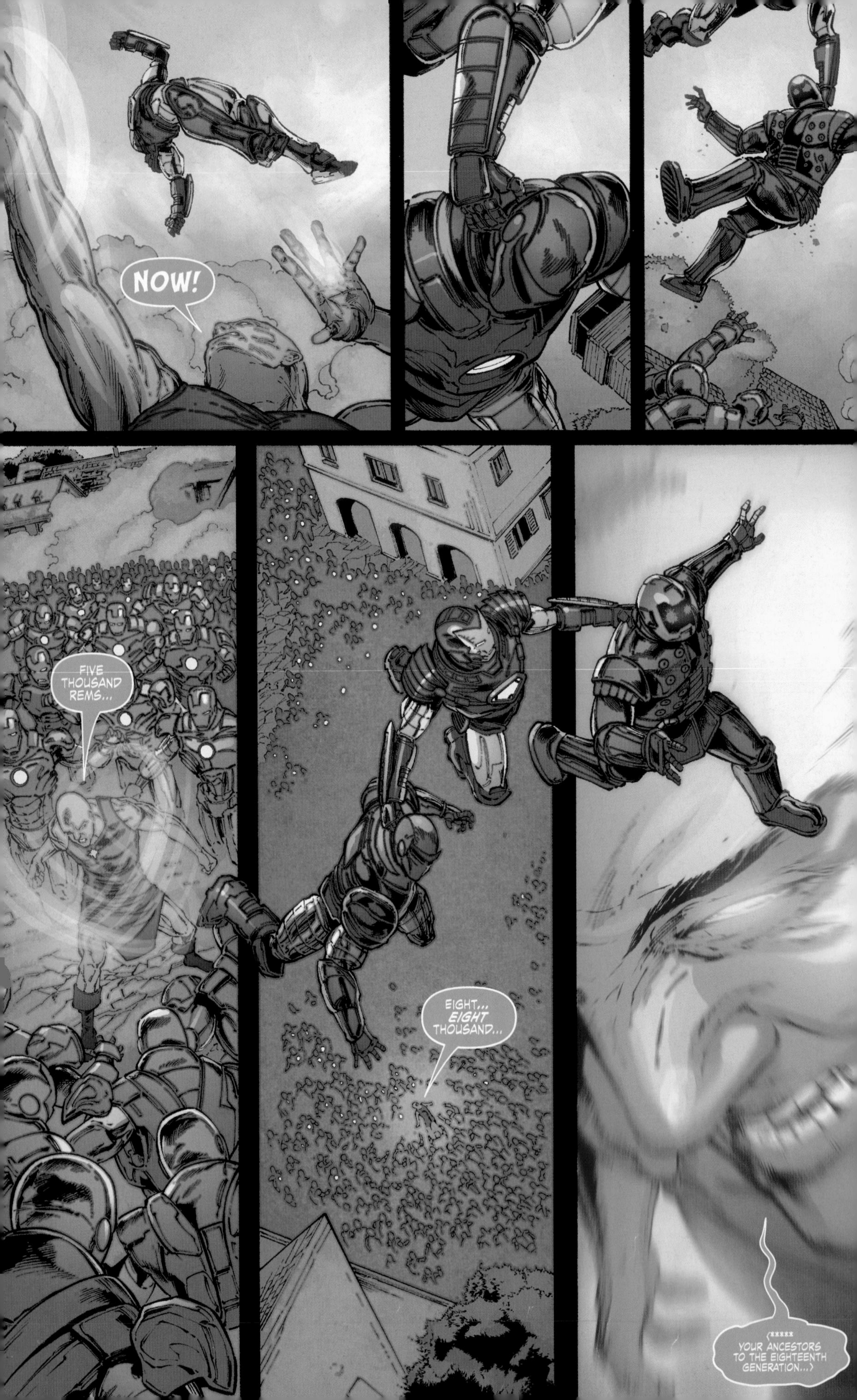
NOW!
FIVE THOUSAND REMS...
EIGHT... EIGHT THOUSAND...
<***** YOUR ANCESTORS TO THE EIGHTEENTH GENERATION...>

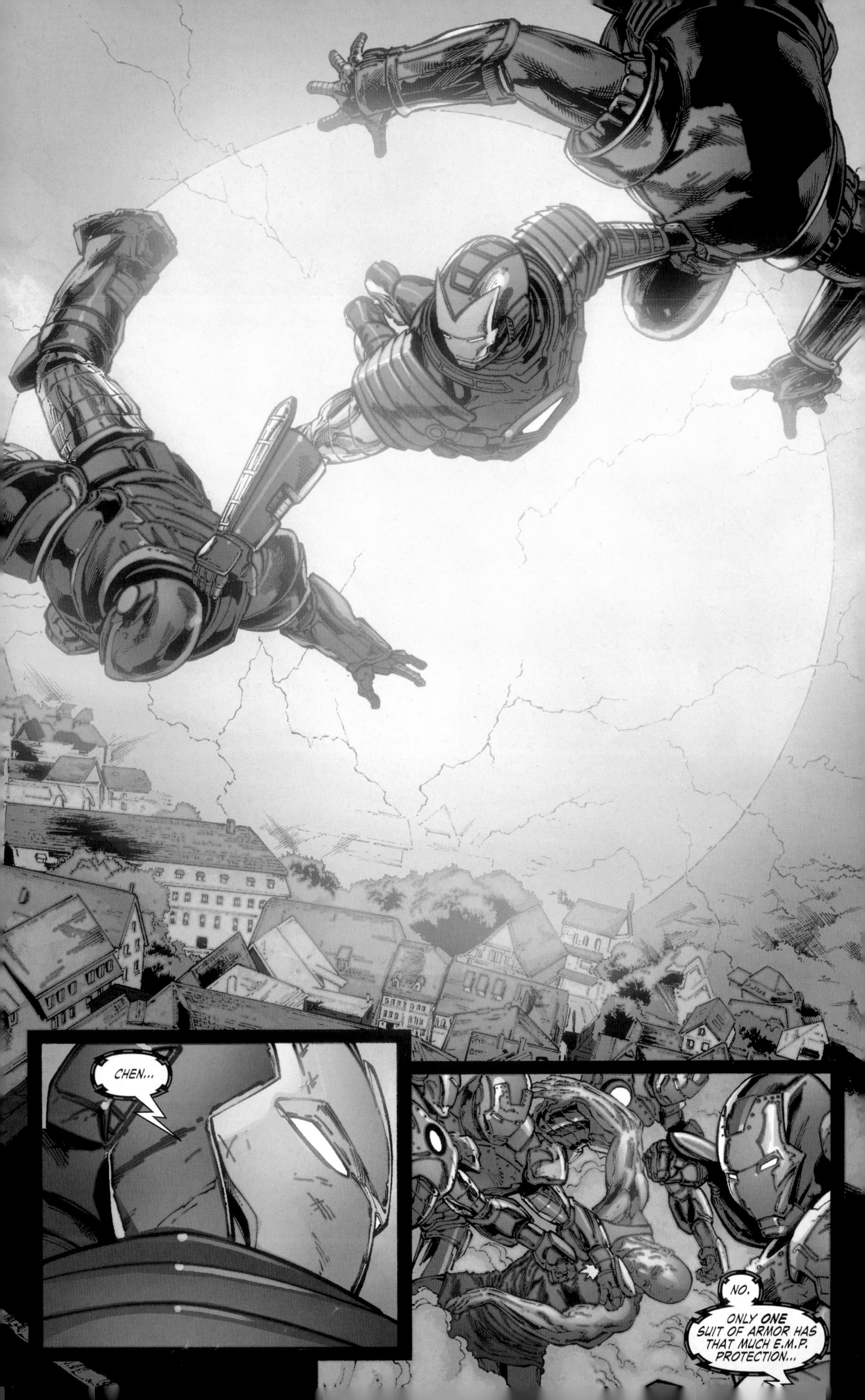
CHEN...
NO.
ONLY ONE
SUIT OF ARMOR HAS
THAT MUCH E.M.P.
PROTECTION...

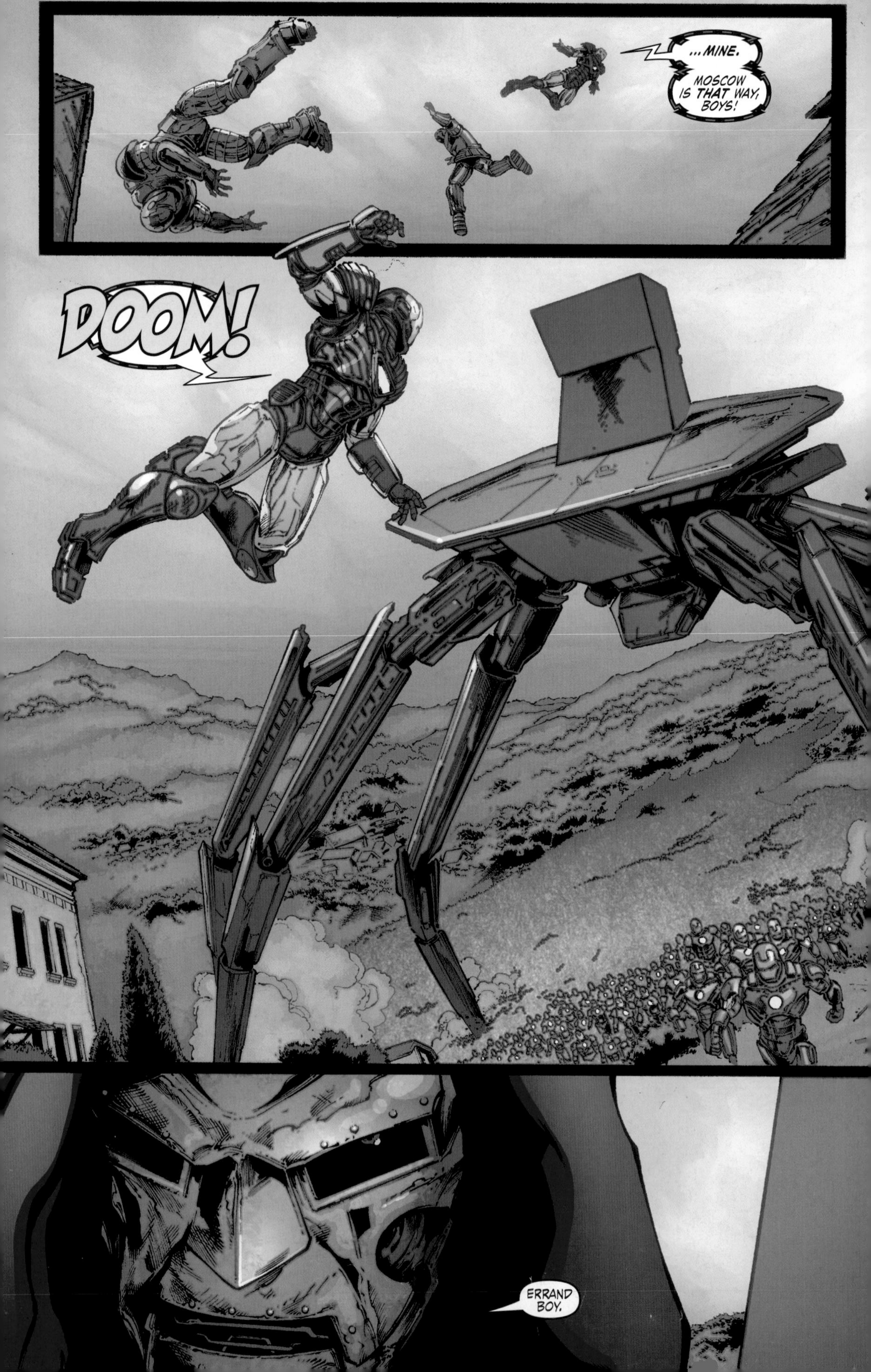
...MINE.
MOSCOW IS THAT WAY, BOYS!
DOOM!
ERRAND BOY.

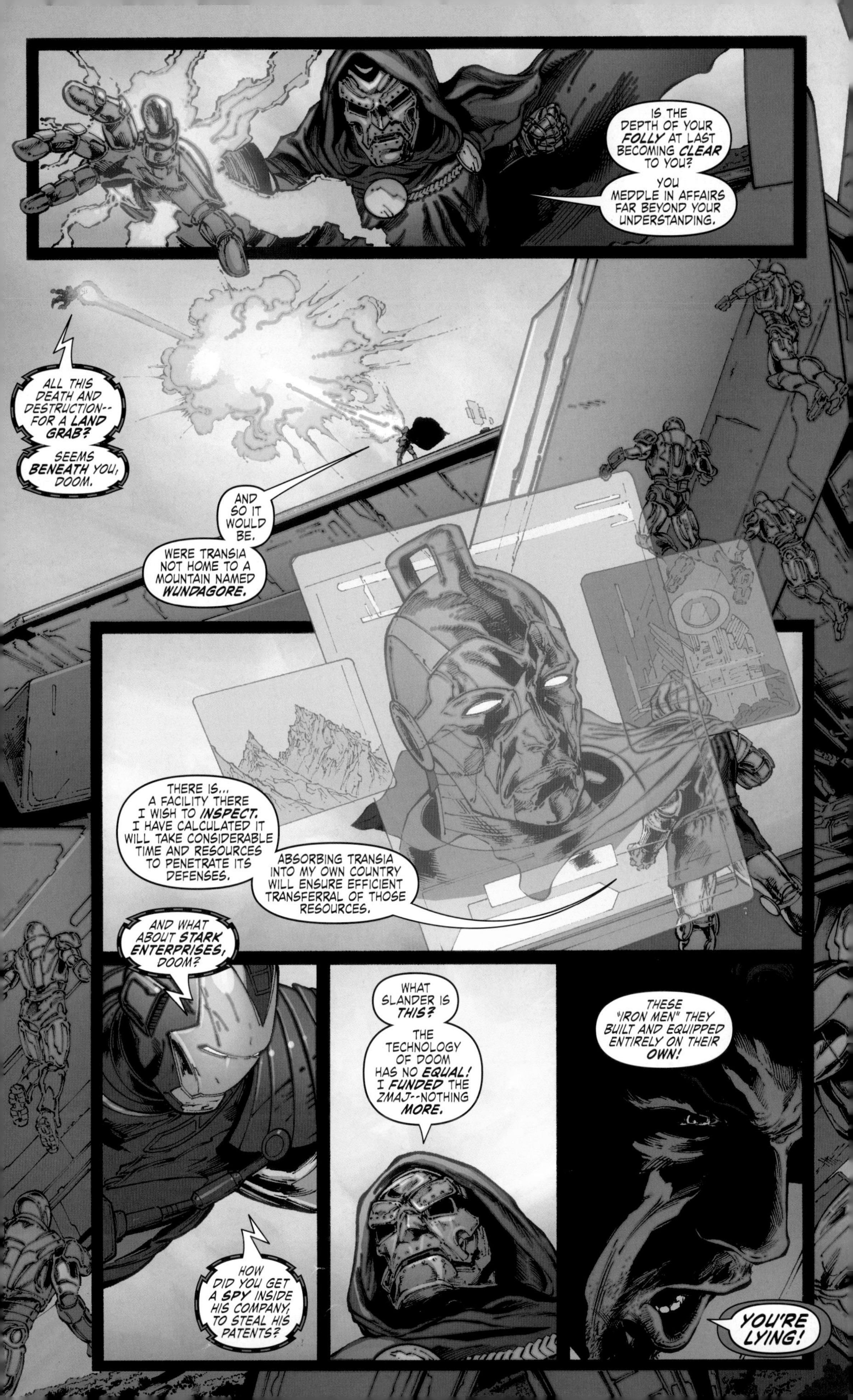
IS THE DEPTH OF YOUR FOLLY AT LAST BECOMING CLEAR TO YOU?
YOU MEDDLE IN AFFAIRS FAR BEYOND YOUR UNDERSTANDING.
ALL THIS DEATH AND DESTRUCTION--FOR A LAND GRAB?
SEEMS BENEATH YOU, DOOM.
AND SO IT WOULD BE.
WERE TRANSIA NOT HOME TO A MOUNTAIN NAMED WUNDAGORE.
THERE IS... A FACILITY THERE I WISH TO INSPECT. I HAVE CALCULATED IT WILL TAKE CONSIDERABLE TIME AND RESOURCES TO PENETRATE ITS DEFENSES.
ABSORBING TRANSIA INTO MY OWN COUNTRY WILL ENSURE EFFICIENT TRANSFERRAL OF THOSE RESOURCES.
AND WHAT ABOUT STARK ENTERPRISES, DOOM?
HOW DID YOU GET A SPY INSIDE HIS COMPANY, TO STEAL HIS PATENTS?
WHAT SLANDER IS THIS?
THE TECHNOLOGY OF DOOM HAS NO EQUAL! I FUNDED THE ZMAJ--NOTHING MORE.
THESE "IRON MEN" THEY BUILT AND EQUIPPED ENTIRELY ON THEIR OWN!
YOU'RE LYING!

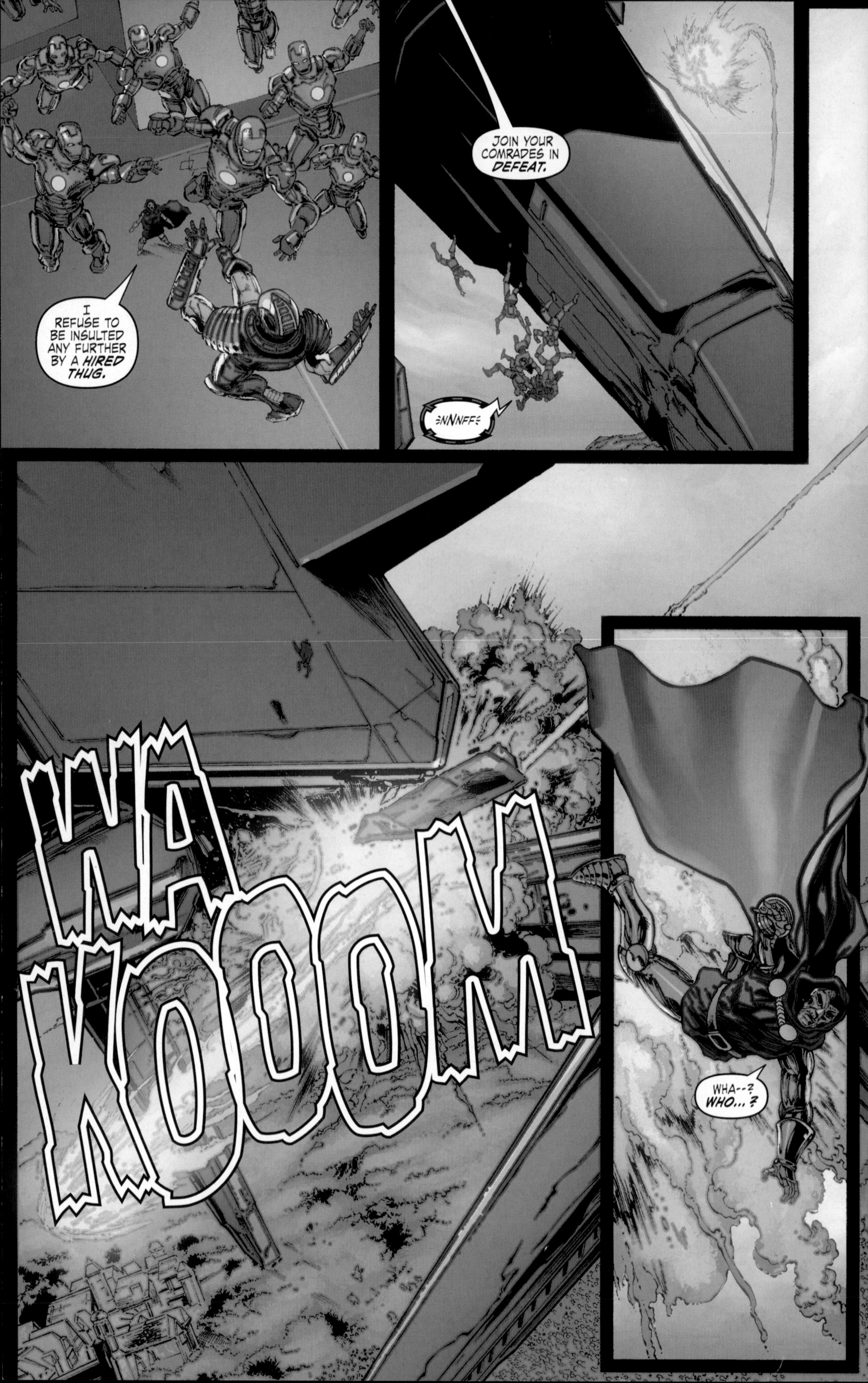

I REFUSE TO BE INSULTED ANY FURTHER BY A *HIRED THUG.*
JOIN YOUR COMRADES IN *DEFEAT.*
NNNFF
WA KOOOM
WHA--? *WHO...?*

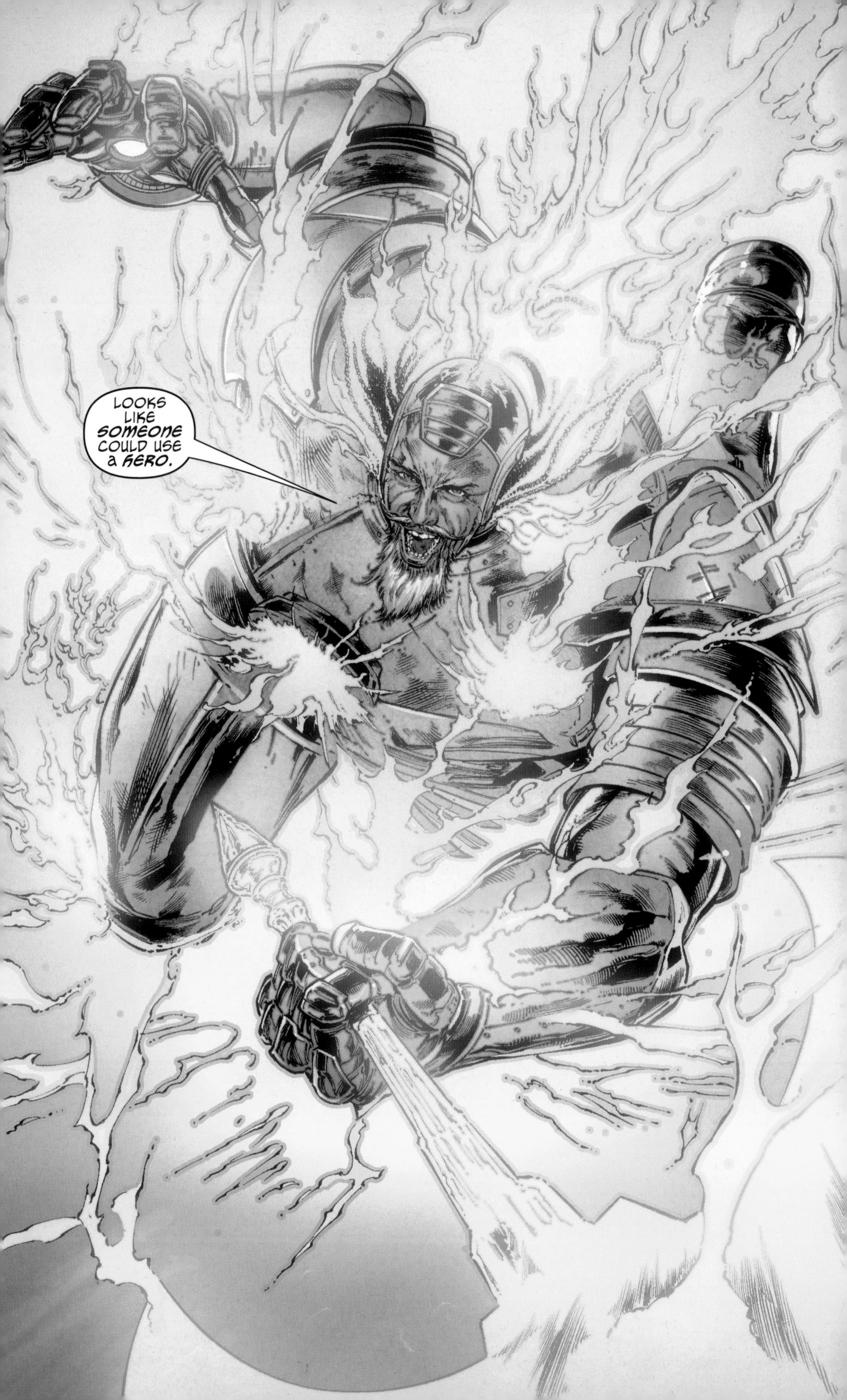
LOOKS LIKE SOMEONE COULD USE A HERO.

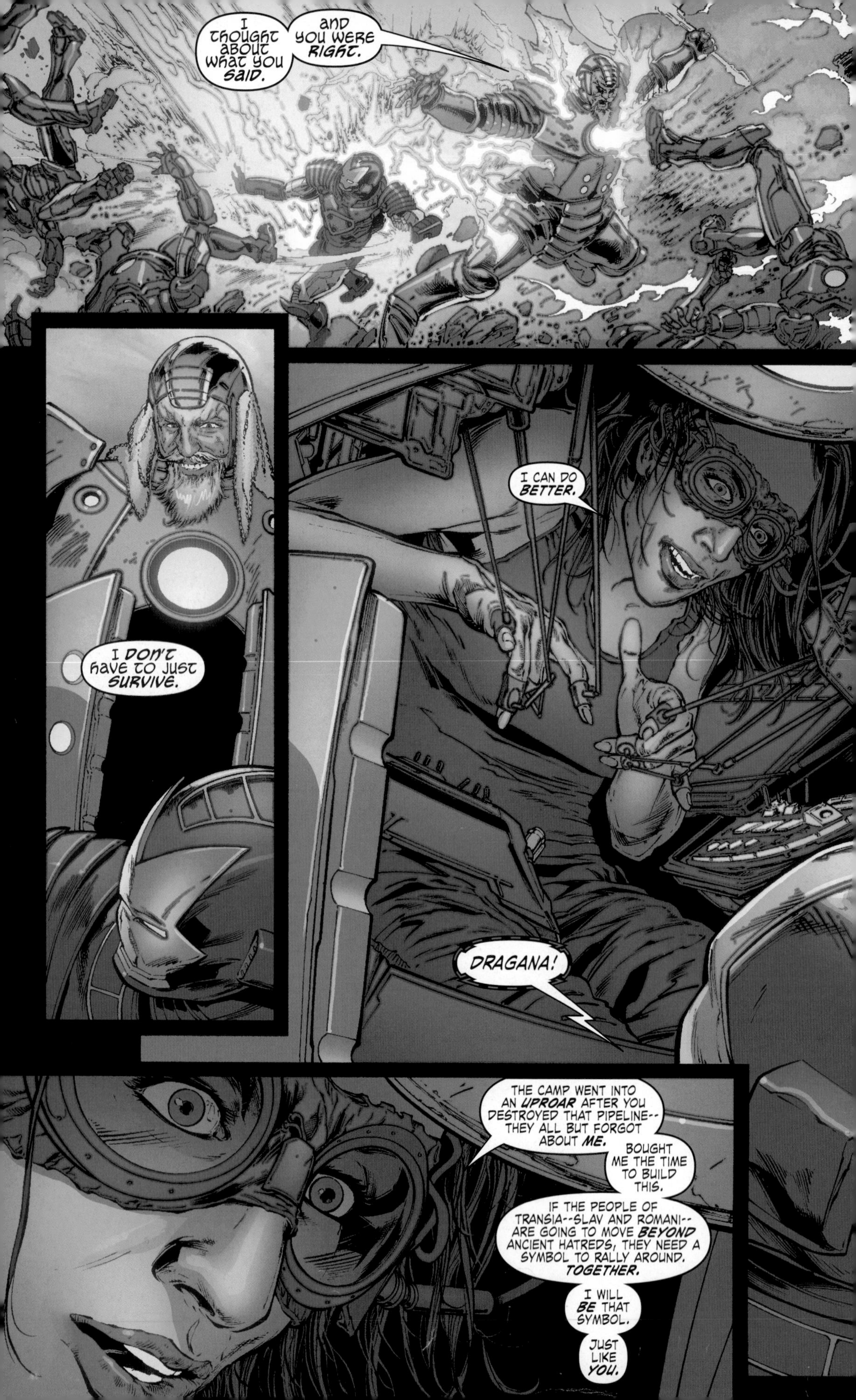
I THOUGHT ABOUT WHAT YOU SAID.
AND YOU WERE RIGHT.
I DON'T HAVE TO JUST SURVIVE.
I CAN DO BETTER.
DRAGANA!
THE CAMP WENT INTO AN UPROAR AFTER YOU DESTROYED THAT PIPELINE-- THEY ALL BUT FORGOT ABOUT ME.
BOUGHT ME THE TIME TO BUILD THIS.
IF THE PEOPLE OF TRANSIA--SLAV AND ROMANI-- ARE GOING TO MOVE BEYOND ANCIENT HATREDS, THEY NEED A SYMBOL TO RALLY AROUND. TOGETHER.
I WILL BE THAT SYMBOL.
JUST LIKE YOU.

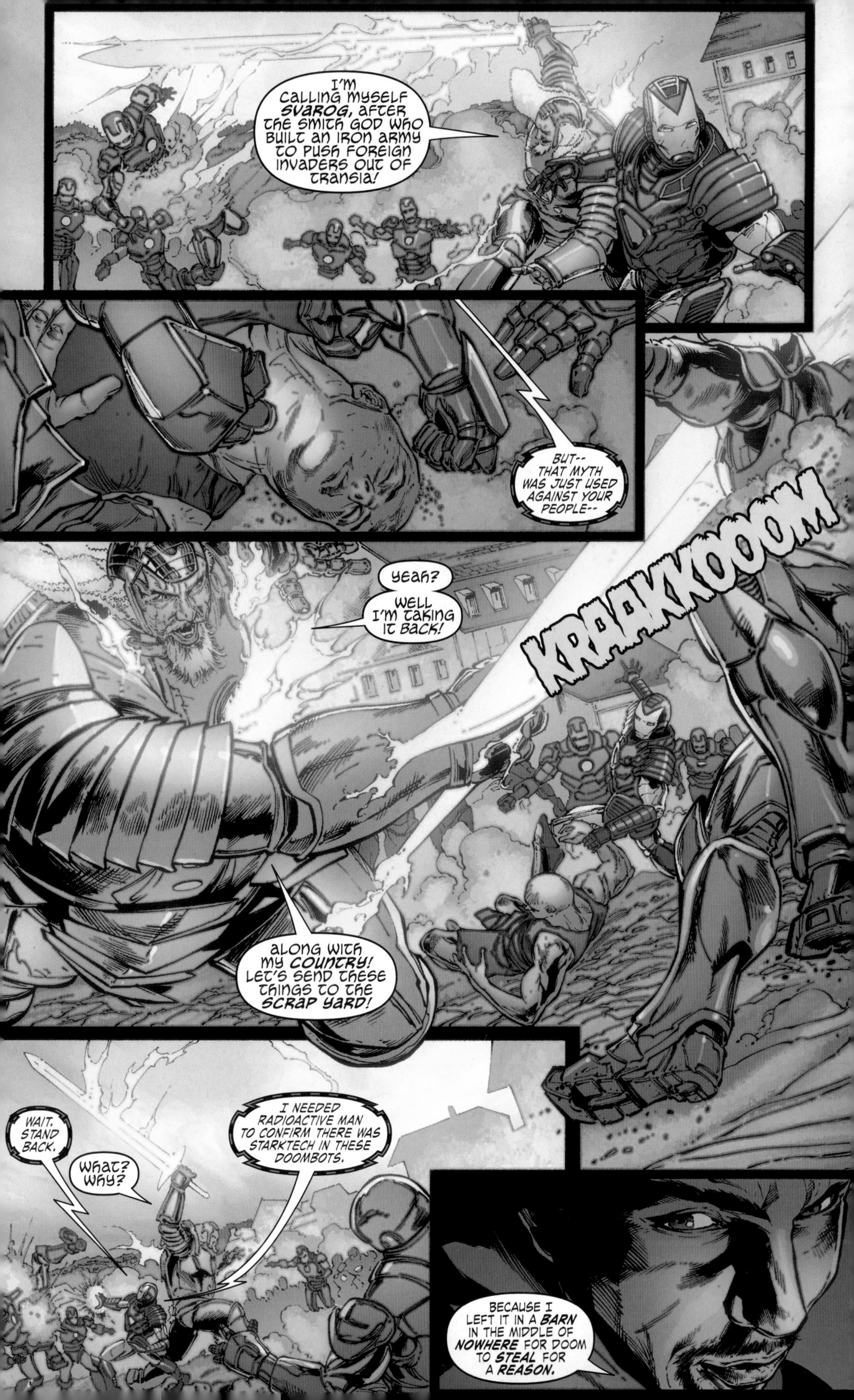
I'M CALLING MYSELF SVAROG, AFTER THE SMITH GOD WHO BUILT AN IRON ARMY TO PUSH FOREIGN INVADERS OUT OF TRANSIA!
BUT-- THAT MYTH WAS JUST USED AGAINST YOUR PEOPLE--
YEAH?
WELL I'M TAKING IT BACK!
KRAAKKOOOM
ALONG WITH MY COUNTRY! LET'S SEND THESE THINGS TO THE SCRAP YARD!
WAIT. STAND BACK.
WHAT? WHY?
I NEEDED RADIOACTIVE MAN TO CONFIRM THERE WAS STARKTECH IN THESE DOOMBOTS.
BECAUSE I LEFT IT IN A BARN IN THE MIDDLE OF NOWHERE FOR DOOM TO STEAL FOR A REASON.

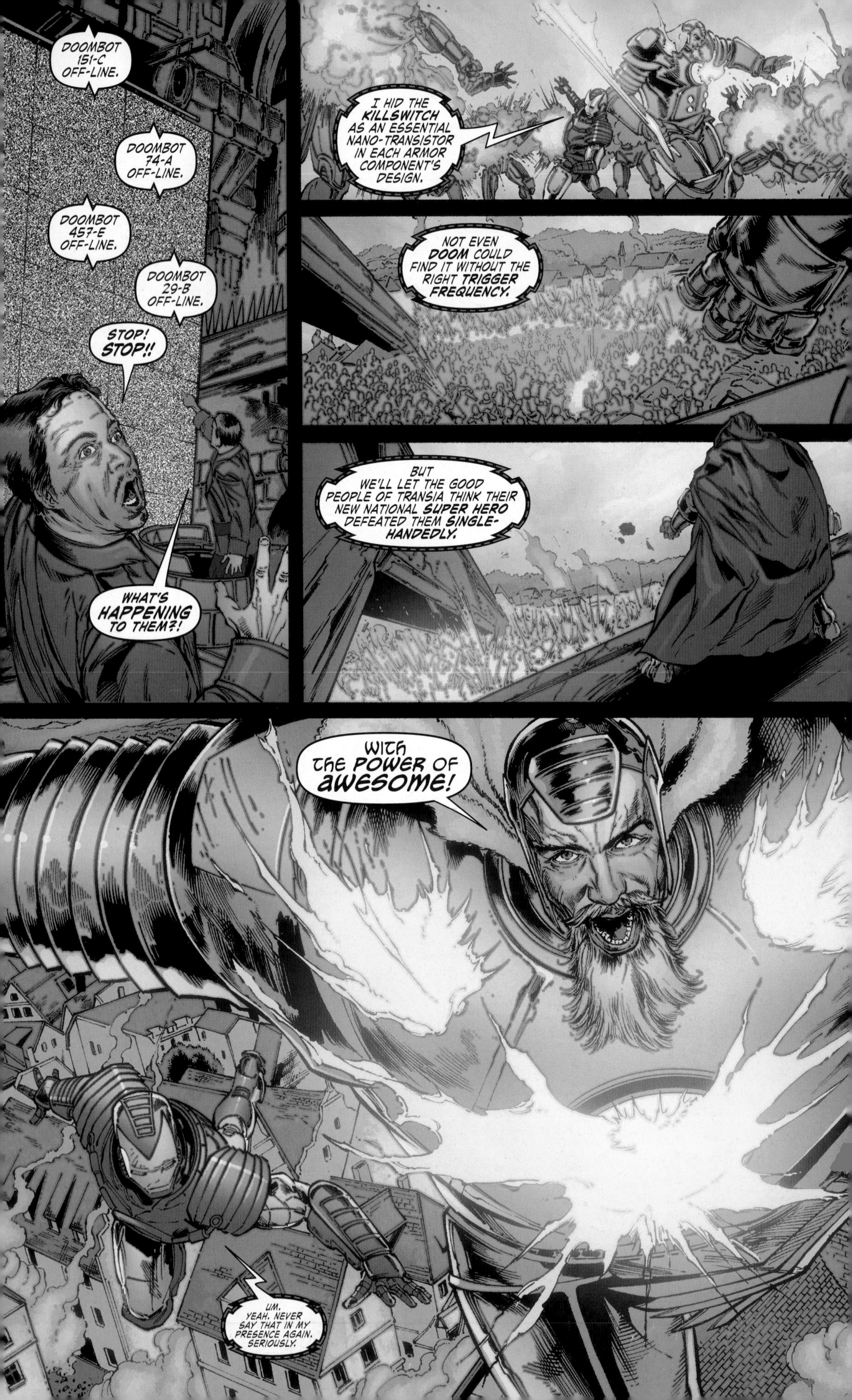
DOOMBOT 151-C OFF-LINE.
DOOMBOT 74-A OFF-LINE.
DOOMBOT 457-E OFF-LINE.
DOOMBOT 29-B OFF-LINE.
STOP! STOP!!
WHAT'S HAPPENING TO THEM?!
I HID THE KILLSWITCH AS AN ESSENTIAL NANO-TRANSISTOR IN EACH ARMOR COMPONENT'S DESIGN.
NOT EVEN DOOM COULD FIND IT WITHOUT THE RIGHT TRIGGER FREQUENCY.
BUT WE'LL LET THE GOOD PEOPLE OF TRANSIA THINK THEIR NEW NATIONAL SUPER HERO DEFEATED THEM SINGLE-HANDEDLY.
WITH THE POWER OF AWESOME!
UM. YEAH. NEVER SAY THAT IN MY PRESENCE AGAIN. SERIOUSLY.

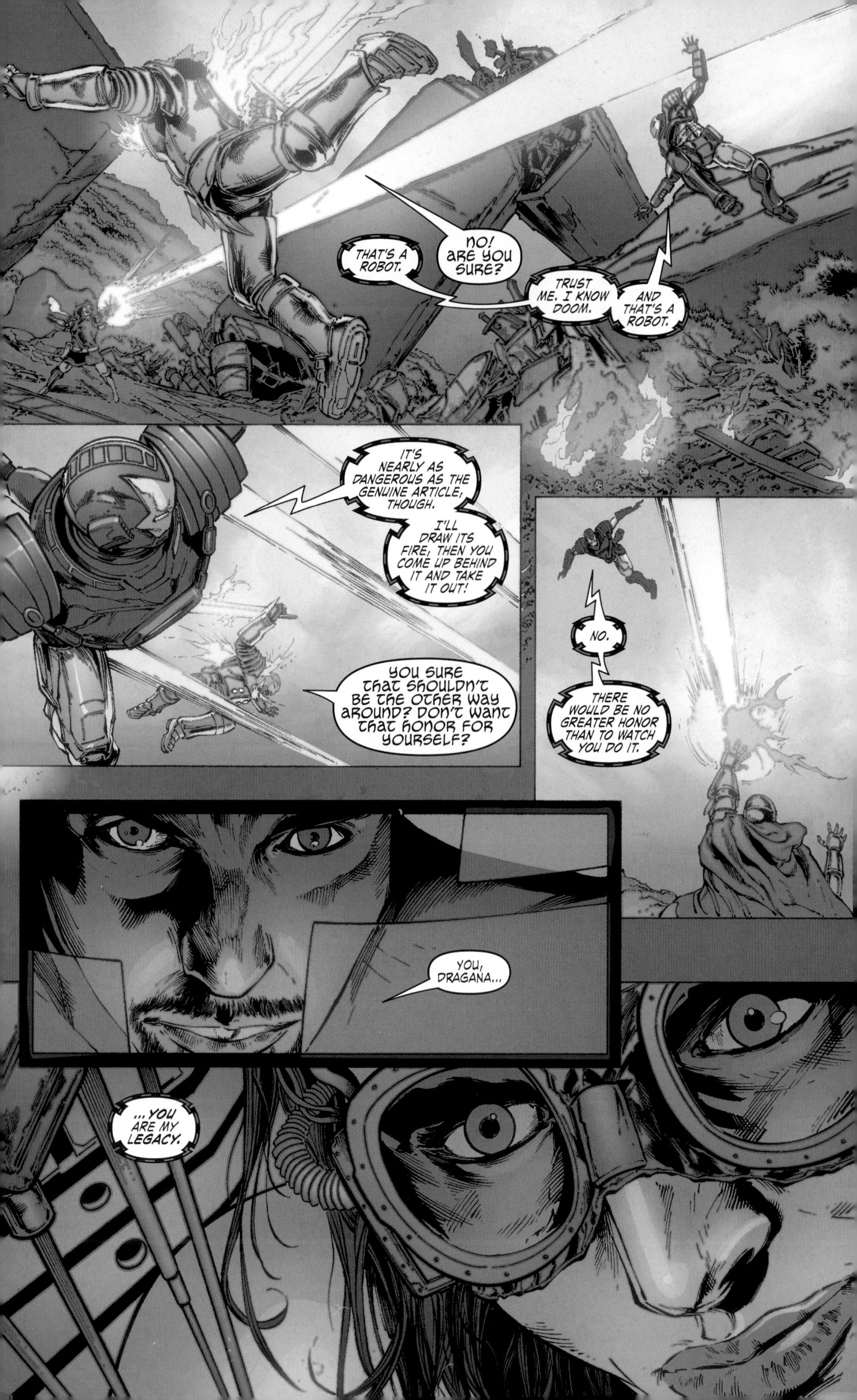
THAT'S A ROBOT.
NO! ARE YOU SURE?
TRUST ME. I KNOW DOOM.
AND THAT'S A ROBOT.
IT'S NEARLY AS DANGEROUS AS THE GENUINE ARTICLE, THOUGH.
I'LL DRAW ITS FIRE, THEN YOU COME UP BEHIND IT AND TAKE IT OUT!
YOU SURE THAT SHOULDN'T BE THE OTHER WAY AROUND? DON'T WANT THAT HONOR FOR YOURSELF?
NO.
THERE WOULD BE NO GREATER HONOR THAN TO WATCH YOU DO IT.
YOU, DRAGANA...
...YOU ARE MY LEGACY.

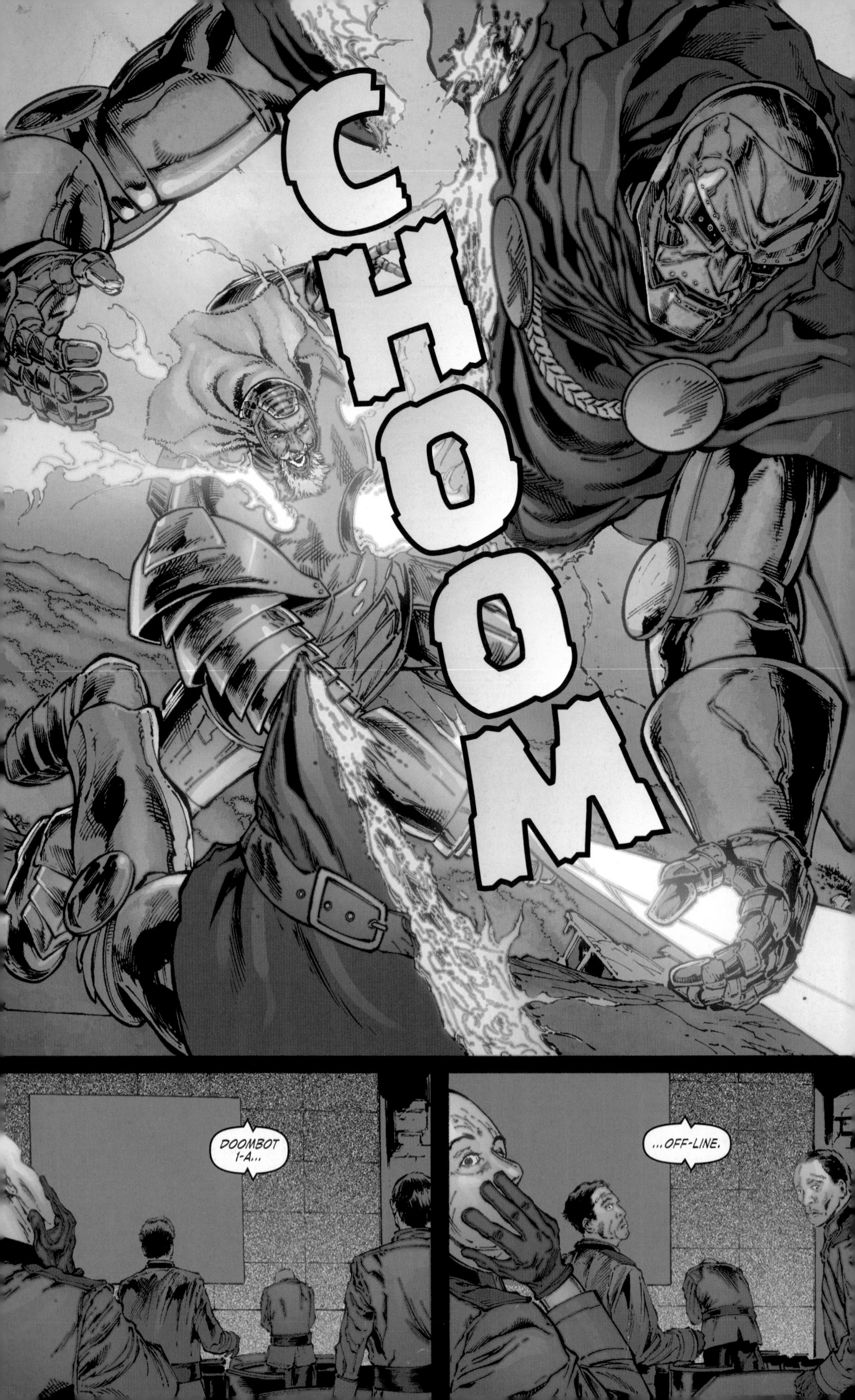
CHOOM
DOOMBOT 1-A...
...OFF-LINE.

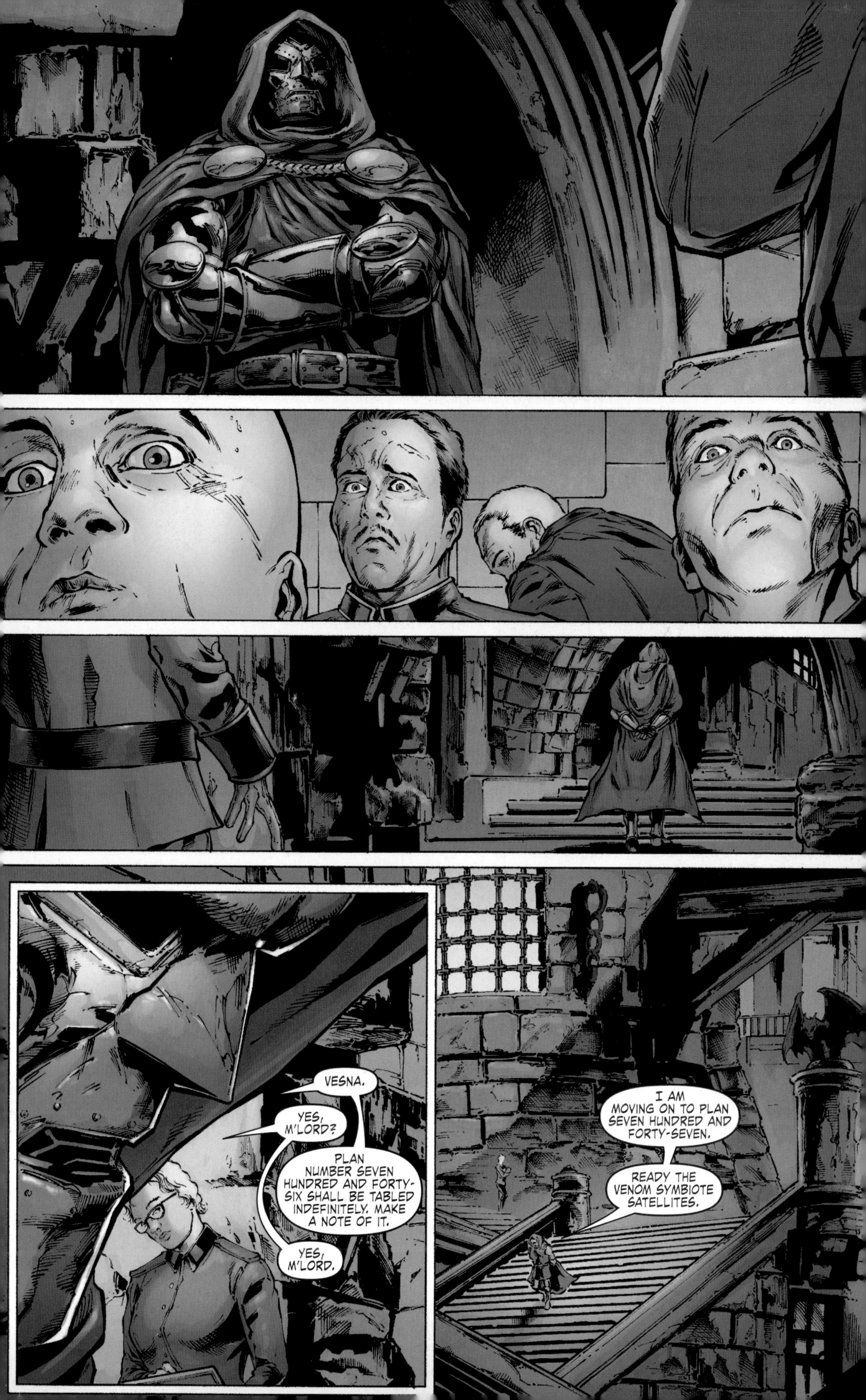
VESNA.
YES, M'LORD?
PLAN NUMBER SEVEN HUNDRED AND FORTY-SIX SHALL BE TABLED INDEFINITELY. MAKE A NOTE OF IT.
YES, M'LORD.
I AM MOVING ON TO PLAN SEVEN HUNDRED AND FORTY-SEVEN.
READY THE VENOM SYMBIOTE SATELLITES.

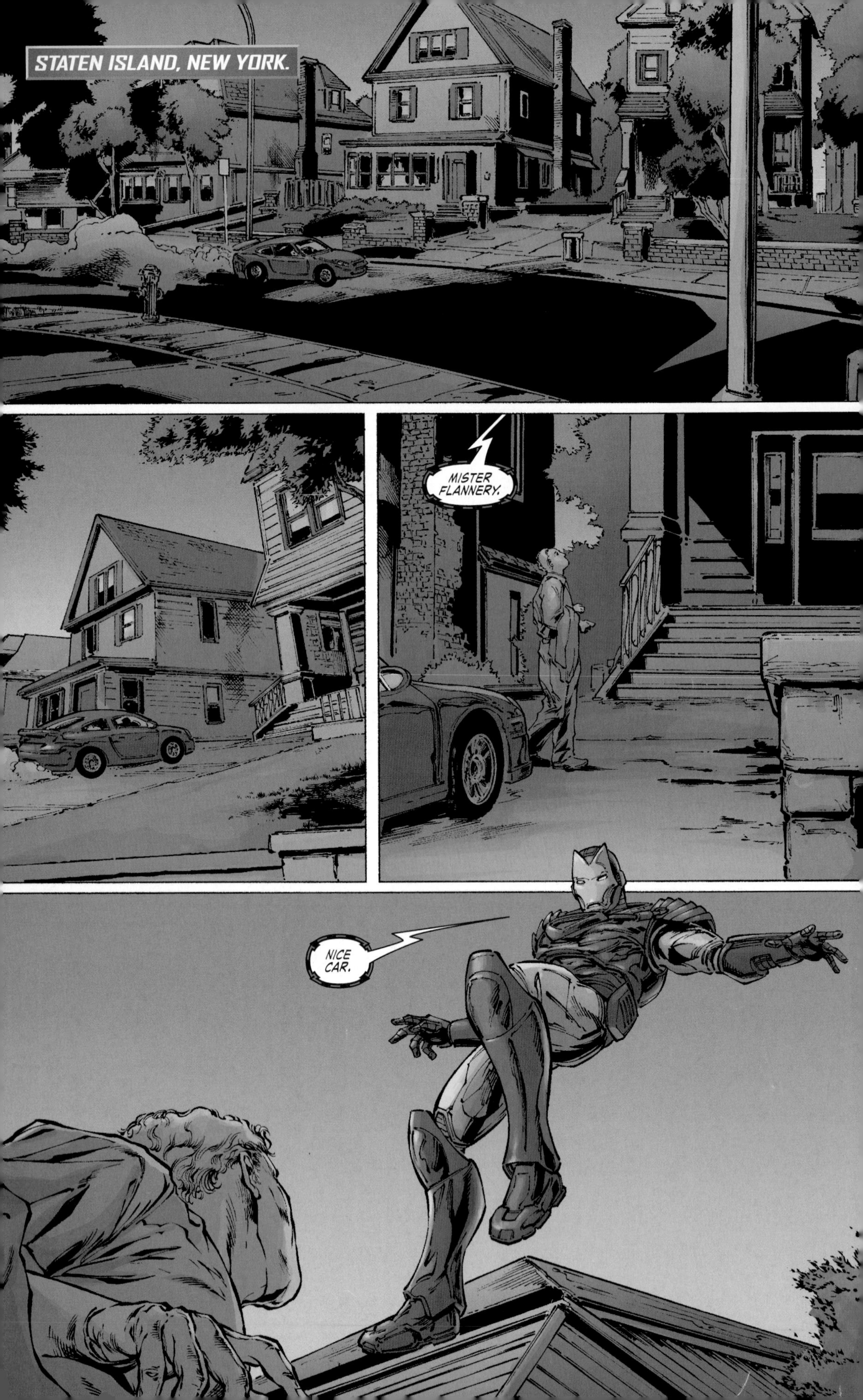
STATEN ISLAND, NEW YORK.
MISTER FLANNERY.
NICE CAR.

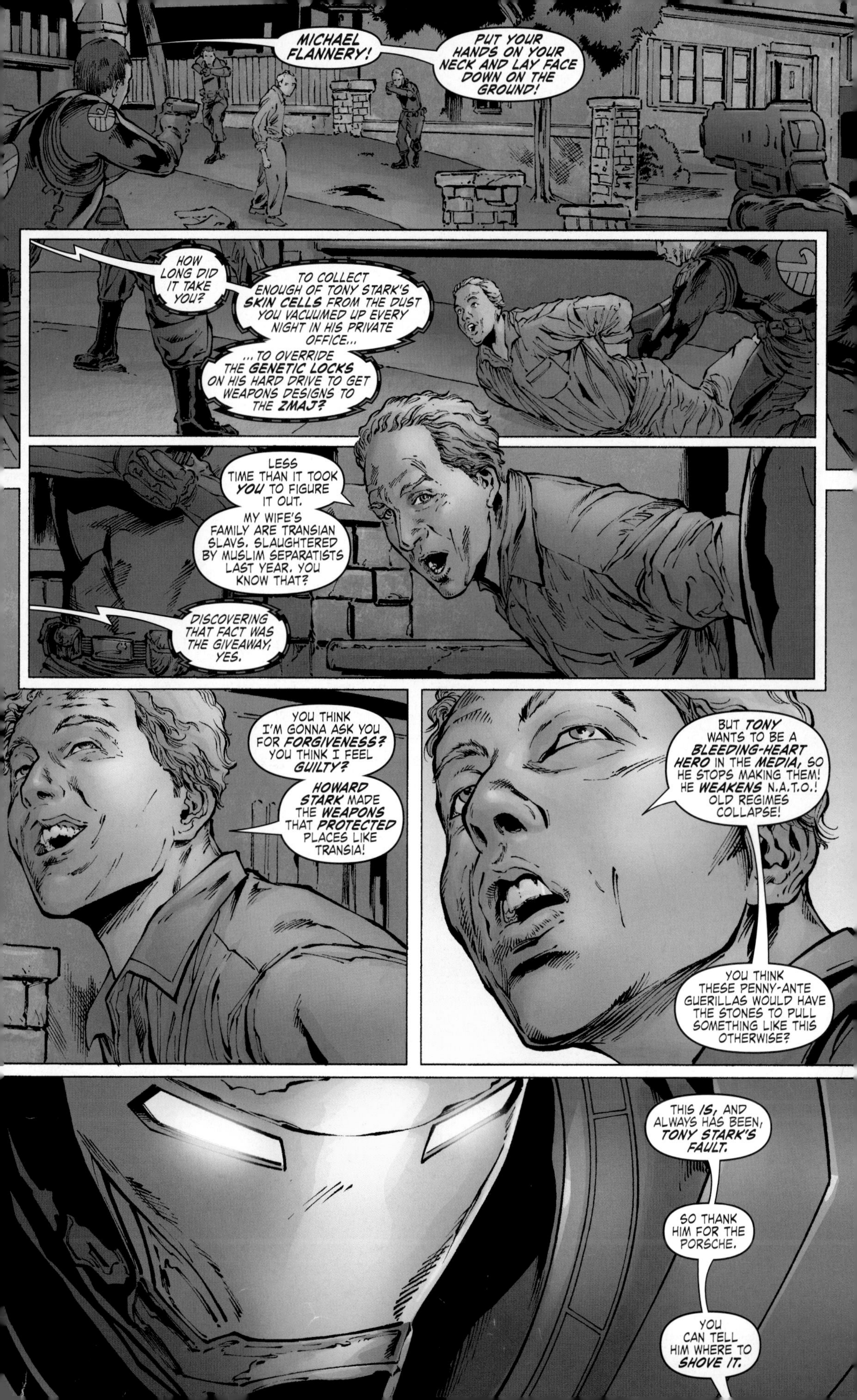
MICHAEL FLANNERY!
PUT YOUR HANDS ON YOUR NECK AND LAY FACE DOWN ON THE GROUND!
HOW LONG DID IT TAKE YOU?
TO COLLECT ENOUGH OF TONY STARK'S SKIN CELLS FROM THE DUST YOU VACUUMED UP EVERY NIGHT IN HIS PRIVATE OFFICE...
...TO OVERRIDE THE GENETIC LOCKS ON HIS HARD DRIVE TO GET WEAPONS DESIGNS TO THE ZMAJ?
LESS TIME THAN IT TOOK YOU TO FIGURE IT OUT.
MY WIFE'S FAMILY ARE TRANSIAN SLAVS. SLAUGHTERED BY MUSLIM SEPARATISTS LAST YEAR. YOU KNOW THAT?
DISCOVERING THAT FACT WAS THE GIVEAWAY, YES.
YOU THINK I'M GONNA ASK YOU FOR FORGIVENESS? YOU THINK I FEEL GUILTY?
HOWARD STARK MADE THE WEAPONS THAT PROTECTED PLACES LIKE TRANSIA!
BUT TONY WANTS TO BE A BLEEDING-HEART HERO IN THE MEDIA, SO HE STOPS MAKING THEM! HE WEAKENS N.A.T.O.! OLD REGIMES COLLAPSE!
YOU THINK THESE PENNY-ANTE GUERILLAS WOULD HAVE THE STONES TO PULL SOMETHING LIKE THIS OTHERWISE?
THIS IS, AND ALWAYS HAS BEEN, TONY STARK'S FAULT.
SO THANK HIM FOR THE PORSCHE.
YOU CAN TELL HIM WHERE TO SHOVE IT.

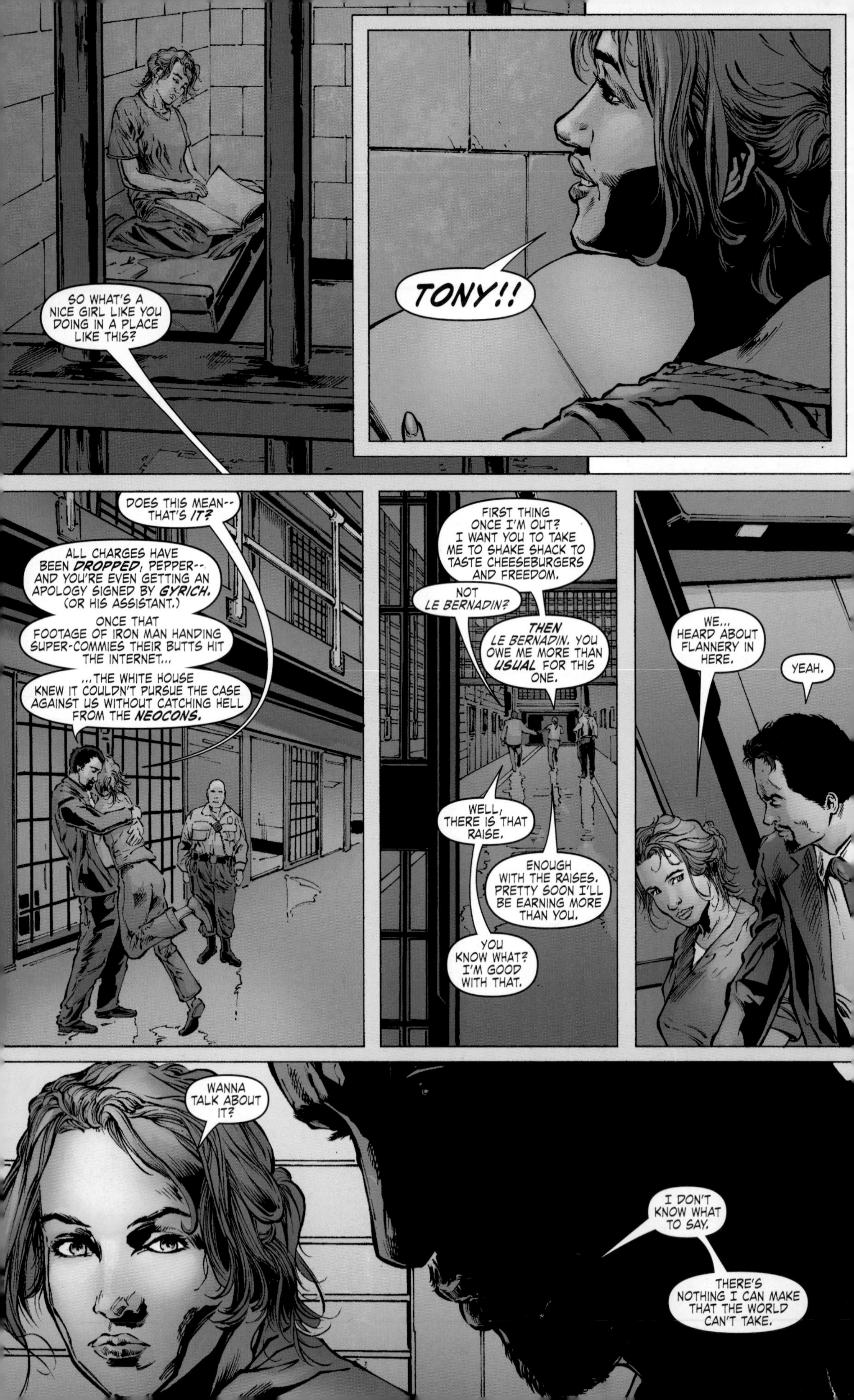
SO WHAT'S A NICE GIRL LIKE YOU DOING IN A PLACE LIKE THIS?
TONY!!
DOES THIS MEAN-- THAT'S IT?
ALL CHARGES HAVE BEEN DROPPED, PEPPER-- AND YOU'RE EVEN GETTING AN APOLOGY SIGNED BY GYRICH. (OR HIS ASSISTANT.)
ONCE THAT FOOTAGE OF IRON MAN HANDING SUPER-COMMIES THEIR BUTTS HIT THE INTERNET...
...THE WHITE HOUSE KNEW IT COULDN'T PURSUE THE CASE AGAINST US WITHOUT CATCHING HELL FROM THE NEOCONS.
FIRST THING ONCE I'M OUT? I WANT YOU TO TAKE ME TO SHAKE SHACK TO TASTE CHEESEBURGERS AND FREEDOM.
NOT LE BERNADIN?
THEN LE BERNADIN. YOU OWE ME MORE THAN USUAL FOR THIS ONE.
WELL, THERE IS THAT RAISE.
ENOUGH WITH THE RAISES. PRETTY SOON I'LL BE EARNING MORE THAN YOU.
YOU KNOW WHAT? I'M GOOD WITH THAT.
WE... HEARD ABOUT FLANNERY IN HERE.
YEAH.
WANNA TALK ABOUT IT?
I DON'T KNOW WHAT TO SAY.
THERE'S NOTHING I CAN MAKE THAT THE WORLD CAN'T TAKE.

"BUT--THROUGH TOTAL *ACCIDENT,* LIKE *MOST* GOOD THINGS--I CREATED ONE THING *WORTH COPYING.*

"I MADE *IRON MAN.*

"NOT THE ARMOR.

"BUT THE IDEAL.

"THE *IDEA* OF IRON MAN WILL BE AROUND MUCH *LONGER* THAN I AM.

"AND THERE WILL COME A DAY WHEN I AM NOT AROUND TO *OPERATE* HIM.

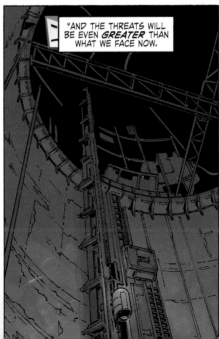

"AND THE THREATS WILL BE EVEN *GREATER* THAN WHAT WE FACE NOW.

"AND ON *THAT* DAY...

"...BY *THAT* TIME...

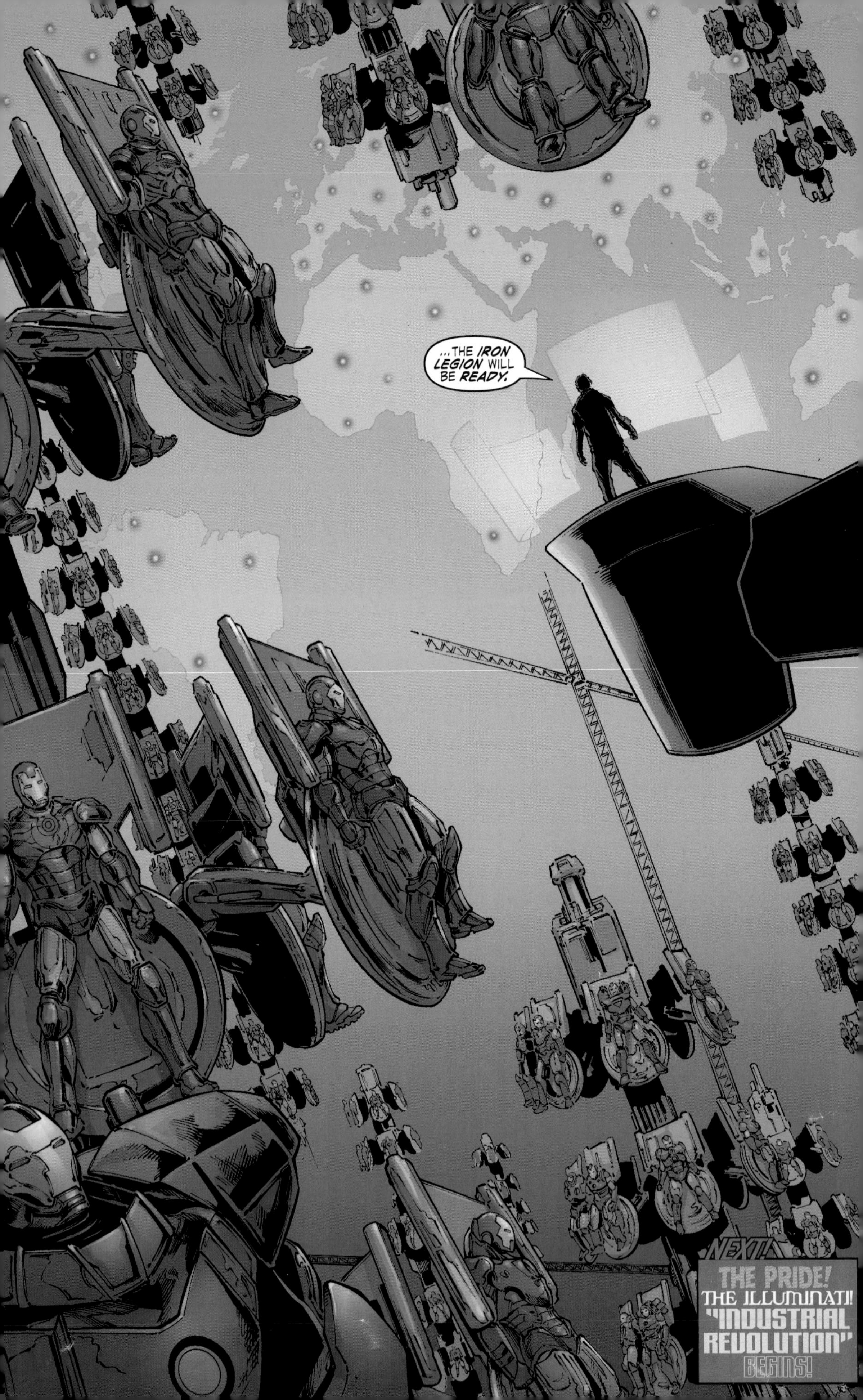
...THE IRON LEGION WILL BE READY.
NEXT:
THE PRIDE!
THE ILLUMINATI!
"INDUSTRIAL REVOLUTION"
BEGINS!

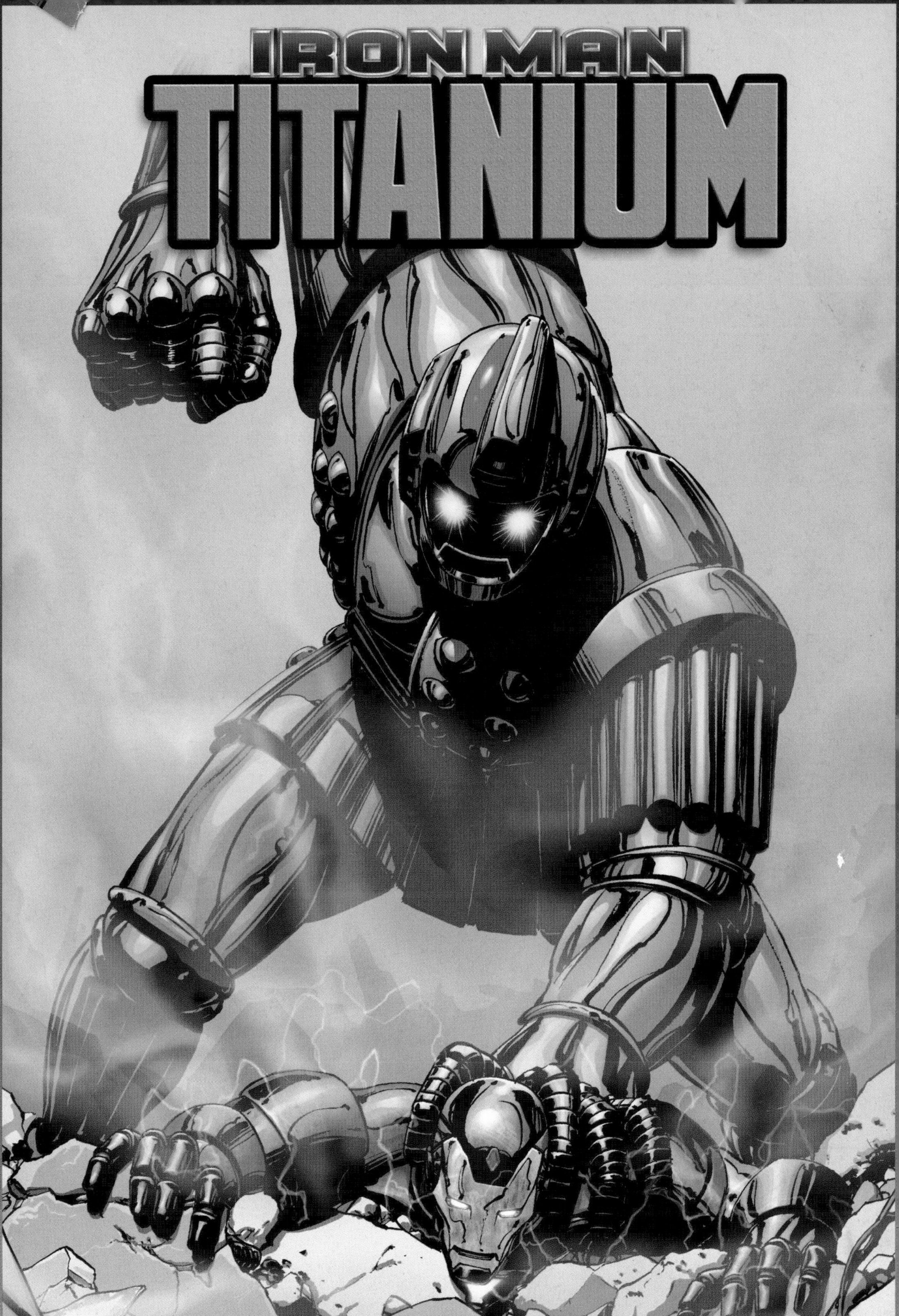
IRON MAN
TITANIUM
YARDIN

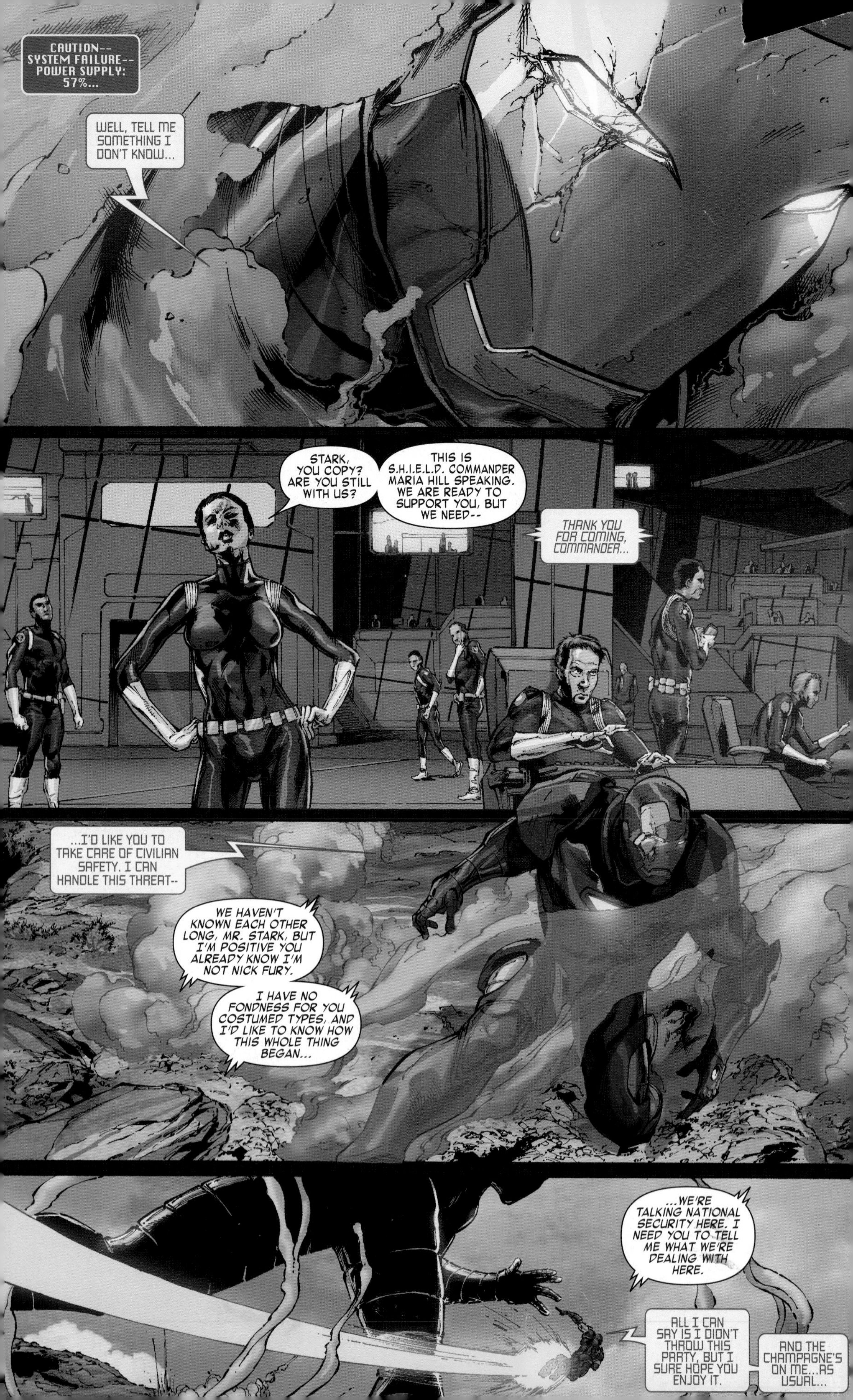
CAUTION-- SYSTEM FAILURE-- POWER SUPPLY: 57%...
WELL, TELL ME SOMETHING I DON'T KNOW...
STARK, YOU COPY? ARE YOU STILL WITH US?
THIS IS S.H.I.E.L.D. COMMANDER MARIA HILL SPEAKING. WE ARE READY TO SUPPORT YOU, BUT WE NEED--
THANK YOU FOR COMING, COMMANDER...
...I'D LIKE YOU TO TAKE CARE OF CIVILIAN SAFETY. I CAN HANDLE THIS THREAT--
WE HAVEN'T KNOWN EACH OTHER LONG, MR. STARK, BUT I'M POSITIVE YOU ALREADY KNOW I'M NOT NICK FURY.
I HAVE NO FONDNESS FOR YOU COSTUMED TYPES, AND I'D LIKE TO KNOW HOW THIS WHOLE THING BEGAN...
...WE'RE TALKING NATIONAL SECURITY HERE. I NEED YOU TO TELL ME WHAT WE'RE DEALING WITH HERE.
ALL I CAN SAY IS I DIDN'T THROW THIS PARTY, BUT I SURE HOPE YOU ENJOY IT.
AND THE CHAMPAGNE'S ON ME...AS USUAL...

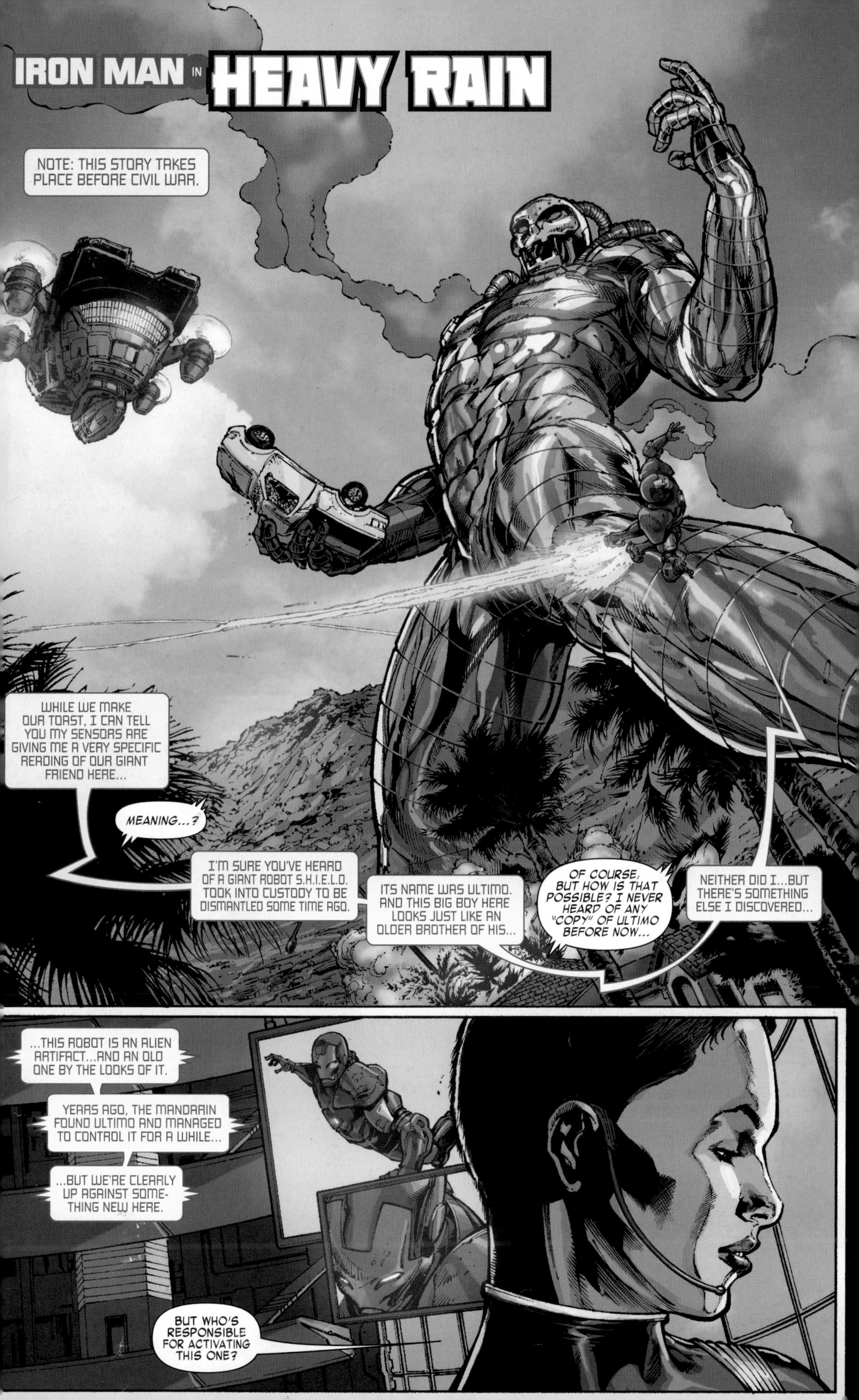
IRON MAN IN HEAVY RAIN
NOTE: THIS STORY TAKES PLACE BEFORE CIVIL WAR.
WHILE WE MAKE OUR TOAST, I CAN TELL YOU MY SENSORS ARE GIVING ME A VERY SPECIFIC READING OF OUR GIANT FRIEND HERE...
MEANING...?
I'M SURE YOU'VE HEARD OF A GIANT ROBOT S.H.I.E.L.D. TOOK INTO CUSTODY TO BE DISMANTLED SOME TIME AGO.
ITS NAME WAS ULTIMO. AND THIS BIG BOY HERE LOOKS JUST LIKE AN OLDER BROTHER OF HIS...
OF COURSE, BUT HOW IS THAT POSSIBLE? I NEVER HEARD OF ANY "COPY" OF ULTIMO BEFORE NOW...
NEITHER DID I...BUT THERE'S SOMETHING ELSE I DISCOVERED...
...THIS ROBOT IS AN ALIEN ARTIFACT...AND AN OLD ONE BY THE LOOKS OF IT.
YEARS AGO, THE MANDARIN FOUND ULTIMO AND MANAGED TO CONTROL IT FOR A WHILE...
...BUT WE'RE CLEARLY UP AGAINST SOMETHING NEW HERE.
BUT WHO'S RESPONSIBLE FOR ACTIVATING THIS ONE?

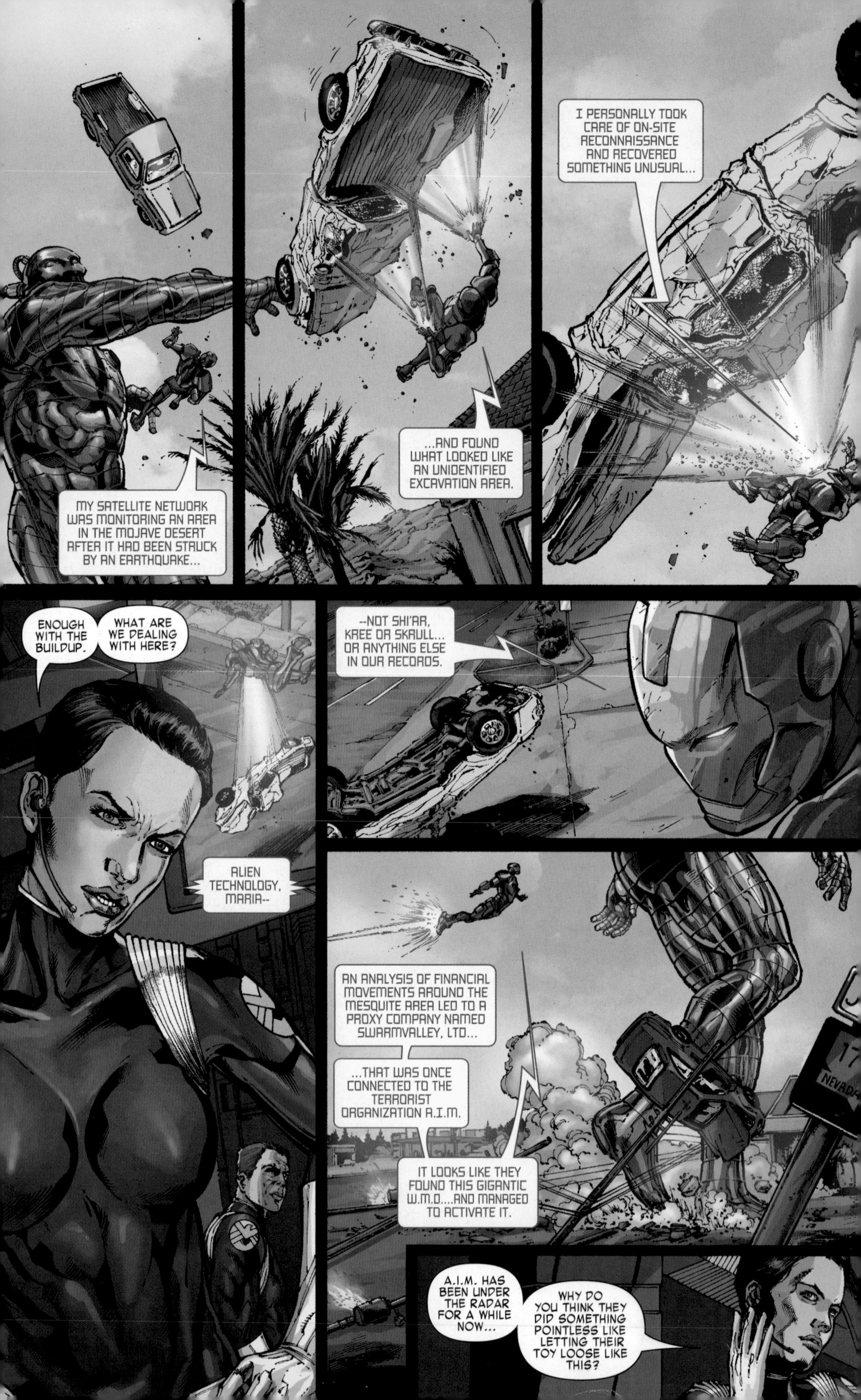
MY SATELLITE NETWORK WAS MONITORING AN AREA IN THE MOJAVE DESERT AFTER IT HAD BEEN STRUCK BY AN EARTHQUAKE...
...AND FOUND WHAT LOOKED LIKE AN UNIDENTIFIED EXCAVATION AREA.
I PERSONALLY TOOK CARE OF ON-SITE RECONNAISSANCE AND RECOVERED SOMETHING UNUSUAL...
ENOUGH WITH THE BUILDUP.
WHAT ARE WE DEALING WITH HERE?
ALIEN TECHNOLOGY, MARIA--
--NOT SHI'AR, KREE OR SKRULL... OR ANYTHING ELSE IN OUR RECORDS.
AN ANALYSIS OF FINANCIAL MOVEMENTS AROUND THE MESQUITE AREA LED TO A PROXY COMPANY NAMED SWARMVALLEY, LTD...
...THAT WAS ONCE CONNECTED TO THE TERRORIST ORGANIZATION A.I.M.
IT LOOKS LIKE THEY FOUND THIS GIGANTIC W.M.D....AND MANAGED TO ACTIVATE IT.
NEVADA
A.I.M. HAS BEEN UNDER THE RADAR FOR A WHILE NOW...
WHY DO YOU THINK THEY DID SOMETHING POINTLESS LIKE LETTING THEIR TOY LOOSE LIKE THIS?

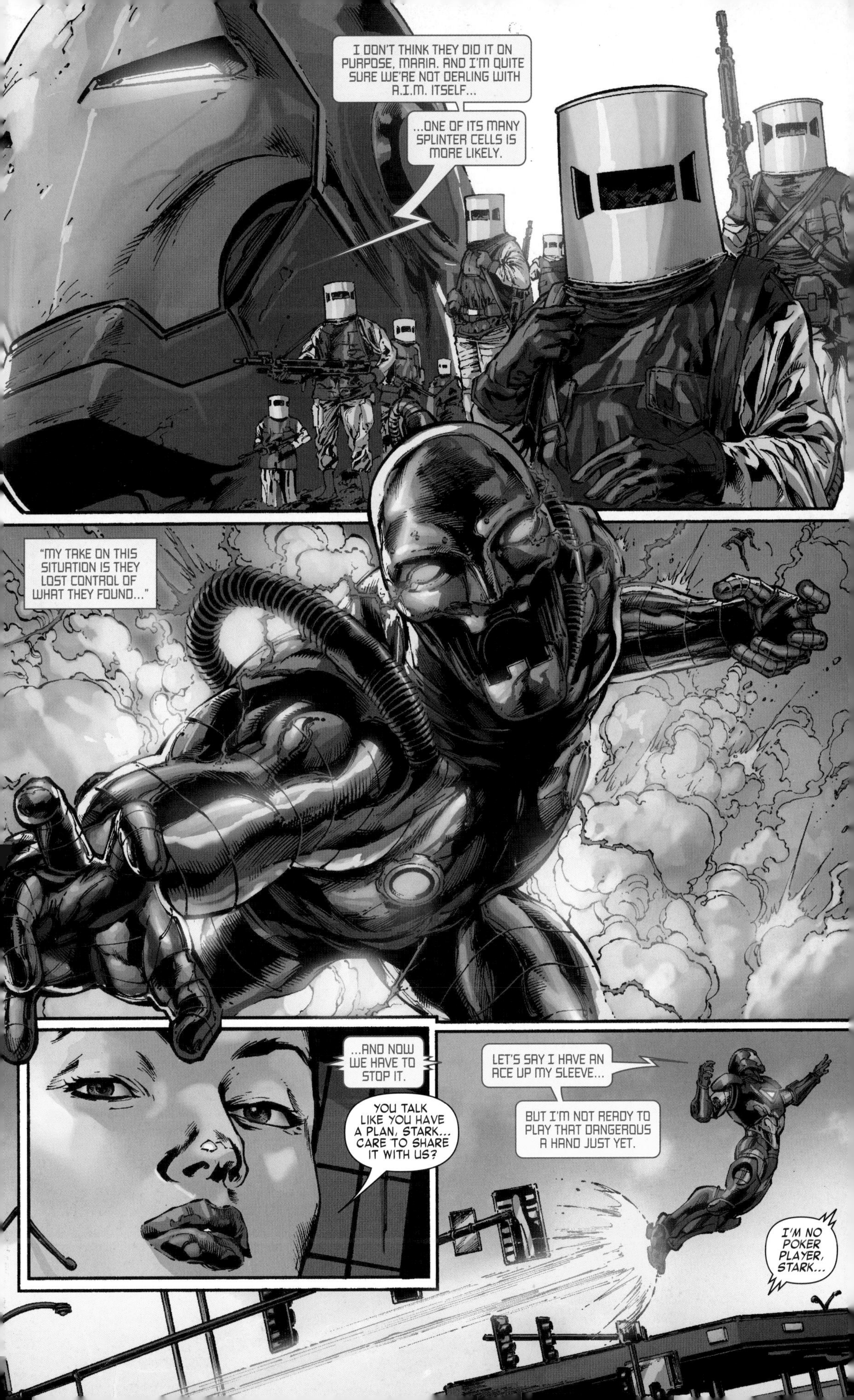
I DON'T THINK THEY DID IT ON PURPOSE, MARIA. AND I'M QUITE SURE WE'RE NOT DEALING WITH A.I.M. ITSELF...
...ONE OF ITS MANY SPLINTER CELLS IS MORE LIKELY.
"MY TAKE ON THIS SITUATION IS THEY LOST CONTROL OF WHAT THEY FOUND..."
...AND NOW WE HAVE TO STOP IT.
YOU TALK LIKE YOU HAVE A PLAN, STARK... CARE TO SHARE IT WITH US?
LET'S SAY I HAVE AN ACE UP MY SLEEVE...
BUT I'M NOT READY TO PLAY THAT DANGEROUS A HAND JUST YET.
I'M NO POKER PLAYER, STARK...

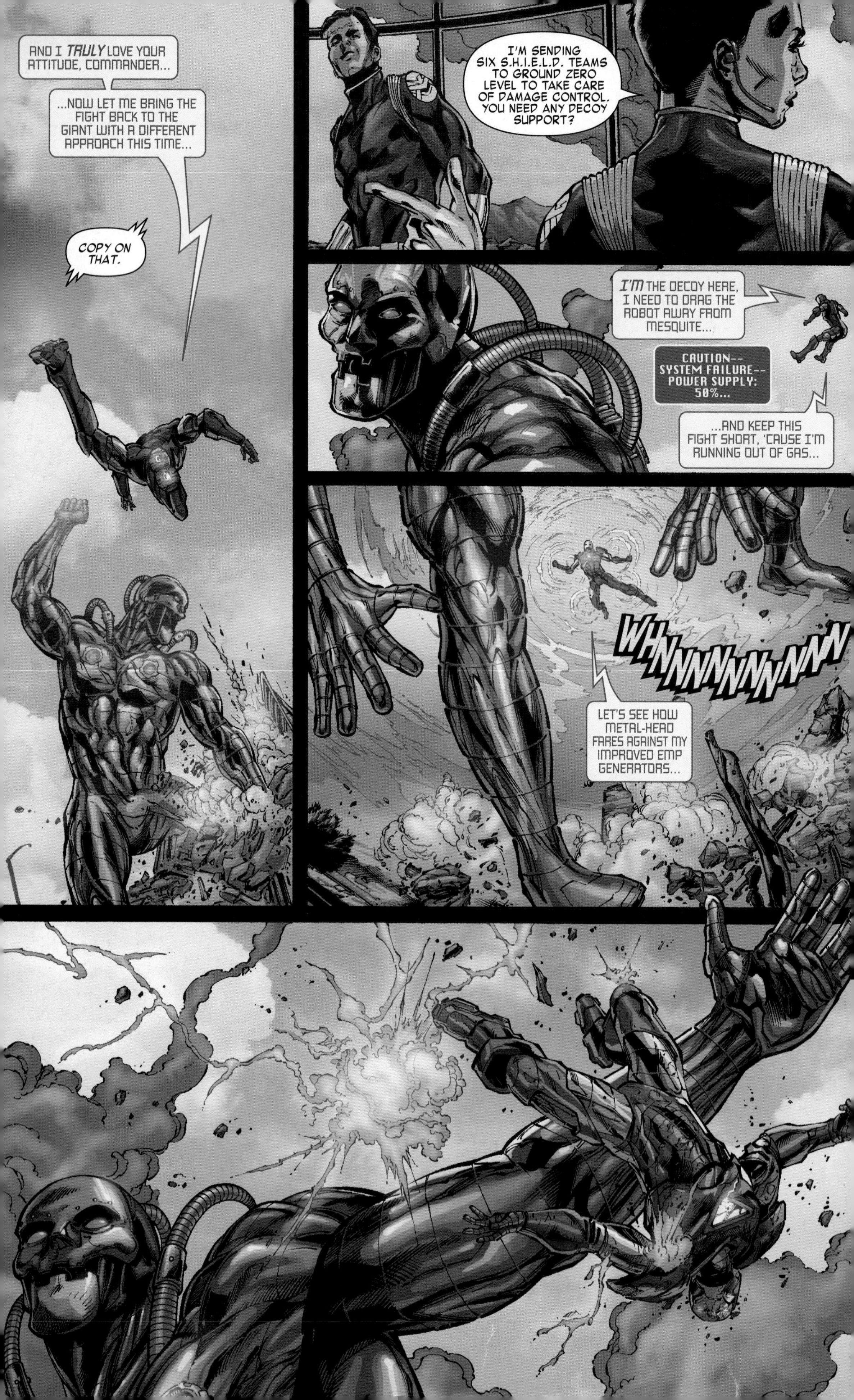

AND I TRULY LOVE YOUR ATTITUDE, COMMANDER...
...NOW LET ME BRING THE FIGHT BACK TO THE GIANT WITH A DIFFERENT APPROACH THIS TIME...
I'M SENDING SIX S.H.I.E.L.D. TEAMS TO GROUND ZERO LEVEL TO TAKE CARE OF DAMAGE CONTROL. YOU NEED ANY DECOY SUPPORT?
COPY ON THAT.
I'M THE DECOY HERE, I NEED TO DRAG THE ROBOT AWAY FROM MESQUITE...
CAUTION-- SYSTEM FAILURE-- POWER SUPPLY: 50%...
...AND KEEP THIS FIGHT SHORT, 'CAUSE I'M RUNNING OUT OF GAS...
WHNNNNNNNNNN
LET'S SEE HOW METAL-HEAD FARES AGAINST MY IMPROVED EMP GENERATORS...

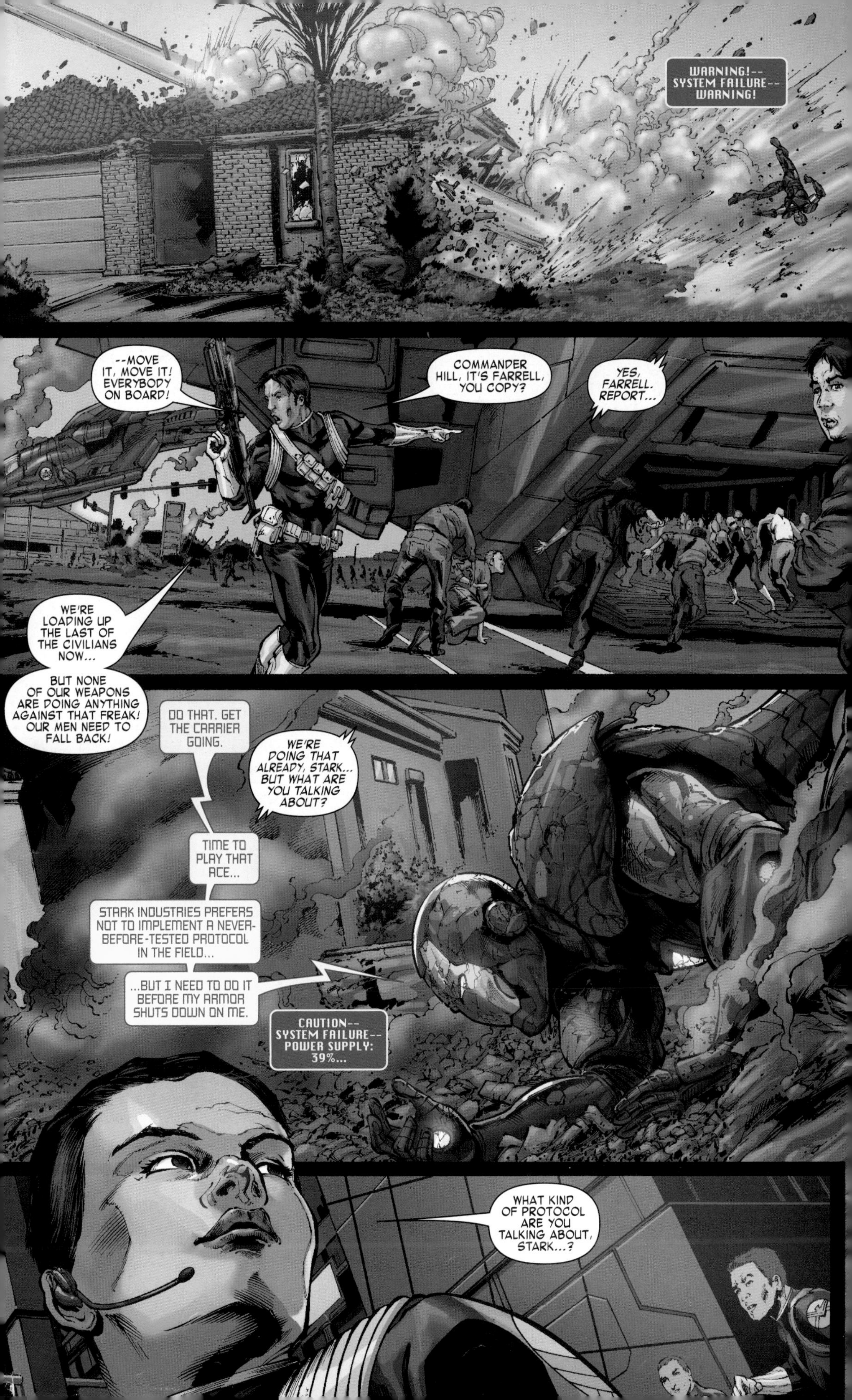
WARNING!--
SYSTEM FAILURE--
WARNING!
--MOVE IT, MOVE IT! EVERYBODY ON BOARD!
COMMANDER HILL, IT'S FARRELL, YOU COPY?
YES, FARRELL. REPORT...
WE'RE LOADING UP THE LAST OF THE CIVILIANS NOW...
BUT NONE OF OUR WEAPONS ARE DOING ANYTHING AGAINST THAT FREAK! OUR MEN NEED TO FALL BACK!
DO THAT. GET THE CARRIER GOING.
WE'RE DOING THAT ALREADY, STARK... BUT WHAT ARE YOU TALKING ABOUT?
TIME TO PLAY THAT ACE...
STARK INDUSTRIES PREFERS NOT TO IMPLEMENT A NEVER-BEFORE-TESTED PROTOCOL IN THE FIELD...
...BUT I NEED TO DO IT BEFORE MY ARMOR SHUTS DOWN ON ME.
CAUTION--
SYSTEM FAILURE--
POWER SUPPLY:
39%...
WHAT KIND OF PROTOCOL ARE YOU TALKING ABOUT, STARK...?

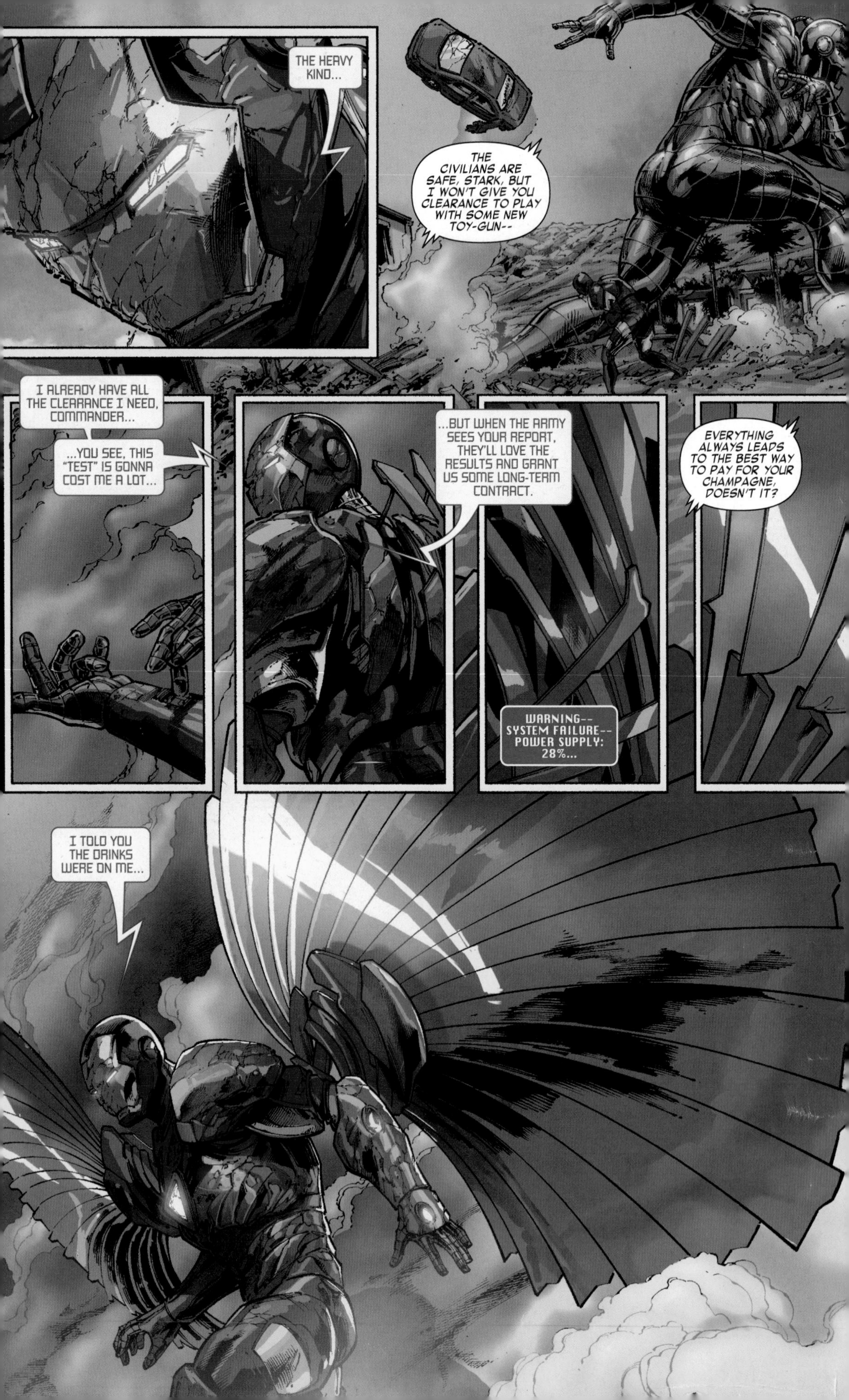
THE HEAVY KIND...
THE CIVILIANS ARE SAFE, STARK, BUT I WON'T GIVE YOU CLEARANCE TO PLAY WITH SOME NEW TOY-GUN--
I ALREADY HAVE ALL THE CLEARANCE I NEED, COMMANDER...
...YOU SEE, THIS "TEST" IS GONNA COST ME A LOT...
...BUT WHEN THE ARMY SEES YOUR REPORT, THEY'LL LOVE THE RESULTS AND GRANT US SOME LONG-TERM CONTRACT.
WARNING-- SYSTEM FAILURE-- POWER SUPPLY: 28%...
EVERYTHING ALWAYS LEADS TO THE BEST WAY TO PAY FOR YOUR CHAMPAGNE, DOESN'T IT?
I TOLD YOU THE DRINKS WERE ON ME...

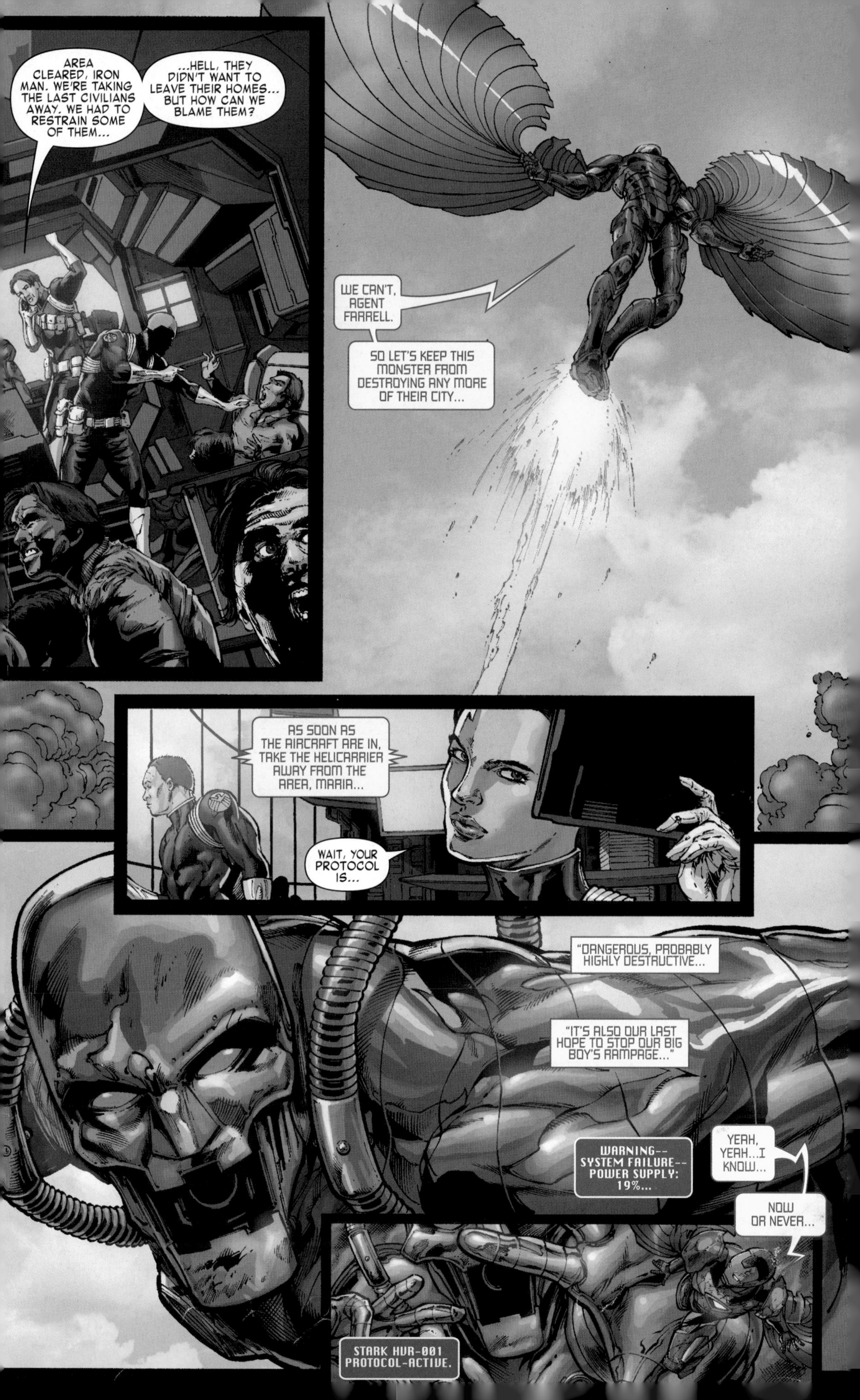
AREA CLEARED, IRON MAN. WE'RE TAKING THE LAST CIVILIANS AWAY. WE HAD TO RESTRAIN SOME OF THEM...
...HELL, THEY DIDN'T WANT TO LEAVE THEIR HOMES... BUT HOW CAN WE BLAME THEM?
WE CAN'T, AGENT FARRELL.
SO LET'S KEEP THIS MONSTER FROM DESTROYING ANY MORE OF THEIR CITY...
AS SOON AS THE AIRCRAFT ARE IN, TAKE THE HELICARRIER AWAY FROM THE AREA, MARIA...
WAIT, YOUR PROTOCOL IS...
"DANGEROUS, PROBABLY HIGHLY DESTRUCTIVE...
"IT'S ALSO OUR LAST HOPE TO STOP OUR BIG BOY'S RAMPAGE..."
WARNING-- SYSTEM FAILURE-- POWER SUPPLY: 19%...
YEAH, YEAH...I KNOW...
NOW OR NEVER...
STARK HVR-001 PROTOCOL-ACTIVE.

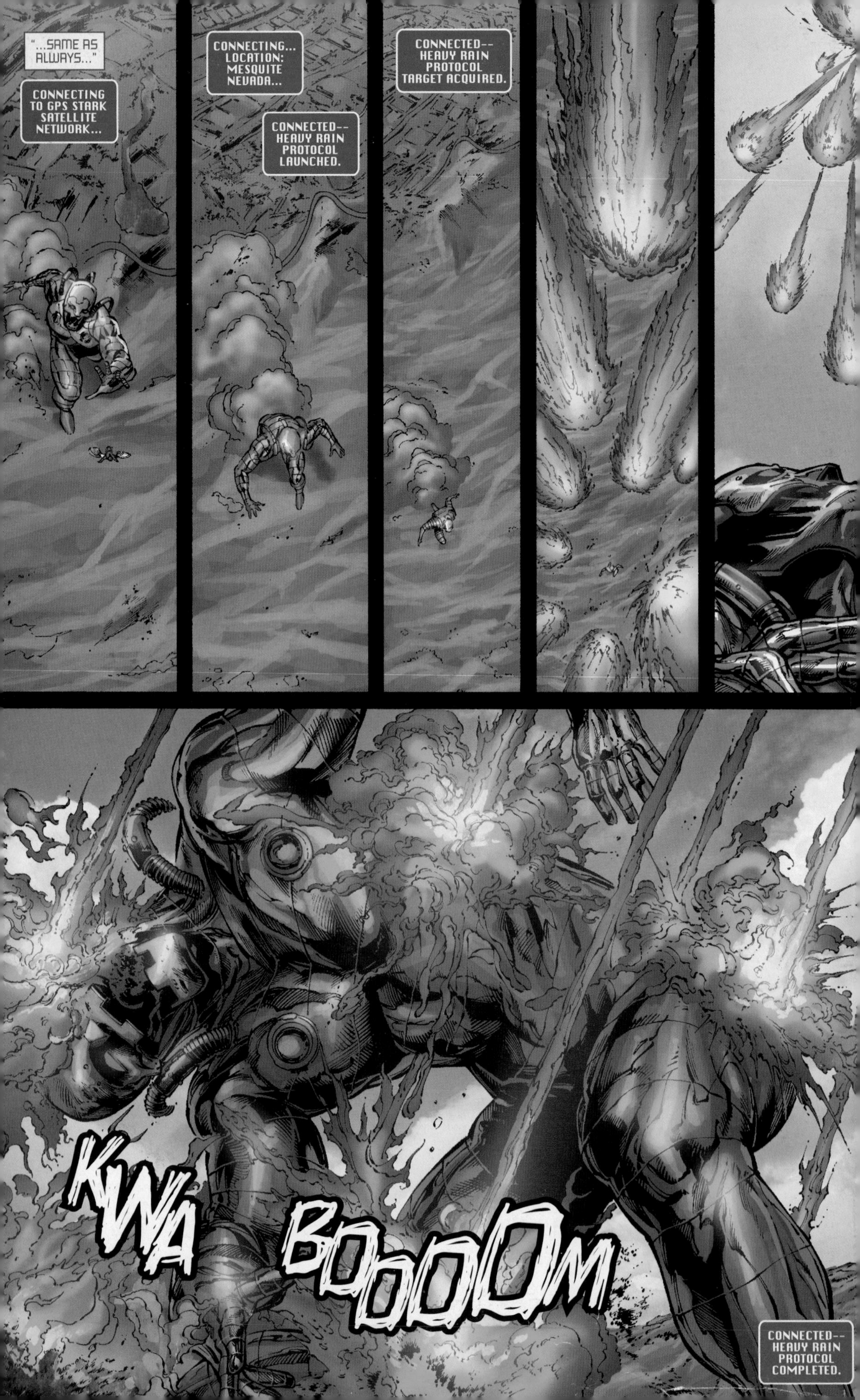
"...SAME AS ALWAYS..."
CONNECTING TO GPS STARK SATELLITE NETWORK...
CONNECTING... LOCATION: MESQUITE NEVADA...
CONNECTED-- HEAVY RAIN PROTOCOL LAUNCHED.
CONNECTED-- HEAVY RAIN PROTOCOL TARGET ACQUIRED.
KWA BOOOOOM
CONNECTED-- HEAVY RAIN PROTOCOL COMPLETED.

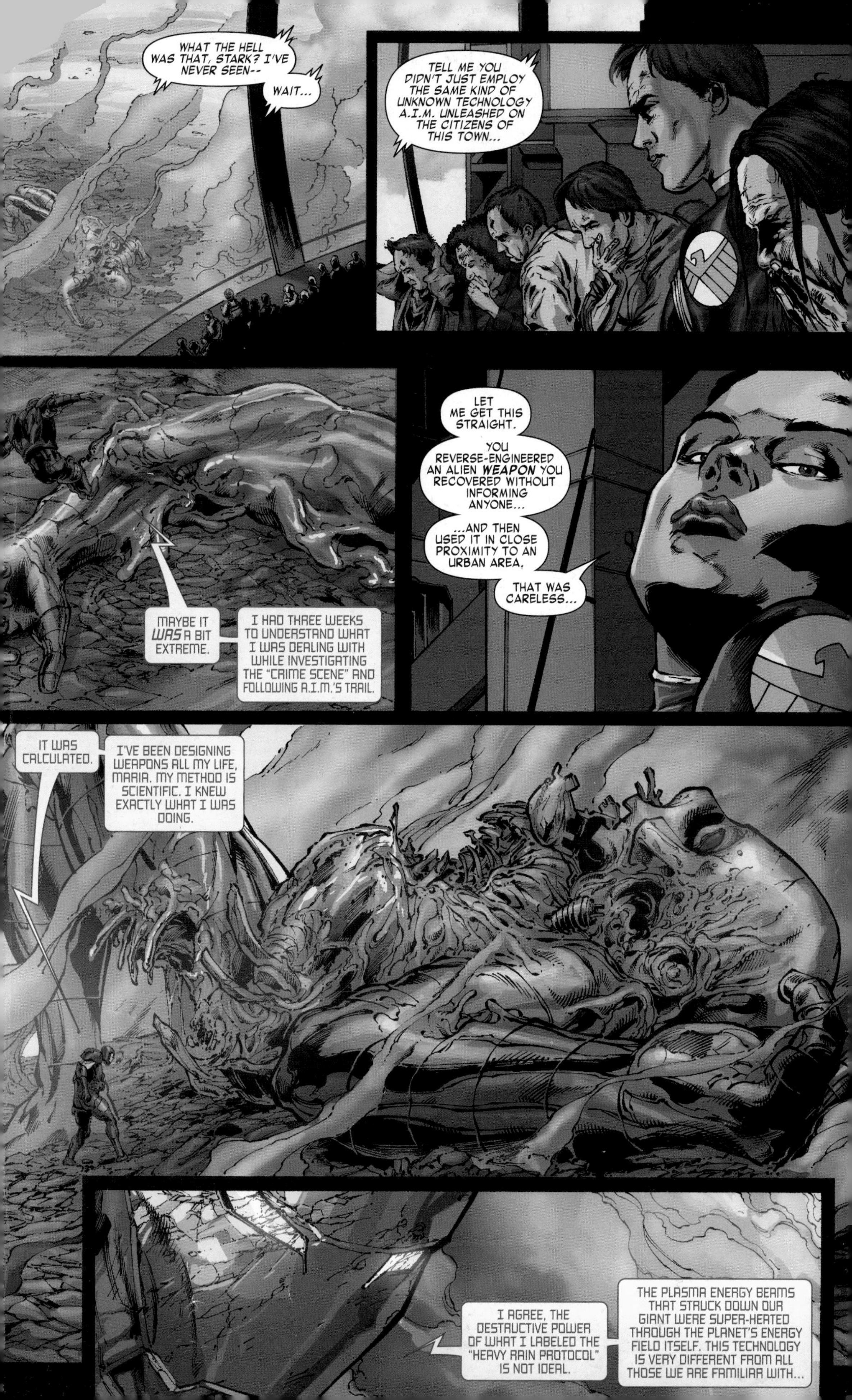
WHAT THE HELL WAS THAT, STARK? I'VE NEVER SEEN--
WAIT...
TELL ME YOU DIDN'T JUST EMPLOY THE SAME KIND OF UNKNOWN TECHNOLOGY A.I.M. UNLEASHED ON THE CITIZENS OF THIS TOWN...
MAYBE IT WAS A BIT EXTREME.
I HAD THREE WEEKS TO UNDERSTAND WHAT I WAS DEALING WITH WHILE INVESTIGATING THE "CRIME SCENE" AND FOLLOWING A.I.M.'S TRAIL.
LET ME GET THIS STRAIGHT.
YOU REVERSE-ENGINEERED AN ALIEN WEAPON YOU RECOVERED WITHOUT INFORMING ANYONE...
...AND THEN USED IT IN CLOSE PROXIMITY TO AN URBAN AREA.
THAT WAS CARELESS...
IT WAS CALCULATED.
I'VE BEEN DESIGNING WEAPONS ALL MY LIFE, MARIA. MY METHOD IS SCIENTIFIC. I KNEW EXACTLY WHAT I WAS DOING.
I AGREE, THE DESTRUCTIVE POWER OF WHAT I LABELED THE "HEAVY RAIN PROTOCOL" IS NOT IDEAL.
THE PLASMA ENERGY BEAMS THAT STRUCK DOWN OUR GIANT WERE SUPER-HEATED THROUGH THE PLANET'S ENERGY FIELD ITSELF. THIS TECHNOLOGY IS VERY DIFFERENT FROM ALL THOSE WE ARE FAMILIAR WITH...

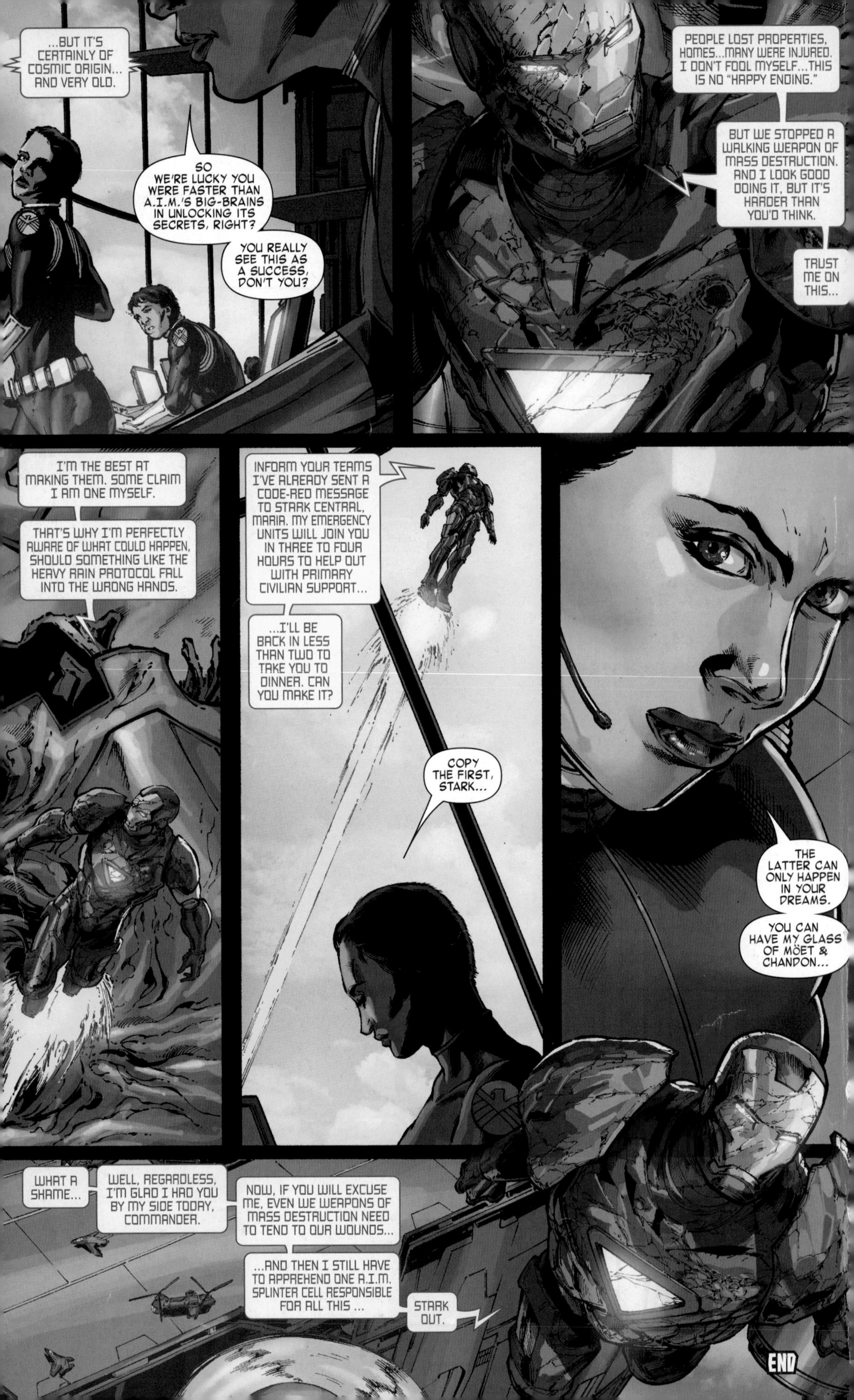
...BUT IT'S CERTAINLY OF COSMIC ORIGIN... AND VERY OLD.
SO WE'RE LUCKY YOU WERE FASTER THAN A.I.M.'S BIG-BRAINS IN UNLOCKING ITS SECRETS, RIGHT?
YOU REALLY SEE THIS AS A SUCCESS, DON'T YOU?
PEOPLE LOST PROPERTIES, HOMES...MANY WERE INJURED. I DON'T FOOL MYSELF...THIS IS NO "HAPPY ENDING."
BUT WE STOPPED A WALKING WEAPON OF MASS DESTRUCTION. AND I LOOK GOOD DOING IT, BUT IT'S HARDER THAN YOU'D THINK.
TRUST ME ON THIS...
I'M THE BEST AT MAKING THEM. SOME CLAIM I AM ONE MYSELF.
THAT'S WHY I'M PERFECTLY AWARE OF WHAT COULD HAPPEN, SHOULD SOMETHING LIKE THE HEAVY RAIN PROTOCOL FALL INTO THE WRONG HANDS.
INFORM YOUR TEAMS I'VE ALREADY SENT A CODE-RED MESSAGE TO STARK CENTRAL, MARIA. MY EMERGENCY UNITS WILL JOIN YOU IN THREE TO FOUR HOURS TO HELP OUT WITH PRIMARY CIVILIAN SUPPORT...
...I'LL BE BACK IN LESS THAN TWO TO TAKE YOU TO DINNER. CAN YOU MAKE IT?
COPY THE FIRST, STARK...
THE LATTER CAN ONLY HAPPEN IN YOUR DREAMS.
YOU CAN HAVE MY GLASS OF MÖET & CHANDON...
WHAT A SHAME...
WELL, REGARDLESS, I'M GLAD I HAD YOU BY MY SIDE TODAY, COMMANDER.
NOW, IF YOU WILL EXCUSE ME, EVEN WE WEAPONS OF MASS DESTRUCTION NEED TO TEND TO OUR WOUNDS...
...AND THEN I STILL HAVE TO APPREHEND ONE A.I.M. SPLINTER CELL RESPONSIBLE FOR ALL THIS ...
STARK OUT.
END